THE NEW FOLGER LIBRARY
SHAKESPEARE

Designed to make Shakespeare's great plays available to all readers, the New Folger Library edition of Shakespeare's plays provides accurate texts in modern spelling and punctuation, as well as scene-by-scene action summaries, full explanatory notes, many pictures clarifying Shakespeare's language, and notes recording all significant departures from the early printed versions. Each play is prefaced by a brief introduction, by a guide to reading Shakespeare's language, and by accounts of his life and theater. Each play is followed by an annotated list of further readings and by a "Modern Perspective" written by an expert on that particular play.

Barbara A. Mowat was Director of Research *emerita* at the Folger Shakespeare Library, Consulting Editor of *Shakespeare Quarterly*, and author of *The Dramaturgy of Shakespeare's Romances* and of essays on Shakespeare's plays and their editing.

Paul Werstine is Professor of English at the Graduate School and at King's University College at Western University. He is a general editor of the New Variorum Shakespeare and author of *Early Modern Playhouse Manuscripts and the Editing of Shakespeare* and of many papers and articles on the printing and editing of Shakespeare's plays.

The Folger Shakespeare Library

The Folger Shakespeare Library in Washington, D.C., a privately funded research library dedicated to Shakespeare and the civilization of early modern Europe, was founded in 1932 by Henry Clay and Emily Jordan Folger, and incorporated as part of Amherst College in Amherst, Massachusetts, one of the nation's oldest liberal arts colleges, from which Henry Folger had graduated in 1879. In addition to its role as the world's preeminent Shakespeare collection and its emergence as a leading center for Renaissance studies, the Folger Shakespeare Library offers a wide array of cultural and educational programs and services for the general public.

EDITORS

BARBARA A. MOWAT
Former Director of Research emerita
Folger Shakespeare Library

PAUL WERSTINE
Professor of English
King's University College
at Western University, Canada

Folger SHAKESPEARE LIBRARY

Henry V

By
WILLIAM SHAKESPEARE

An Updated Edition

Edited by Barbara A. Mowat
and Paul Werstine

Simon & Schuster Paperbacks
New York London Toronto Sydney New Delhi

Simon & Schuster
1230 Avenue of the Americas
New York, NY 10020

This Simon & Schuster trade paperback edition February 2020

SIMON & SCHUSTER and colophon are registered trademarks of Simon & Schuster, Inc.

For information about special discounts for bulk purchases, please contact Simon & Schuster Special Sales at 1-866-506-1949 or business@simonandschuster.com.

The Simon & Schuster Speakers Bureau can bring authors to your live event. For more information or to book an event, contact the Simon & Schuster Speakers Bureau at 1-866-248-3049 or visit our website at www.simonspeakers.com.

Manufactured in the United States of America

10   9   8

ISBN 978-1-9821-0941-7
ISBN 978-1-5011-2657-4 (ebook)

From the Director of the Folger Shakespeare Library

It is hard to imagine a world without Shakespeare. Since their composition more than four hundred years ago, Shakespeare's plays and poems have traveled the globe, inviting those who see and read his works to make them their own.

Readers of the New Folger Editions are part of this ongoing process of "taking up Shakespeare," finding our own thoughts and feelings in language that strikes us as old or unusual and, for that very reason, new. We still struggle to keep up with a writer who could think a mile a minute, whose words paint pictures that shift like clouds. These expertly edited texts, presented here with accompanying explanatory notes and up-to-date critical essays, are distinctive because of what they do: they allow readers not simply to keep up, but to engage deeply with a writer whose works invite us to think, and think again.

These New Folger Editions of Shakespeare's plays are also special because of where they come from. The Folger Shakespeare Library in Washington, D.C., where the Editions are produced, is the single greatest documentary source of Shakespeare's works. An unparalleled collection of early modern books, manuscripts, and artwork connected to Shakespeare, the Folger's holdings have been consulted extensively in the preparation of these texts. The Editions also reflect the expertise gained through the regular performance of Shakespeare's works in the Folger's Elizabethan Theatre.

I want to express my deep thanks to editors Barbara
Mowat and Paul Werstine for creating these indispens-
able editions of Shakespeare's works, which incorporate the best of textual scholarship with a richness of
commentary that is both inspired and engaging. Readers who want to know more about Shakespeare and his
plays can follow the paths these distinguished scholars
have trod by visiting the Folger itself, where a range of
physical and digital resources (available online) exists
to supplement the material in these texts. I commend
to you these words, and hope that they inspire.

Michael Witmore
Director, Folger Shakespeare Library

Contents

Editors' Preface

In recent years, ways of dealing with Shakespeare's texts and with the interpretation of his plays have been undergoing significant change. This edition, while retaining many of the features that have always made the Folger Shakespeare so attractive to the general reader, at the same time reflects these current ways of thinking about Shakespeare. For example, modern readers, actors, and teachers have become interested in the differences between, on the one hand, the early forms in which Shakespeare's plays were first published and, on the other hand, the forms in which editors through the centuries have presented them. In response to this interest, we have based our edition on what we consider the best early printed version of a particular play (explaining our rationale in a section called "An Introduction to This Text") and have marked our changes in the text—unobtrusively, we hope, but in such a way that the curious reader can be aware that a change has been made and can consult the "Textual Notes" to discover what appeared in the early printed version.

Current ways of looking at the plays are reflected in our brief introductions, in many of the commentary notes, in the annotated lists of "Further Reading," and especially in each play's "Modern Perspective," an essay written by an outstanding scholar who brings to the reader his or her fresh assessment of the play in the light of today's interests and concerns.

As in the Folger Library General Reader's Shakespeare, which this edition replaces, we include explanatory notes designed to help make Shakespeare's language clearer to a modern reader, and we place the

notes on the page facing the text that they explain. We
also follow the earlier edition in including illustrations—
of objects, of clothing, of mythological figures—from
books and manuscripts in the Folger Shakespeare
Library collection. We provide fresh accounts of the life
of Shakespeare, of the publishing of his plays, and of
the theaters in which his plays were performed, as well
as an introduction to the text itself. We also include a
section called "Reading Shakespeare's Language," in
which we try to help readers learn to "break the code"
of Elizabethan poetic language.

For each section of each volume, we are indebted
to a host of generous experts and fellow scholars. The
"Reading Shakespeare's Language" sections, for example, could not have been written had not Arthur King,
of Brigham Young University, and Randal Robinson,
author of *Unlocking Shakespeare's Language,* led the
way in untangling Shakespearean language puzzles
and generously shared their insights and methodolo-
gies with us. "Shakespeare's Life" profited by the careful reading given it by S. Schoenbaum, "Shakespeare's
Theater" was read and strengthened by Andrew Gurr,
John Astington, and William Ingram, and "The Publication of Shakespeare's Plays" is indebted to the comments of Peter W. M. Blayney. We, as editors, take sole
responsibility for any errors in our editions.

We are grateful to the authors of the "Modern Perspectives"; to Leeds Barroll and David Bevington for
their generous encouragement; to the Huntington and
Newberry Libraries for fellowship support; to King's
University College for the grants it has provided to
Paul Werstine; to the Social Sciences and Humanities Research Council of Canada, which provided him
with Research Time Stipends; to Penny Gill and Eva
Mary Hooker for insightful conversations about the
language of *Henry V*; to Skiles Howard and Scott Reiss

for advice on Renaissance music and dance; and to the Folger Institute's Center for Shakespeare Studies for its fortuitous sponsorship of a workshop on "Shakespeare's Texts for Students and Teachers" (funded by the National Endowment for the Humanities and led by Richard Knowles of the University of Wisconsin), a workshop from which we learned an enormous amount about what is wanted by college and high-school teachers of Shakespeare today.

In preparing this preface for the publication of *Henry V* in 1995, we wrote: "Our biggest debt is to the Folger Shakespeare Library—to Werner Gundersheimer, Director of the Library, who made possible our edition; to Jean Miller, the Library's Art Curator, who combs the Library holdings for illustrations, and to Julie Ainsworth, Head of the Photography Department, who carefully photographs them; to Peggy O'Brien, Director of Education, and her assistant, Molly Haws, who continue to give us expert advice about the needs being expressed by Shakespeare teachers and students (and to Martha Christian and other 'master teachers' who used our texts in manuscript in their classrooms); to Jessica Hymowitz, who provides expert computer support; to the staff of the Academic Programs Division, especially Mary Tonkinson, Lena Cowen Orlin, Jean Feerick, Amy Adler, Kathleen Lynch, and Carol Brobeck; and, finally, to the staff of the Library Reading Room, whose patience and support are invaluable."

As we revise the play for publication in 2019, we add to the above our gratitude to Michael Witmore, Director of the Folger Shakespeare Library, who brings to our work a gratifying enthusiasm and vision; to Eric Johnson, the Folger's Director of Digital Access, who expertly manages our editions in both their paper and their many electronic forms; to Gail Kern Paster, Director of the Library from 2002 until July 2011, whose interest and support have been unfailing and whose scholarly expertise continues to be an invaluable resource; to Jonathan Evans and Alysha Bullock, our production editors at Simon & Schuster, whose expertise, attention to detail, and wisdom are essential to this project; to the Folger's Photography Department; to Deborah Curren-Aquino for continuing superb editorial assistance and for her exceptionally fine Further Reading annotations; to Alice Falk for her expert copyediting; to Michael Poston for unfailing computer support; to Jessica Roberts Frazier, Sophie Byvik, Gabrielle Linnell, and Stacey Redick; and to Rebecca Niles (whose help is crucial). Finally, we once again express our thanks to Stephen Llano for twenty-five years of support as our invaluable production editor, to the late Jean Miller for the wonderful images she unearthed, and to the ever-supportive staff of the Library Reading Room.

Barbara A. Mowat died on Thanksgiving Day 2017. Her knowledge, wisdom, and great care of Shakespeare's texts will be sorely missed.

Paul Werstine
2020

Shakespeare's *Henry V*

Henry V is Shakespeare's most famous "war play," perhaps because it represents war in such a variety of ways and thereby tests whatever understanding of war we may bring to it. Some of the play glorifies war, especially the play's Choruses and Henry's speeches urging his troops into battle: "Once more unto the breach, dear friends, once more, / Or close the wall up with our English dead!" During this first engagement between the invading English army and the French at Harfleur, Henry tells his men that they can never be more truly and gloriously the sons of their fathers than in making war. The play's Chorus urges us to join the invasion by grappling our imaginations to the sterns of Henry's ships as they set sail for France, and then to join with the Chorus in praise of Henry on the eve of his greatest battle, Agincourt: "Praise and glory on his head!" Repeatedly the Chorus glorifies the warlike king, calling him "the mirror," or paragon, "of all Christian kings" and "this star of England."

But when the Chorus is offstage we hear other voices of war that are far less alluring. We hear bishops conniving for war so that they can postpone a bill in Parliament that would heavily tax the Church's wealth. Then we hear soldiers in a tavern enthusiastic for war, not in the hope of winning glory but in the expectation of reaping profits ("To suck, to suck, the very blood to suck"). Even in the impressive speeches of Henry and his nobles threatening the French, there are many chilling references to the human cost of war, to "the widows' tears, the orphans' cries, / . . . the privèd maidens' groans" for dead combatants, as well as to the horrors awaiting the noncombatants: "the filthy and

"Henry the Fifth, King of England, and France,
Lord of Ireland."
From John Taylor, *All the workes of . . .* (1630).

contagious clouds / Of heady murder, spoil," rape, and infanticide.

After you read this range of different voices that make up the text of *Henry V,* we invite you to read "A Modern Perspective" on the play written by Professor Michael Neill of the University of Auckland, printed at the back of this book.

Henry V's French Descent

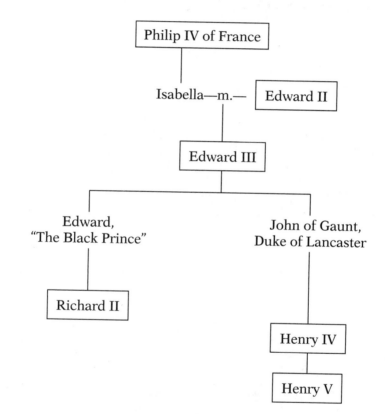

Reading Shakespeare's Language:
Henry V

For many people today, reading Shakespeare's language can be a problem—but it is a problem that can be solved. Those who have studied Latin (or even French or German or Spanish) and those who are used to reading poetry will have little difficulty understanding the language of Shakespeare's poetic drama. Others, however, need to develop the skills of untangling unusual sentence structures and of recognizing and understanding poetic compressions, omissions, and wordplay. And even those skilled in reading unusual sentence structures may have occasional trouble with Shakespeare's words. More than four hundred years of "static"—caused by changes in language and life—intervene between his speaking and our hearing. Most of his vocabulary is still in use, but a few of his words are no longer used, and many of his words now have meanings quite different from those they had in the sixteenth century. In the theater, most of these difficulties are solved for us by actors who study the language and articulate it for us so that the essential meaning is heard—or, when combined with stage action, is at least *felt*. When reading on one's own, one must do what each actor does: go over the lines (often with a dictionary close at hand) until the puzzles are solved and the lines yield up their poetry and the characters speak in words and phrases that are, suddenly, rewarding and wonderfully memorable.

Shakespeare's Words

As you begin to read the opening scenes of a play by Shakespeare, you may notice occasional unfamiliar words. Some are unfamiliar simply because we no longer use them. In the opening scenes of *Henry V,* for example, you will find the words *casques* (i.e., helmets), *fain* (i.e., gladly), *severals* (i.e., particulars), and *naught* (i.e., worthless). Words of this kind are explained in notes to the text and will become familiar the more of Shakespeare's plays you read.

In *Henry V,* as in all of Shakespeare's writing, the more problematic are the words that are still in use but that now have different meanings. In the opening scenes of *Henry V,* for example, the word *nicely* has the meaning of "subtly," *floods* is used where we would say "rivers," *dishonest* where we would say "unchaste," and *happy* where we would say "fortunate." Such words will be explained in the notes to the text, but they, too, will become familiar as you continue to read Shakespeare's language.

Some words are strange not because of the "static" introduced by changes in language over the past centuries but because these are words that Shakespeare is using to build a dramatic world that has its own space, time, and history. In *Henry V,* within the larger world of early fifteenth-century Europe that the play creates, Shakespeare uses one set of words to construct Henry V's court (and then his royal pavilion on the battlefield); a second set to fashion the court of the King of France and the French camp; yet a third to mark King Henry's former tavern companions who are now following him to war; and, finally, a fourth to present Henry's captains, who are drawn from Wales, Scotland, and Ireland, as well as from England.

Henry V's court is built through early references in the play to "chivalry," "esquires," "exhibitors," "commonwealth affairs," the "cause of policy," "the main intendment of the Scot," and ambassadors' "embassies" (or messages), as well as to the earlier history of Edward III and Edward the Black Prince. The French court shares with the English court some reference to their common history of past English victories over France; but the language of the French court is richer, with names exotic to English speakers—"the Dukes of Berri and of Brittany, / Of Brabant and of Orléans"— and with an ornamental style of expression in such phrasing as "means defendant" and "our quick blood, spirited with wine," and, especially, with its use of French words—*"les dames d'honneur," "les seigneurs de France,"* and *"Ô Dieu vivant"*—words that we translate rather literally on the facing page.

In the tavern peopled by Bardolph, Nym, Pistol, Hostess Quickly, and the Boy, we enter yet another world; it is a place constructed of an odd medley of language: "shaked of a burning quotidian-tertian," "thou prick-eared cur of Iceland," "that's the humor of it"—including even some broken French: *Couple à gorge.* Still more unusual is the language used to stage the Welsh, Scots, and Irish captains who serve under Henry V: "Kill the poys and the luggage," "ay'll de gud service," "By Chrish, la, 'tish ill done." However strange such expressions appear at first, the words and phrases that create these language worlds will become increasingly familiar as you read further into the play.

Shakespeare's Sentences

In an English sentence, meaning is quite dependent on the place given each word. "The dog bit the boy" and

> For *I have made an offer to his Majesty*—
> Upon our spiritual convocation
> And in regard of causes now in hand,
> Which I have opened to his Grace at large,
> As touching France—*to give a greater sum*
> *Than ever at one time the clergy yet*
> *Did to his predecessors part withal.* (1.1.80–86)

Here the basic sentence elements ("I have made an offer to his Majesty to give a greater sum") are interrupted by several sweeping phrases that characterize the formal rhetoric of the Bishop. A similar pattern occurs in the Chorus to Act 2. There a space is opened up between subject and verb for an epiclike catalog of names and titles, and then opened up a second time between the two parts of the verb for wordplay on *gilt/guilt:*

> . . . *three corrupted men*—
> One, Richard, Earl of Cambridge, and the second,
> Henry, Lord Scroop of Masham, and the third,
> Sir Thomas Grey, knight, of Northumberland—
> *Have,* for the gilt of France (O guilt indeed!),
> *Confirmed* conspiracy with fearful France,
> And by their hands this grace of kings must die[.]
>   (2.Chor.22–28)

In *Henry V,* as in many other of Shakespeare's plays (*Hamlet,* for instance), long interrupted sentences are used frequently, sometimes to catch the audience up in the narrative and sometimes as a characterizing device.

In some of his plays (again, *Hamlet* is a good example), rather than separating basic sentence elements, Shakespeare simply holds them back, delaying them until subordinate material to which he wants to give greater emphasis has been presented. This kind of

delaying structure is used in the public speeches of
Henry V, as, for example, Exeter's when he presents
the King of France with Henry's claim to the French
throne:

> That you may know
> 'Tis no sinister nor no awkward claim
> Picked from the wormholes of long-vanished days
> Nor from the dust of old oblivion raked,
> *He sends you this most memorable line,*
> In every branch truly demonstrative,
> Willing you overlook this pedigree,
> *And* when you find him evenly derived
> From his most famed of famous ancestors,
> Edward the Third, *he bids you then resign*
> *Your crown and kingdom,* indirectly held
> From him, the native and true challenger.
>   (2.4.91–102)

Here the subject and verb of the first main clause are
delayed for three and a half lines, and then the subject and verb of the second main clause are held back
for two lines after the conjunction "And," which marks
the beginning of this second main clause. Stripped
down to its basic elements, the sentence would read, in
"normal" word order: "He sends you this most memorable line, and he bids you then resign your crown and
kingdom." King Henry uses a simpler version of the
same word order when he is threatening Harfleur with
destruction:

> For, as I am a soldier,
> A name that in my thoughts becomes me best,
> If I begin the batt'ry once again,
> *I will not leave the half-achieved Harfleur*
> *Till in her ashes she lie burièd.*   (3.3.5–9)

This time, as the subject and verb are again delayed, the emphasis at the beginning of the sentence falls on Henry's self-characterization as a soldier inclined to begin the battery again.

Finally, in many of Shakespeare's plays, sentences are sometimes complicated not because of unusual structures or interruptions or delays, but because he omits words and parts of words that English sentences normally require. (In conversation, we, too, often omit words. We say "Heard from him yet?" and our hearer supplies the missing "Have you.") Frequent reading of Shakespeare—and of other poets—trains us to supply such missing words. In his later plays, Shakespeare uses omissions both of verbs and of nouns to great dramatic effect. In *Henry V* omissions are extremely rare and seem to be used to affect the tone of the speech or for the sake of speech rhythm. For example, when Ely asks Canterbury, as they are discussing how to stop Parliament from appropriating the Church's wealth, "But what prevention?" the words "is there" are omitted from the end of his question, which thereby seems breathless and all the more anxious. Or, to take another example, in response to Henry's question "May I with right and conscience make this claim [to the French throne]?" Canterbury appears to express utter decisiveness and great conviction with the words "The sin upon my head, dread sovereign." This mood is established through the omission of much of the familiar saying that Canterbury is here made to employ, a saying that in fuller form would exceed iambic pentameter: "If your claim be sinful, may the sin be upon my head [i.e., may it be my responsibility], not upon yours."

Shakespearean Wordplay

Shakespeare plays with language so often and so variously that entire books are written on the topic. Here we will mention only two kinds of wordplay, puns and similes. A pun is a play on words that sound the same but that have different meanings, or—as is sometimes the case in *Henry V*—on a single word that has more than one meaning. In the Chorus to Act 2, as we have already noticed, there is an example of the first kind of pun in the line "for the gilt of France (O guilt indeed!)." Here "gilt" refers to the French gold used to bribe the conspirators to attempt Henry's assassination, while the identical sounding "guilt" is the Chorus's moral condemnation of their treason. The second kind of pun is used extensively by Henry himself when the French ambassador presents him with the Dauphin's gift of a barrel filled with tennis balls:

> When we have matched our rackets to these balls,
> We will in France, by God's grace, play a set
> Shall strike his father's crown into the hazard.
> Tell him he hath made a match with such a wrangler
> That all the courts of France will be disturbed
> With chases.   (1.2.272–78)

In the first lines of this excerpt, Henry is made to speak only of playing a game (or "set") of royal tennis, a sport played inside a walled court. But as the excerpt continues, the terms used become puns in their reference both to tennis and to the war that Henry plans to make in France to win the French crown. For example, "hazard" can mean a hole in the wall of a royal tennis court through which the ball can be hit; but "hazard" can also mean the peril and jeopardy into which Henry intends to put the French crown. In further puns, "courts" are both (1) royal courts and (2) tennis courts; "chases" both (1) winning strokes in tennis and (2) routs of enemies in battles. Thus the language needs to be listened to carefully if one is to catch all its meanings.

A simile is a play on words in which one object or idea is explicitly compared to something else, something with which it is said to share common features. One speech in the play's first scene is entirely devoted to a single simile comparing the growth of plants to the early life of King Henry, whose youthful "wildness" is said to be weedlike in contrast to the "wholesome"-ness of his mature "contemplation":

> The strawberry grows underneath the nettle,
> And wholesome berries thrive and ripen best
> Neighbored by fruit of baser quality;
> And so the Prince obscured his contemplation
> Under the veil of wildness, which [i.e., his
>   contemplation], no doubt,
> Grew like the summer grass, fastest by night,
> Unseen yet crescive in his faculty [i.e., growing
>   according to its own nature]. (1.1.63–69)

This simile characterizes the Bishop of Ely by identifying him with an old-fashioned way of writing called euphuism, named after John Lyly's book *Euphues*, published in 1579, about twenty years before *Henry V* was staged. As a euphuist, Ely is made to explain human behavior by reference to a little-known "fact" from natural history (or science): that summer grass grows at night according to its own nature, without benefit of sunlight.

The most famous simile in *Henry V* is the bee simile given to Canterbury in the second scene, a simile that was already famous before its appearance here.

Its fame arose from its use by the Roman poet Virgil, who, in the century before the birth of Christ, wrote, among other poems, the *Georgics,* a poem celebrating rural life, and the *Aeneid,* an epic poem offering a fictional account of the founding of Rome. Although Virgil developed his discussion of bees most prominently in the *Georgics,* he also employed a bee simile in the first book of the *Aeneid.* Since Canterbury is encouraging Henry to undertake a war of conquest of the kind often celebrated in epics, this simile is appropriate to his speech. The Duke of Exeter has just explained that "government, though high and low and lower," works all to one mutual goal. Canterbury replies,

> Therefore doth heaven divide
> The state of man in divers functions,
> Setting endeavor in continual motion,
> To which is fixèd as an aim or butt
> Obedience; for so work the honeybees,
> Creatures that by a rule in nature teach
> The act of order to a peopled kingdom.
> They have a king and officers of sorts,
> Where some like magistrates correct at home,
> Others like merchants venture trade abroad,
> Others like soldiers armèd in their stings
> Make boot upon the summer's velvet buds,
> Which pillage they with merry march bring home
> To the tent royal of their emperor,
> Who, busied in his majesty, surveys
> The singing masons building roofs of gold,
> The civil citizens kneading up the honey,
> The poor mechanic porters crowding in
> Their heavy burdens at his narrow gate,
> The sad-eyed justice with his surly hum
> Delivering o'er to executors pale
> The lazy yawning drone.   (1.2.191–212)

In Canterbury's simile, the kingdom of the bee is a model for a human kingdom: the bees, he claims, have social ranks in which all work happily—king bees, magistrate bees, soldier bees, mason bees who sing as they build, citizen bees who knead up the honey, porter bees who carry the heavy loads, even executioner bees who slaughter the lazy drones. In *Henry V*, simile is most often used to lift a character's rhetoric to a "high style," demonstrating his linguistic powers, his control over language.

Implied Stage Action

Finally, in reading Shakespeare's plays we should always remember that what we are reading is a performance script. The dialogue is written to be spoken by actors who, at the same time, are moving, gesturing, picking up objects, weeping, shaking their fists. Some stage action is described in what are called "stage directions"; some is suggested within the dialogue itself. We must learn to be alert to such signals as we stage the play in our imaginations. For example, in 2.1, where Pistol and Nym play a game in which they repeatedly challenge each other and draw and then sheathe their swords, there are almost no stage directions in the early printed text to indicate this action. Nevertheless, the dialogue often clearly indicates that swords have been drawn and then that they have been put away. Hostess Quickly's plea to "Good Corporal Nym, show your valor, and put up your sword" announces to reader and editor alike that Nym—and, presumably, Pistol, too—has already drawn. And Pistol's offer to shake hands with Nym—"Give me thy fist, thy forefoot to me give"—is a signal that Pistol himself, and very likely Nym as well, have put away their swords. Like other editors, we include fairly complete stage directions indicating this action, but these directions have no authority beyond our own judgment based upon our reading of the early printed text. (This is one of the reasons we always mark such additions to the text with brackets.) The precise points in the dialogue at which the drawing and sheathing of swords is to take place is at the discretion of readers, as well as directors and actors, to imagine.

Of much greater significance to readers' imaginings of the play on stage is a recent debate about the end of 4.6. This scene begins with a stage direction calling for the entrance of King Henry with *"his train, with prisoners."* The scene ends with Henry's order "every soldier kill his prisoners. / Give the word through. *Exit.*" It has been argued that this combination—the stage direction announcing the entrance of prisoners and the dialogue ordering their deaths—indicates that the prisoners be killed onstage by their captors. It has also been argued that they should *not* be killed onstage: that the stage direction for the English to enter with French prisoners may merely signal stage action to indicate that the English are prevailing in battle, and that Henry's order is that the command be given through the army—*not* that the prisoners before him be instantly slain. This debate points up for the reader a particularly bloody alternative for imagining stage action.

Henry V is unique among Shakespeare's plays in relentlessly keeping before its readers the tasks of the imagination. Each Chorus apologizes for the inadequacy of the stage and of mere actors to represent the scope of the action that is the play's subject; each Chorus urges upon us the imaginative effort of conjuring up from the bare stage with its clutch of actors an immense national conflict. The Chorus thus confronts us with the complex operation of figuring forth to ourselves the look of the play on stage and, at the same time, the horror and, for the Chorus, the glory of the war that is the play's subject.

It is immensely rewarding to work carefully with Shakespeare's language—with the words, the sentences, the wordplay, and the implied stage action—as readers for the past four centuries have discovered. It may be more pleasurable to attend a good performance of a play—though not everyone has thought so. But the joy of being able to stage one of Shakespeare's plays in one's imagination, to return to passages that continue to yield further meanings (or further questions) the more one reads them—these are pleasures that, for many, rival (or at least augment) those of the performed text, and certainly make it worth considerable effort to "break the code" of Elizabethan poetic drama and let free the remarkable language that makes up a Shakespeare text.

Shakespeare's Life

Surviving documents that give us glimpses into the life of William Shakespeare show us a playwright, poet, and actor who grew up in the market town of Stratford-upon-Avon, spent his professional life in London, and returned to Stratford a wealthy landowner. He was born in April 1564, died in April 1616, and is buried inside the chancel of Holy Trinity Church in Stratford.

We wish we could know more about the life of the world's greatest dramatist. His plays and poems are testaments to his wide reading—especially to his knowledge of Virgil, Ovid, Plutarch, Holinshed's *Chronicles*, and the Bible—and to his mastery of the English language, but we can only speculate about his education. We know that the King's New School in Stratford-upon-Avon was considered excellent. The school was one of the English "grammar schools" established to educate young men, primarily in Latin grammar and literature. As in other schools of the time, students began their studies at the age of four or five in the attached "petty school," and there learned to read and write in English, studying primarily the catechism from the Book of Common Prayer. After two years in the petty school, students entered the lower form (grade) of the grammar school, where they began the serious study of Latin grammar and Latin texts that would occupy most of the remainder of their school days. (Several Latin texts that Shakespeare used repeatedly in writing his plays and poems were texts that schoolboys memorized and recited.) Latin comedies were introduced early in the lower form; in the upper form, which the boys entered at age ten or eleven, students wrote their own Latin orations and

CATECHISMVS

paruus pueris primùm Latinè
qui ediscatur, proponendus
in Scholis.

LONDINI
Apud Iohannem Dayum Typo-
graphum. An. 1573.

Cum Priuilegio Regiæ Maieſtatis.

A catechism.
Title page of *Catechismus paruus pueris primum Latine . . .* (1573).

declamations, studied Latin historians and rhetoricians, and began the study of Greek using the Greek New Testament.

Since the records of the Stratford "grammar school" do not survive, we cannot prove that William Shakespeare attended the school; however, every indication (his father's position as an alderman and bailiff of Stratford, the playwright's own knowledge of the Latin classics, scenes in the plays that recall grammar-school experiences—for example, *The Merry Wives of Windsor,* 4.1) suggests that he did. We also lack generally accepted documentation about Shakespeare's life after his schooling ended and his professional life in London began. His marriage in 1582 (at age eighteen) to Anne Hathaway and the subsequent births of his daughter Susanna (1583) and the twins Judith and Hamnet (1585) are recorded, but how he supported himself and where he lived are not known. Nor do we know when and why he left Stratford for the London theatrical world, nor how he rose to be the important figure in that world that he had become by the early 1590s.

We do know that by 1592 he had achieved some prominence in London as both an actor and a playwright. In that year was published a book by the playwright Robert Greene attacking an actor who had the audacity to write blank-verse drama and who was "in his own conceit [i.e., opinion] the only Shake-scene in a country." Since Greene's attack includes a parody of a line from one of Shakespeare's early plays, there is little doubt that it is Shakespeare to whom he refers, a "Shake-scene" who had aroused Greene's fury by successfully competing with university-educated dramatists like Greene himself. It was in 1593 that Shakespeare became a published poet. In that year he published his long narrative poem *Venus and Adonis;* in 1594, he followed it with *Lucrece.* Both poems were dedicated to the young earl of Southampton (Henry Wriothesley), who may have become Shakespeare's patron.

It seems no coincidence that Shakespeare wrote these narrative poems at a time when the theaters were closed because of the plague, a contagious epidemic disease that devastated the population of London. When the theaters reopened in 1594, Shakespeare apparently resumed his double career of actor and playwright and began his long (and seemingly profitable) service as an acting-company shareholder. Records for December of 1594 show him to be a leading member of the Lord Chamberlain's Men. It was this company of actors, later named the King's Men, for whom he would be a principal actor, dramatist, and shareholder for the rest of his career.

So far as we can tell, that career spanned about twenty years. In the 1590s, he wrote his plays on English history as well as several comedies and at least two tragedies (*Titus Andronicus* and *Romeo and Juliet*). These histories, comedies, and tragedies are the plays credited to him in 1598 in a work, *Palladis Tamia*, that in one chapter compares English writers with "Greek, Latin, and Italian Poets." There the author, Francis Meres, claims that Shakespeare is comparable to the Latin dramatists Seneca for tragedy and Plautus for comedy, and calls him "the most excellent in both kinds for the stage." He also names him "Mellifluous and honey-tongued Shakespeare": "I say," writes Meres, "that the Muses would speak with Shakespeare's fine filed phrase, if they would speak English." Since Meres also mentions Shakespeare's "sugared sonnets among his private friends," it is assumed that many of Shakespeare's sonnets (not published until 1609) were also written in the 1590s.

In 1599, Shakespeare's company built a theater

for themselves across the river from London, naming it the Globe. The plays that are considered by many to be Shakespeare's major tragedies (*Hamlet, Othello, King Lear,* and *Macbeth*) were written while the company was resident in this theater, as were such comedies as *Twelfth Night* and *Measure for Measure.* Many of Shakespeare's plays were performed at court (both for Queen Elizabeth I and, after her death in 1603, for King James I), some were presented at the Inns of Court (the residences of London's legal societies), and some were doubtless performed in other towns, at the universities, and at great houses when the King's Men went on tour; otherwise, his plays from 1599 to 1608 were, so far as we know, performed only at the Globe. Between 1608 and 1612, Shakespeare wrote several plays—among them *The Winter's Tale* and *The Tempest*—presumably for the company's new indoor Blackfriars theater, though the plays were performed also at the Globe and at court. Surviving documents describe a performance of *The Winter's Tale* in 1611 at the Globe, for example, and performances of *The Tempest* in 1611 and 1613 at the royal palace of Whitehall.

Shakespeare seems to have written very little after 1612, the year in which he probably wrote *King Henry VIII.* (It was at a performance of *Henry VIII* in 1613 that the Globe caught fire and burned to the ground.) Sometime between 1610 and 1613, according to many biographers, he returned to live in Stratford-upon-Avon, where he owned a large house and considerable property, and where his wife and his two daughters lived. (His son Hamnet had died in 1596.) However, other biographers suggest that Shakespeare did not leave London for good until much closer to the time of his death. During his professional years in London, Shakespeare had presumably derived income from the acting company's profits as well as from his own career as an actor, from the sale of his play manuscripts to the acting company, and, after 1599, from his shares as an owner of the Globe. It was presumably that income, carefully invested in land and other property, that made him the wealthy man that surviving documents show him to have become. It is also assumed that William Shakespeare's growing wealth and reputation played some part in inclining the Crown, in 1596, to grant John Shakespeare, William's father, the coat of arms that he had so long sought. William Shakespeare died in Stratford on April 23, 1616 (according to the epitaph carved under his bust in Holy Trinity Church) and was buried on April 25. Seven years after his death, his collected plays were published as *Mr. William Shakespeares Comedies, Histories, & Tragedies* (the work now known as the First Folio).

The years in which Shakespeare wrote were among the most exciting in English history. Intellectually, the discovery, translation, and printing of Greek and Roman classics were making available a set of works and worldviews that interacted complexly with Christian texts and beliefs. The result was a questioning, a vital intellectual ferment, that provided energy for the period's amazing dramatic and literary output and that fed directly into Shakespeare's plays. The Ghost in *Hamlet,* for example, is wonderfully complicated in part because he is a figure from Roman tragedy— the spirit of the dead returning to seek revenge—who at the same time inhabits a Christian hell (or purgatory); Hamlet's description of humankind reflects at one moment the Neoplatonic wonderment at mankind ("What a piece of work is a man!") and, at the next, the Christian view of the human condition ("And yet, to me, what is this quintessence of dust?").

As intellectual horizons expanded, so also did geographical and cosmological horizons. New worlds—

Ptolemaic universe.
From Marcus Manilius, *The sphere of* . . . (1675).

both North and South America—were explored, and in them were found human beings who lived and worshipped in ways radically different from those of Renaissance Europeans and Englishmen. The universe during these years also seemed to shift and expand. Copernicus had earlier theorized that the Earth was not the center of the cosmos but revolved as a planet around the sun. Galileo's telescope, created in 1609, allowed scientists to see that Copernicus had been correct: the universe was not organized with the Earth at the center, nor was it so nicely circumscribed as people had, until that time, thought. In terms of expanding horizons, the impact of these discoveries on people's beliefs—religious, scientific, and philosophical—cannot be overstated.

London, too, rapidly expanded and changed during the years (from the early 1590s to 1610 or somewhat later) that Shakespeare lived there. London—the center of England's government, its economy, its royal court, its overseas trade—was, during these years, becoming an exciting metropolis, drawing to it thousands of new citizens every year. Troubled by overcrowding, by poverty, by recurring epidemics of the plague, London was also a mecca for the wealthy and the aristocratic, and for those who sought advancement at court, or power in government or finance or trade. One hears in Shakespeare's plays the voices of London—the struggles for power, the fear of venereal disease, the language of buying and selling. One hears as well the voices of Stratford-upon-Avon—references to the nearby Forest of Arden, to sheepherding, to small-town gossip, to village fairs and markets. Part of the richness of Shakespeare's work is the influence felt there of the various worlds in which he lived: the world of metropolitan London, the world of small-town and rural England, the world of the theater, and the worlds of craftsmen and shepherds.

That Shakespeare inhabited such worlds we know from surviving London and Stratford documents, as well as from the evidence of the plays and poems themselves. From such records we can sketch the dramatist's life. We know from his works that he was a voracious reader. We know from legal and business documents that he was a multifaceted theater man who became a wealthy landowner. We know a bit about his family life and a fair amount about his legal and financial dealings. Most scholars today depend upon such evidence as they draw their picture of the world's greatest playwright. Such, however, has not always been the case. Until the late eighteenth century, the William Shakespeare who lived in most biographies was the creation of legend and tradition. This was the Shakespeare who was supposedly caught poaching deer at Charlecote, the estate of Sir Thomas Lucy close by Stratford; this was the Shakespeare who fled from Sir Thomas's vengeance and made his way in London by taking care of horses outside a playhouse; this was the Shakespeare who reportedly could barely read, but whose natural gifts were extraordinary, whose father was a butcher who allowed his gifted son sometimes to help in the butcher shop, where William supposedly killed calves "in a high style," making a speech for the occasion. It was this legendary William Shakespeare whose Falstaff (in *1* and *2 Henry IV*) so pleased Queen Elizabeth that she demanded a play about Falstaff in love, and demanded that it be written in fourteen days (hence the existence of *The Merry Wives of Windsor*). It was this legendary Shakespeare who reached the top of his acting career in the roles of the Ghost in *Hamlet* and old Adam in *As You Like It*—and who died of a fever con-

tracted by drinking too hard at "a merry meeting" with
the poets Michael Drayton and Ben Jonson. This legendary Shakespeare is a rambunctious, undisciplined
man, as attractively "wild" as his plays were seen by
earlier generations to be. Unfortunately, there is no
trace of evidence to support these wonderful stories.

Perhaps in response to the disreputable Shakespeare of legend—or perhaps in response to the fragmentary and, for some, all-too-ordinary Shakespeare
documented by surviving records—some people since
the mid-nineteenth century have argued that William
Shakespeare could not have written the plays that bear
his name. These persons have put forward some dozen
names as more likely authors, among them Queen
Elizabeth, Sir Francis Bacon, Edward de Vere (earl of
Oxford), and Christopher Marlowe. Such attempts to
find what for these people is a more believable author
of the plays is a tribute to the regard in which the plays
are held. Unfortunately for their claims, the documents
that exist that provide evidence for the facts of Shakespeare's life tie him inextricably to the body of plays
and poems that bear his name. Unlikely as it seems
to those who want the works to have been written by
an aristocrat, a university graduate, or an "important"
person, the plays and poems seem clearly to have been
produced by a man from Stratford-upon-Avon with a
very good "grammar-school" education and a life of
experience in London and in the world of the London theater. How this particular man produced the
works that dominate the cultures of much of the world
more than four hundred years after his death is one of
life's mysteries—and one that will continue to tease our
imaginations as we continue to delight in his plays and
poems.

Shakespeare's Theater

The actors of Shakespeare's time are known to have performed plays in a great variety of locations. They played at court (that is, in the great halls of such royal residences as Whitehall, Hampton Court, and Greenwich); they played in halls at the universities of Oxford and Cambridge, and at the Inns of Court (the residences in London of the legal societies); and they also played in the private houses of great lords and civic officials. Sometimes acting companies went on tour from London into the provinces, often (but not only) when outbreaks of bubonic plague in the capital forced the closing of theaters to reduce the possibility of contagion in crowded audiences. In the provinces the actors usually staged their plays in churches (until around 1600), in guildhalls, or in the great houses of individual patrons. While surviving records show only a handful of occasions when actors played at inns while on tour, London inns were important playing places up until the 1590s.

The building of theaters in London had begun only shortly before Shakespeare wrote his first plays in the 1590s. These theaters were of two kinds: outdoor or public playhouses that could accommodate large numbers of playgoers, and indoor or private theaters for much smaller audiences. What is usually regarded as the first London outdoor public playhouse was called simply the Theatre. James Burbage—the father of Richard Burbage, who was perhaps the most famous actor in Shakespeare's company—built it in 1576 in an area north of the city of London called Shoreditch. Among the more famous of the other public playhouses that capitalized on the new fashion were the Curtain and

A stylized representation of the Globe theater.
From Claes Jansz Visscher, *Londinum florentissima
Britanniae urbs* ... [c. 1625].

the Fortune (both also built north of the city), the Rose, the Swan, the Globe, and the Hope (all located on the Bankside, a region just across the Thames south of the city of London). All these playhouses had to be built outside the jurisdiction of the city of London because many civic officials were hostile to the performance of drama and repeatedly petitioned the royal council to abolish it.

The theaters erected on the Bankside (a region under the authority of the Church of England, whose head was the monarch) shared the neighborhood with houses of prostitution and with the Paris Garden, where the blood sports of bearbaiting and bullbaiting were carried on. There may have been no clear distinction between playhouses and buildings for such sports, for we know that the Hope was used for both plays and baiting and that Philip Henslowe, owner of the Rose and, later, partner in the ownership of the Fortune, was also a partner in a monopoly on baiting. All these forms of entertainment were easily accessible to Londoners by boat across the Thames or over London Bridge.

Evidently Shakespeare's company prospered on the Bankside. They moved there in 1599. Threatened by difficulties in renewing the lease on the land where their first theater (the Theatre) had been built, Shakespeare's company took advantage of the Christmas holiday in 1598 to dismantle the Theatre and transport its timbers across the Thames to the Bankside, where, in 1599, these timbers were used in the building of the Globe. The weather in late December 1598 is recorded as having been especially harsh. It was so cold that the Thames was "nigh [nearly] frozen," and there was heavy snow. Perhaps the weather aided Shakespeare's company in eluding their landlord, the snow hiding their activity and the freezing of the Thames allowing them to slide the timbers across to the Bankside without paying tolls for repeated trips over London Bridge. Attractive as this narrative is, it remains just as likely that the heavy snow hampered transport of the timbers in wagons through the London streets to the river. It also must be remembered that the Thames was, according to report, only "nigh frozen," and therefore did not necessarily provide solid footing. Whatever the precise circumstances of this fascinating event in English theater history, Shakespeare's company was able to begin playing at their new Globe theater on the Bankside in 1599. After this theater burned down in 1613 during the staging of Shakespeare's *Henry VIII* (its thatch roof set alight by cannon fire called for in performance), Shakespeare's company immediately rebuilt on the same location. The second Globe seems to have been a grander structure than its predecessor. It remained in use until 1642, when Parliament officially closed the theaters. Soon thereafter it was pulled down.

The public theaters of Shakespeare's time were very different buildings from our theaters today. First of all, they were open-air playhouses. As recent excavations of the Rose and the Globe confirm, some were polygonal or roughly circular in shape; the Fortune, however, was square. The most recent estimates of their size put the diameter of these buildings at 72 feet (the Rose) to 100 feet (the Globe), but we know that they held vast audiences of two or three thousand, who must have been squeezed together quite tightly. Some of these spectators paid extra to sit or stand in the two or three levels of roofed galleries that extended, on the upper levels, all the way around the theater and surrounded an open space. In this space were the stage and, perhaps, the tiring house (what we would call dressing rooms), as well as the so-called yard. In the yard stood the spectators who chose to pay less, the ones whom Hamlet contemptuously called "groundlings." For a roof they had only the sky, and so they were exposed to all kinds of weather. They stood on a floor that was sometimes made of mortar and sometimes of ash mixed with the shells of hazelnuts, which, it has recently been discovered, were standard flooring material in the period.

Unlike the yard, the stage itself was covered by a roof. Its ceiling, called "the heavens," is thought to have been elaborately painted to depict the sun, moon, stars, and planets. The exact size of the stage remains hard to determine. We have a single sketch of part of the interior of the Swan. A Dutchman named Johannes de Witt visited this theater around 1596 and sent a sketch of it back to his friend, Arend van Buchel. Because van Buchel found de Witt's letter and sketch of interest, he copied both into a book. It is van Buchel's copy, adapted, it seems, to the shape and size of the page in his book, that survives. In this sketch, the stage appears to be a large rectangular platform that thrusts far out into the yard, perhaps even as far as the center of the circle formed by the surrounding galleries. This drawing, combined with the specifications for the size of the stage in the building contract for the Fortune, has led scholars to conjecture that the stage on which Shakespeare's plays were performed must have measured approximately 43 feet in width and 27 feet in depth, a vast acting area. But the digging up of a large part of the Rose by late twentieth-century archaeologists has provided evidence of a quite different stage design. The Rose stage was a platform tapered at the corners and much shallower than what seems to be depicted in the van Buchel sketch. Indeed, its measurements seem to be about 37.5 feet across at its widest point and only 15.5 feet deep. Because the surviving indications of stage size and design differ from each other so much, it is possible that the stages in other theaters, like the Theatre, the Curtain, and the Globe (the outdoor playhouses where we know that Shakespeare's plays were performed), were different from those at both the Swan and the Rose.

After about 1608 Shakespeare's plays were staged not only at the Globe but also at an indoor or private playhouse in Blackfriars. This theater had been constructed in 1596 by James Burbage in an upper hall of a former Dominican priory or monastic house. Although Henry VIII had dissolved all English monasteries in the 1530s (shortly after he had founded the Church of England), the area remained under church, rather than hostile civic, control. The hall that Burbage had purchased and renovated was a large one in which Parliament had once met. In the private theater that he constructed, the stage, lit by candles, was built across the narrow end of the hall, with boxes flanking it. The rest of the hall offered seating room only. Because there was no provision for standing room, the largest audience it could hold was less than a thousand, or about a quarter of what the Globe could accommodate. Admission to Blackfriars was correspondingly more expensive. Instead of a penny to stand in the yard at the Globe, it cost a minimum of sixpence to get into Blackfriars. The best seats at the Globe (in the Lords' Room in the gallery above and behind the stage) cost sixpence; but the boxes flanking the stage at Blackfriars were half a crown, or five times sixpence. Some spectators who were particularly interested in displaying themselves paid even more to sit on stools on the Blackfriars stage.

Whether in the outdoor or indoor playhouses, the stages of Shakespeare's time were different from ours. They were not separated from the audience by the dropping of a curtain between acts and scenes. Therefore the playwrights of the time had to find other ways of signaling to the audience that one scene (to be imagined as occurring in one location at a given time) had ended and the next (to be imagined at perhaps a different location at a later time) had begun. The customary way used by Shakespeare and many of his contemporaries was to have everyone on stage exit at the end of one scene and have one or more different characters enter to begin the next. In a few cases, where characters remain onstage from one scene to another, the dialogue or stage action makes the change of location clear, and the characters are generally to be imagined as having moved from one place to another. For example, in *Romeo and Juliet,* Romeo and his friends remain onstage in Act 1 from scene 4 to scene 5, but they are represented as having moved between scenes from the street that leads to Capulet's house into Capulet's house itself. The new location is signaled in part by the appearance onstage of Capulet's servingmen carrying table napkins, something they would not take into the streets. Playwrights had to be quite resourceful in the use of hand properties, like the napkin, or in the use of dialogue to specify where the action was taking place in their plays because, in contrast to most of today's theaters, the playhouses of Shakespeare's time did not fill the stage with scenery to make the setting precise. A consequence of this difference was that the playwrights of Shakespeare's time did not have to specify exactly where the action of their plays was set when they did not choose to do so, and much of the action of their plays is tied to no specific place.

Usually Shakespeare's stage is referred to as a "bare stage," to distinguish it from the stages of the past two or three centuries with their elaborate sets. But the stage in Shakespeare's time was not completely bare. Philip Henslowe, owner of the Rose, lists in his inventory of stage properties a rock, three tombs, and two mossy banks. Stage directions in plays of the time also call for such things as thrones (or "states"), banquets (presumably tables with plaster replicas of food on them), and beds and tombs to be pushed onto the stage. Thus the stage often held more than the actors.

The actors did not limit their performing to the stage alone. Occasionally they went beneath the stage, as the Ghost appears to do in the first act of *Hamlet.* From there they could emerge onto the stage through a trapdoor. They could retire behind the hangings across the back of the stage, as, for example, the actor playing Polonius does when he hides behind the arras. Sometimes the hangings could be drawn back during a performance to "discover" one or more actors behind them. When performance required that an actor appear "above," as when Juliet is imagined to stand at the window of her chamber in the famous and misnamed "balcony scene," then the actor probably climbed the stairs to the gallery over the back of the stage and temporarily shared it with some of the spectators. The stage was also provided with ropes and winches so that actors could descend from, and reascend to, the "heavens."

Perhaps the greatest difference between dramatic performances in Shakespeare's time and ours was that in Shakespeare's England the roles of women were played by boys. (Some of these boys grew up to take male roles in their maturity.) There were no women in the acting companies. It was not so in Europe, and it had not always been so in the history of the English stage. There are records of women on English stages in the thirteenth and fourteenth centuries, two hundred years before Shakespeare's plays were performed. After the accession of James I in 1603, the queen of England and her ladies took part in entertainments at court called masques, and with the reopening of the theaters in 1660 at the restoration of Charles II, women again took their place on the public stage.

The chief competitors of such acting companies as the one to which Shakespeare belonged and for which he wrote were companies of exclusively boy actors. The competition was most intense in the early 1600s. There were then two principal children's companies: the Children of Paul's (the choirboys from St. Paul's Cathedral, whose private playhouse was near the cathedral), and the Children of the Chapel Royal (the choirboys from the monarch's private chapel, who performed at the Blackfriars theater built by Burbage in 1596). In *Hamlet* Shakespeare writes of "an aerie [nest] of children, little eyases [hawks], that cry out on the top of question and are most tyrannically clapped for 't. These are now the fashion and . . . berattle the common stages [attack the public theaters]." In the long run, the adult actors prevailed. The Children of Paul's dissolved around 1606. By about 1608 the Children of the Chapel Royal had been forced to stop playing at the Blackfriars theater, which was then taken over by the King's Men, Shakespeare's own troupe.

Acting companies and theaters of Shakespeare's time seem to have been organized in various ways. For example, with the building of the Globe, Shakespeare's company apparently managed itself, with the principal actors, Shakespeare among them, having the status of "sharers" and the right to a share in the takings, as well as the responsibility for a part of the expenses. Five of the sharers, including Shakespeare, owned the Globe. As actor, as sharer in an acting company and in ownership of theaters, and as playwright, Shakespeare was about as involved in the theatrical industry as one could imagine. Although Shakespeare and his fellows prospered, their status under the law was conditional upon the protection of powerful patrons. "Common players"—those who did not have patrons or masters—were classed in the language of the law with "vagabonds and sturdy beggars." So the actors had to secure for themselves the official rank of servants of patrons. Among the patrons under whose protection Shakespeare's company worked were the lord chamberlain and, after the accession of King James in 1603, the king himself.

In the early 1990s we began to learn a great deal more about the theaters in which Shakespeare and his contemporaries performed—or, at least, began to open up new questions about them. At that time about 70 percent of the Rose had been excavated, as had about 10 percent of the second Globe, the one built in 1614. Excavation was halted at that point, but London has come to value the sites of its early playhouses, and takes what opportunities it can to explore them more deeply, both on the Bankside and in Shoreditch. Information about the playhouses of Shakespeare's London is therefore a constantly changing resource.

The Publication of Shakespeare's Plays

Eighteen of Shakespeare's plays found their way into print during the playwright's lifetime, but there is nothing to suggest that he took any interest in their publication. These eighteen appeared separately in editions in quarto or, in the case of *Henry VI, Part 3*, octavo format. The quarto pages are not much larger than a modern mass-market paperback book, and the octavo pages are even smaller; these little books were sold unbound for a few pence. The earliest of the quartos that still survive were printed in 1594, the year that both *Titus Andronicus* and a version of the play now called *Henry VI, Part 2* became available. While almost every one of these early quartos displays on its title page the name of the acting company that performed the play, only about half provide the name of the playwright, Shakespeare. The first quarto edition to bear the name Shakespeare on its title page is *Love's Labor's Lost* of 1598. A few of the quartos were popular with the book-buying public of Shakespeare's lifetime; for example, quarto *Richard II* went through five editions between 1597 and 1615. But most of the quartos were far from best sellers; *Love's Labor's Lost* (1598), for instance, was not reprinted in quarto until 1631. After Shakespeare's death, two more of his plays appeared in quarto format: *Othello* in 1622 and *The Two Noble Kinsmen*, coauthored with John Fletcher, in 1634.

In 1623, seven years after Shakespeare's death, *Mr. William Shakespeares Comedies, Histories, & Tragedies* was published. This printing offered readers in a single book thirty-six of the thirty-eight plays now

thought to have been written by Shakespeare, including eighteen that had never been printed before. And
it offered them in a style that was then reserved for
serious literature and scholarship. The plays were
arranged in double columns on pages nearly a foot
high. This large page size is called "folio," as opposed
to the smaller "quarto," and the 1623 volume is usually called the Shakespeare First Folio. It is reputed to
have sold for the lordly price of a pound. (One copy
at the Folger Shakespeare Library is marked fifteen
shillings—that is, three-quarters of a pound.)

In a preface to the First Folio titled "To the great
Variety of Readers," two of Shakespeare's former fellow actors in the King's Men, John Heminge and Henry
Condell, wrote that they themselves had collected their
dead companion's plays. They suggested that they had
seen his own papers: "we have scarce received from
him a blot in his papers." The title page of the Folio
declared that the plays within it had been printed
"according to the True Original Copies." Comparing the
Folio to the quartos, Heminge and Condell disparaged
the quartos, advising their readers that "before you
were abused with divers stolen and surreptitious copies, maimed, and deformed by the frauds and stealths
of injurious impostors." Many Shakespeareans of the
eighteenth and nineteenth centuries believed Heminge
and Condell and regarded the Folio plays as superior to
anything in the quartos.

Once we begin to examine the Folio plays in detail,
it becomes less easy to take at face value the word of
Heminge and Condell about the superiority of the
Folio texts. For example, of the first nine plays in the
Folio (one-quarter of the entire collection), four were
essentially reprinted from earlier quarto printings that
Heminge and Condell had disparaged, and four have
now been identified as printed from copies written in

the hand of a professional scribe of the 1620s named Ralph Crane; the ninth, *The Comedy of Errors*, was apparently also printed from a manuscript, but one whose origin cannot be readily identified. Evidently, then, eight of the first nine plays in the First Folio were not printed, in spite of what the Folio title page announces, "according to the True Original Copies," or Shakespeare's own papers, and the source of the ninth is unknown. Since today's editors have been forced to treat Heminge and Condell's pronouncements with skepticism, they must choose whether to base their own editions upon quartos or the Folio on grounds other than Heminge and Condell's story of where the quarto and Folio versions originated.

Editors have often fashioned their own narratives to explain what lies behind the quartos and Folio. They have said that Heminge and Condell meant to criticize only a few of the early quartos, the ones that offer much shorter and sometimes quite different, often garbled, versions of plays. Among the examples of these are the 1600 quarto of *Henry V* (the Folio offers a much fuller version) or the 1603 *Hamlet* quarto. (In 1604 a different, much longer form of the play got into print as a quarto.) Early twentieth-century editors and some scholars in the present century have speculated that these questionable texts were produced when someone in the audience took notes from the plays' dialogue during performances and then employed "hack poets" to fill out the notes. The poor results were then sold to a publisher and presented in print as Shakespeare's plays. For much of the twentieth century this story gave way to another in which the shorter versions are said to be re-creations from memory of Shakespeare's plays by actors who wanted to stage them in the provinces but lacked manuscript copies. Most of the quartos offer much better texts than these so-called bad quartos. Indeed, in most of the quartos we find texts that are at least equal to or better than what is printed in the Folio. Many Shakespeare enthusiasts persuaded themselves that most of the quartos were set into type directly from Shakespeare's own papers, although there is nothing on which to base this conclusion except the desire for it to be true. Thus speculation continues about how the Shakespeare plays got to be printed. All that we have are the printed texts.

The book collector who was most successful in bringing together copies of the quartos and the First Folio was Henry Clay Folger, founder of the Folger Shakespeare Library in Washington, D.C. While it is estimated that there survive around the world only about 230 copies of the First Folio, Mr. Folger was able to acquire more than seventy-five copies, as well as a large number of fragments, for the library that bears his name. He also amassed a substantial number of quartos. For example, only fourteen copies of the First Quarto of *Love's Labor's Lost* are known to exist, and three are at the Folger Shakespeare Library. As a consequence of Mr. Folger's labors, scholars visiting the Folger Shakespeare Library have been able to learn a great deal about sixteenth- and seventeenth-century printing and, particularly, about the printing of Shakespeare's plays. And Mr. Folger did not stop at the First Folio, but collected many copies of later editions of Shakespeare, beginning with the Second Folio (1632), the Third (1663–64), and the Fourth (1685). Each of these later folios was based on its immediate predecessor and was edited anonymously. The first editor of Shakespeare whose name we know was Nicholas Rowe, whose first edition came out in 1709. Mr. Folger collected this edition and many, many more by Rowe's successors, and the collecting and scholarship continue.

An Introduction to This Text

The play we call *The Life of Henry V* was printed in two quite different versions in the first quarter of the seventeenth century.

The first version appeared in 1600 as *The Cronicle History of Henry the fift, With his battell fought at Agin Court in France. Togither with Auntient Pistoll. As it hath bene sundry times playd by the Right honorable the Lord Chamberlaine his seruants*. This printing was a quarto or pocket-size book known today as "Q1." Q1 differs extensively from the play familiar to modern readers: it is only about half as long; it omits whole scenes and all the choruses; and it prints some scenes in a different order. A striking difference is the fact that the Duke of Bourbon, rather than the Dauphin, appears in the scenes set at Agincourt. Twentieth-century textual critics and editors usually dubbed Q1 a "bad quarto" but nonetheless, as will be noticed shortly, tried to make use of it in preparing editions of the play. Q1 was reprinted first in 1602 (as "Q2"), with no remarkable changes. Its second reprinting, in 1619 (as "Q3"), is unusual: first, because as one of the so-called Pavier Quartos, Q3 is misdated 1608; and, second, because it contains a handful of departures from Q1 that seem beyond the skill of a typesetter to introduce. These new readings in Q3 anticipate what is printed in the Folio version of 1623 and have given rise to editorial conjecture that either during the typesetting of the Folio its printers consulted Q3 or that the printers of Q3 had access to a manuscript that in some respects resembled the one used to print the Folio. Neither explanation is convincing, and the source of the Q3 readings in question remains a mystery.

The second version of the play, the one in the Folio of 1623, is titled simply *The Life of Henry the Fift*. It was printed from a manuscript containing a much fuller text of the play than the manuscript used for Q1.

Throughout the editorial tradition, editions of the play have been based on the Folio. In the latter half of the twentieth century, it was even widely assumed that the Folio version is based directly on Shakespeare's own manuscript. In contrast, Q1 was said to reproduce an abridged version put together from memory by actors who had roles in the play as it was performed outside London. A few recent editors were so convinced of the truth of such stories about Q1 as to depend on it for a record of what was acted. These editors, for example, not only incorporated into their editions as many lines unique to Q1 as can be managed, but also substituted Q1 variants in dialogue and stage directions for their Folio counterparts, replacing, for example, the Folio's Dauphin with Q1's Bourbon in the Agincourt scenes. Nevertheless, as today's scholars reexamine the narratives about the origins of the printed texts, we discover that these narratives are based either on questionable evidence or sometimes on none at all, and we become more skeptical about ever identifying how the play assumed the forms in which it came to be printed.

The present edition is based upon a fresh examination of the early printed texts, rather than upon any modern edition.* It offers its readers the Folio printing of *Henry V.* But it offers an *edition* of the Folio because it prints such editorial changes and such readings from other early printed versions as are, in the editors' judgment, needed to repair what may be errors and defi-

_____

*We have also consulted a computerized text of the First Folio provided by the Text Archive of the Oxford University Computing Centre, to which we are grateful.

ciencies in the Folio. Except for occasional readings, this edition excludes Q1 from its text because Q1 is, for the most part, so widely different from the Folio. However, when there has been editorial agreement about incorporating a line from Q1 into the Folio version, that line (and an accompanying discussion) is printed in the explanatory notes.

In this edition, whenever we change the wording of the Folio or add anything to its stage directions, we mark the change by enclosing it in superior half brackets ($\ulcorner$ $\urcorner$). We want our readers to be immediately aware when we have intervened. (Only when we correct an obvious typographical error in the Folio does the change not get marked.) Whenever we change either the Folio's wording or its punctuation so that meaning changes, we list the change in the textual notes at the back of the book, even if all we have done is fix an obvious error.

One major exception to this editorial policy is the French dialogue that is so extensive in *Henry V*, a feature that makes this play unique among plays attributed to Shakespeare. The quality of the French is very poor in the Folio (and a great deal worse in Q1). To mark every correction of this French would be to litter pages of the play with brackets, and so we have corrected it silently. The Folio's French may be studied in the textual notes, which often include (in an appendix) whole speeches and even one whole scene. We have corrected the French of the characters who, in the play's fiction, are native French speakers much more heavily than that of nonnative speakers, who appear to be given deliberately fractured French. However, without departing widely from the Folio, we have found it impossible to reduce to standard French even all the dialogue of the fictional native speakers. We therefore retain some of the mistakes in French that mark the

Folio; these seem to indicate that no one involved in preparing this play, Shakespeare included, knew how to write French very well.

For the convenience of the reader, we have generally modernized the punctuation and the spelling of the Folio. Sometimes we go so far as to modernize certain old forms of words; for example, when *a* means "he," we change it to *he;* we change *mo* to *more* and *ye* to *you.* But it is not our practice in editing any of the plays to modernize words that sound distinctly different from modern forms. For example, when the early printed texts read *sith* or *apricocks* or *porpentine,* we have not modernized to *since, apricots, porcupine.* When the forms *an, and,* or *and if* appear instead of the modern form *if,* we have reduced *and* to *an* but have not changed any of these forms to their modern equivalent, *if.*

We correct or regularize a large number of proper names, especially French ones, as is the usual practice in editions of the play. For example, the Folio's spelling "Britaine" becomes "Brittany"; "Dolphin" becomes "Dauphin"; "Harflew" becomes "Harfleur," and "Calis" "Calais"; there are many other comparable adjustments in the names.

This edition differs from many earlier ones in its efforts to aid the reader in imagining the play as a performance. Thus stage directions are written with reference to the stage, except in cases where the stage directions of the Folio (which was and is a book designed to be read rather than acted) refer to the fictional circumstances of the play rather than to its staging. In those cases, we retain the Folio's stage direction. For example, 3.3 opens in the Folio with the stage direction *"Enter the King and all his Traine before the Gates."* In the fiction of the play, the "Gates" are the town gates of Harfleur, but these, almost certainly, would not have been replicated on the stage of

Shakespeare's time. Even though this Folio direction has no reference to the stage, we keep it, but we do not embellish it (as is done in many editions) by adding to it town walls with citizens standing on top of them.

Whenever it is reasonably certain, in our view, that a speech is accompanied by a particular action, we provide a stage direction describing the action. (Occasional exceptions to this rule occur when the action is so obvious that to add a stage direction would insult the reader.) Stage directions for the entrance of characters in mid-scene are, with rare exceptions, placed so that they immediately precede the characters' participation in the scene, even though these entrances may appear somewhat earlier in the early printed texts. Whenever we move a stage direction, we record this change in the textual notes. Latin stage directions (e.g., *Exeunt*) are translated into English (e.g., *They exit*).

We expand the often severely abbreviated forms of names used as speech headings in early printed texts into the full names of the characters. We also regularize the speakers' names in speech headings, using only a single designation for each character, even though the early printed texts sometimes use a variety of designations. Variations in the speech headings of the early printed texts are recorded in the textual notes.

In the present edition, as well, we mark with a dash any change of address within a speech, unless a stage direction intervenes. When the *-ed* ending of a word is to be pronounced, we mark it with an accent. Like editors for the past two centuries, we print metrically linked lines in the following way:

BISHOP OF ELY
     This would drink deep.
BISHOP OF CANTERBURY   'Twould drink the cup
     and all.

However, when there are a number of short verse lines that can be linked in more than one way, we do not, with rare exceptions, indent any of them.

The Explanatory Notes

The notes that appear on the pages facing the text are designed to provide readers with the help that they may need to enjoy the play. Whenever the meaning of a word in the text is not readily accessible in a good contemporary dictionary, we offer the meaning in a note. Sometimes we provide a note even when the relevant meaning is to be found in the dictionary but when the word has acquired since Shakespeare's time other potentially confusing meanings. In our notes, we try to offer modern synonyms for Shakespeare's words. We also try to indicate to the reader the connection between the word in the play and the modern synonym. For example, Shakespeare sometimes uses the word *head* to mean "source," but, for modern readers, there may be no connection evident between these two words. We provide the connection by explaining Shakespeare's usage as follows: "**head:** fountainhead, source." On some occasions, a whole phrase or clause needs explanation. Then, if space allows, we rephrase in our own words the difficult passage, and add at the end synonyms for individual words in the passage. When scholars have been unable to determine the meaning of a word or phrase, we acknowledge the uncertainty. Unless otherwise noted, biblical quotations are from the Geneva Bible (1560), with spelling modernized.

The Life of

HENRY V

The Line of Edward III

[Characters in *Henry V* appear in bold]

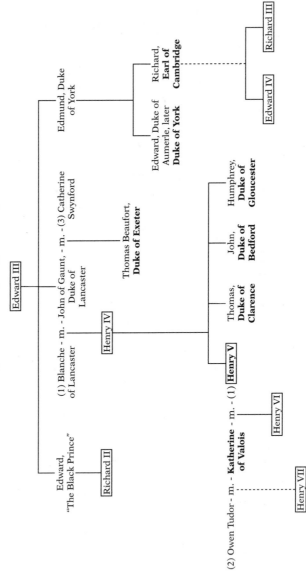

Characters in the Play

CHORUS

HENRY V, KING OF ENGLAND

THOMAS, DUKE OF EXETER, uncle to the King

HUMPHREY, DUKE OF GLOUCESTER
JOHN, DUKE OF BEDFORD
THOMAS, DUKE OF CLARENCE
} *brothers to the King*

DUKE OF YORK
EARL OF WESTMORELAND
EARL OF CAMBRIDGE
} *cousins to the King*

EARL OF WARWICK
EARL OF SALISBURY
EARL OF HUNTINGTON
LORD SCROOP OF MASHAM
SIR THOMAS GREY
} *English nobles*

HOSTESS QUICKLY

PISTOL
NYM
BARDOLPH
} *former companions of Henry, now in his army*
BOY, their servant

SIR THOMAS ERPINGHAM
CAPTAIN FLUELLEN
CAPTAIN GOWER
CAPTAIN MACMORRIS
CAPTAIN JAMY
} *officers in Henry's army*

3

English heralds

JOHN BATES
ALEXANDER COURT ⎫ *soldiers in Henry's army*
MICHAEL WILLIAMS ⎭

BISHOP OF CANTERBURY
BISHOP OF ELY

KING OF FRANCE
QUEEN ISABEL OF FRANCE
KATHERINE, Princess of France
ALICE, a gentlewoman attending on Katherine
DAUPHIN (i.e., Prince) of France

DUKE OF BERRI
DUKE OF BRITTANY
DUKE OF ORLÉANS
DUKE OF BOURBON
DUKE OF BURGUNDY   *French nobles*
CONSTABLE OF FRANCE
LORD GRANDPRÉ
LORD RAMBURES
LORD BEAUMONT

MONTJOY, French herald
French ambassadors to England

MONSIEUR LE FER, a French soldier

Governor of Harfleur

Lords, Attendants, Soldiers, French Prisoners, Messengers

The Life of

HENRY V

ACT 1

Prologue. The Chorus wishes for a far greater stage, actors, and audience. He apologizes for the scanty resources that are available and urges the audience to use its imagination to make up for them.

---

0 SD. **Chorus:** a character who tells the audience what they are about to see, or who comments on the action

1. **a muse:** an inspiring goddess (In mythology, the Muses were nine sister-goddesses who preside over the arts and sciences.) **fire:** the element that rose highest above the other elements of earth, water, and air

2. **invention:** inventiveness, creativity

3. **A kingdom for a stage:** i.e., I wish we had a whole **kingdom** as our **stage**

4. **swelling:** stately, majestic

5. **like himself:** i.e., represented in a fashion worthy of him

6. **port:** bearing; **Mars:** the Roman god of war (See picture, page 114.)

9. **for employment:** ready to do service; **gentles:** i.e., ladies and gentlemen (a polite, perhaps ingratiating, address to the audience)

10. **flat unraisèd:** dull, lifeless (in contrast to the **muse of fire** [line 1]); **spirits:** i.e., actors and, perhaps, their playwright; **hath:** i.e., have

11. **scaffold:** platform, stage

12. **object:** sight, spectacle; **cockpit:** the open space (including the stage) enclosed by the theater's

(continued)

PROLOGUE

Enter ⌜Chorus as⌝ Prologue.

⌜CHORUS⌝
  O, for a muse of fire that would ascend
  The brightest heaven of invention!
  A kingdom for a stage, princes to act,
  And monarchs to behold the swelling scene!
  Then should the warlike Harry, like himself,   5
  Assume the port of Mars, and at his heels,
  Leashed in like hounds, should famine, sword, and
     fire
  Crouch for employment. But pardon, gentles all,
  The flat unraisèd spirits that hath dared   10
  On this unworthy scaffold to bring forth
  So great an object. Can this cockpit hold
  The vasty fields of France? Or may we cram
  Within this wooden O the very casques
  That did affright the air at Agincourt?   15
  O pardon, since a crookèd figure may
  Attest in little place a million,
  And let us, ciphers to this great account,
  On your imaginary forces work.
  Suppose within the girdle of these walls   20
  Are now confined two mighty monarchies,
  Whose high uprearèd and abutting fronts

7

galleries (see "Shakespeare's Theater," pages xli–l); literally, a small pit used for cockfighting

13. **vasty:** i.e., vast

14. **wooden O:** i.e., theater (For the generally "round" shapes of the public theaters, see "Shakespeare's Theater," page xliv, and the picture on page xxxii.) **the very casques:** i.e., even the helmets (of the knights) See picture, page 54.

15. **Agincourt:** site of Henry's most famous battle

16–17. **a crookèd ... million:** i.e., a zero (or **cipher**), placed on the right in a number (100,000), may multiply the number even to the value of **a million   crookèd:** curved (i.e., round)

18. **account:** (1) sum; (2) story

19. **imaginary forces:** powers of imagination

22. **uprearèd:** erected; **abutting:** adjacent; **fronts:** (1) cliffs (of Dover and Calais); (2) frontiers

23. **narrow ocean:** i.e., English Channel

24. **Piece out:** extend with extra pieces

26. **puissance:** armed forces

29. **deck:** adorn

31. **times:** i.e., periods of time

32. **th' accomplishment of:** i.e., what was done in

33. **for ... supply:** i.e., for support in doing all this

34. **Admit me chorus to this history:** i.e., allow me to serve as commentator on this story

35. **your ... pray:** perhaps meaning "humbly **pray your patience**" (Andrew Gurr)

36. **Gently, kindly:** in a gentle, kind manner (with wordplay on *gentle* and *kind* as "well-born, gentlemanly")

The perilous narrow ocean parts asunder.
Piece out our imperfections with your thoughts.
Into a thousand parts divide one man,   25
And make imaginary puissance.
Think, when we talk of horses, that you see them
Printing their proud hoofs i' th' receiving earth,
For 'tis your thoughts that now must deck our
    kings,   30
Carry them here and there, jumping o'er times,
Turning th' accomplishment of many years
Into an hourglass; for the which supply,
Admit me chorus to this history,
Who, prologue-like, your humble patience pray   35
Gently to hear, kindly to judge our play.

                                      He exits.

1.1 The Bishop of Canterbury informs the Bishop of Ely of a bill threatening Church revenues and of a plan to postpone it by justifying King Henry's invasion of France to claim the French throne. Canterbury also reports his offer of a most generous contribution to the King to help finance the war.

---

0 SD. **Bishops:** To be historically accurate, the Folio should have given Canterbury the title "archbishop."

1. **self:** selfsame; **bill:** proposed act of Parliament
2. **th' eleventh . . . reign:** 1410
3. **like:** i.e., likely (to have passed)
4. **scambling:** contentious
5. **farther question:** further debate
8. **better:** i.e., greater; **our possession:** what we own
9–11. **For . . . valued thus:** i.e., they would take as much land bequeathed **to the Church** as would pay the following expenses   **temporal:** i.e., used for worldly, rather than spiritual, purposes
13. **Full:** i.e., no fewer than
14. **esquires:** gentry, just below the rank of knight
15. **to relief:** for the **relief; lazars:** lepers
16. **indigent:** poor; **faint souls:** weak people; **past:** no longer capable of; **corporal toil:** manual labor
17. **almshouses:** houses for the support or accommodation of the poor; **right:** properly

ACT 1

Scene 1
Enter the two Bishops of Canterbury and Ely.

BISHOP OF CANTERBURY
　My lord, I'll tell you that self bill is urged
　Which in th' eleventh year of the last king's reign
　Was like, and had indeed against us passed
　But that the scambling and unquiet time
　Did push it out of farther question.　　　　　5
BISHOP OF ELY
　But how, my lord, shall we resist it now?
BISHOP OF CANTERBURY
　It must be thought on. If it pass against us,
　We lose the better half of our possession,
　For all the temporal lands which men devout
　By testament have given to the Church　　　　10
　Would they strip from us, being valued thus:
　"As much as would maintain, to the King's honor,
　Full fifteen earls and fifteen hundred knights,
　Six thousand and two hundred good esquires;
　And, to relief of lazars and weak age　　　　15
　Of indigent faint souls past corporal toil,
　A hundred almshouses right well supplied;
　And to the coffers of the King besides,
　A thousand pounds by th' year." Thus runs the bill.

24. **grace:** virtue; or, perhaps, heaven's **grace; fair regard:** kindly purposes

26. **courses:** i.e., behavior (The story of Henry's wild youth is told in Shakespeare's *Henry IV, Parts 1* and *2*.)

28. **his:** i.e., Henry V's; **mortified:** brought under control

30. **Consideration:** (1) spiritual meditation; (2) thoughtfulness

31. **th' offending Adam:** i.e., original sin (literally, **Adam** after he had sinned in the garden of Eden, or **paradise**)

35. **reformation:** correction, improvement

36. **heady currance:** powerful flow

37. **Hydra-headed:** In mythology, the **Hydra** was a many-headed monster; when one head was cut off, two grew back. (See picture, page 164.)

38. **his:** i.e., its; **seat:** position of authority

41. **divinity:** theology

44. **commonwealth affairs:** i.e., public welfare

46. **List:** listen to

47. **fearful:** frightening

48. **cause of policy:** political concern

49. **Gordian knot:** in mythology, a knot that could not be untied because it was so intricately knotted (The Macedonian Alexander the Great, who conquered Asia in the fourth century B.C.E., according to legend cut through the knot with his sword. See picture, page 182.)

50. **Familiar:** i.e., as if it were **as familiar; that:** i.e., so that

BISHOP OF ELY
This would drink deep.   20
BISHOP OF CANTERBURY   'Twould drink the cup and
all.
BISHOP OF ELY   But what prevention?
BISHOP OF CANTERBURY
The King is full of grace and fair regard.
BISHOP OF ELY
And a true lover of the holy Church.   25
BISHOP OF CANTERBURY
The courses of his youth promised it not.
The breath no sooner left his father's body
But that his wildness, mortified in him,
Seemed to die too. Yea, at that very moment
Consideration like an angel came   30
And whipped th' offending Adam out of him,
Leaving his body as a paradise
T' envelop and contain celestial spirits.
Never was such a sudden scholar made,
Never came reformation in a flood   35
With such a heady currance scouring faults,
Nor never Hydra-headed willfulness
So soon did lose his seat, and all at once,
As in this king.
BISHOP OF ELY   We are blessèd in the change.   40
BISHOP OF CANTERBURY
Hear him but reason in divinity
And, all-admiring, with an inward wish
You would desire the King were made a prelate;
Hear him debate of commonwealth affairs,
You would say it hath been all in all his study;   45
List his discourse of war, and you shall hear
A fearful battle rendered you in music;
Turn him to any cause of policy,
The Gordian knot of it he will unloose
Familiar as his garter; that, when he speaks,   50

51. **a chartered libertine:** i.e., one licensed to go his own way

53. **sentences:** wise sayings

54–55. **art . . . theoric:** i.e., practical experience must have taught him theoretical discourse

56. **his Grace:** i.e., King Henry

57. **courses vain:** worthless behavior

58. **rude:** (1) uneducated; (2) unmannerly

59. **riots:** dissipation, extravagance

60. **And never:** i.e., and no one ever

61. **retirement, sequestration:** withdrawal

62. **open . . . popularity:** public places and people

63. **nettle:** i.e., weed

67. **which:** i.e., his contemplation

69. **crescive . . . faculty:** i.e., growing according to its own nature

70. **miracles are ceased:** i.e., God no longer performs **miracles**

71–72. **admit the means / How:** acknowledge the natural ways by which

72. **perfected:** accented on the first syllable

74. **How now for mitigation:** i.e., what can be done to reduce the severity

77. **indifferent:** impartial

78. **upon our part:** i.e., toward our side

79. **exhibitors:** i.e., sponsors of the bill

81. **Upon:** following upon; **spiritual convocation:** assembly of clergy

82. **in regard of:** with respect to; **causes now in hand:** matters now under discussion

83. **opened:** explained; **at large:** in general

84. **As touching:** concerning

The air, a chartered libertine, is still,
And the mute wonder lurketh in men's ears
To steal his sweet and honeyed sentences;
So that the art and practic part of life
Must be the mistress to this theoric;   55
Which is a wonder how his Grace should glean it,
Since his addiction was to courses vain,
His companies unlettered, rude, and shallow,
His hours filled up with riots, banquets, sports,
And never noted in him any study,   60
Any retirement, any sequestration
From open haunts and popularity.

BISHOP OF ELY
The strawberry grows underneath the nettle,
And wholesome berries thrive and ripen best
Neighbored by fruit of baser quality;   65
And so the Prince obscured his contemplation
Under the veil of wildness, which, no doubt,
Grew like the summer grass, fastest by night,
Unseen yet crescive in his faculty.

BISHOP OF CANTERBURY
It must be so, for miracles are ceased,   70
And therefore we must needs admit the means
How things are perfected.

BISHOP OF ELY   But, my good lord,
How now for mitigation of this bill
Urged by the Commons? Doth his Majesty   75
Incline to it or no?

BISHOP OF CANTERBURY   He seems indifferent,
Or rather swaying more upon our part
Than cherishing th' exhibitors against us;
For I have made an offer to his Majesty—   80
Upon our spiritual convocation
And in regard of causes now in hand,
Which I have opened to his Grace at large,
As touching France—to give a greater sum

86. **withal:** with
88. **of:** i.e., by
89. **Save:** except
90. **fain:** gladly
91. **severals:** particulars; **unhidden passages:** i.e., clear lines of descent
93. **seat:** throne
94. **Edward:** i.e., Edward III, whose mother, Isabella, was the daughter of Philip IV of France (Henry is thus a direct descendant of the French king Philip IV, but through the female line. See "Henry V's French Descent," page xvi.)
96. **ambassador:** official messenger
100. **his embassy:** the French ambassador's message
103. **wait upon:** attend

1.2 At the King's request, Canterbury provides an extensive interpretation of French law to support Henry's claim to the French throne. After the court discusses ways of preventing a Scottish invasion of England while Henry is in France, Henry decides to go to war against France. The French ambassadors present Henry with a token of the Dauphin's insulting refusal to take seriously Henry's claims in France.

———

Than ever at one time the clergy yet 85
Did to his predecessors part withal.

BISHOP OF ELY
How did this offer seem received, my lord?

BISHOP OF CANTERBURY
With good acceptance of his Majesty—
Save that there was not time enough to hear,
As I perceived his Grace would fain have done, 90
The severals and unhidden passages
Of his true titles to some certain dukedoms,
And generally to the crown and seat of France,
Derived from Edward, his great-grandfather.

BISHOP OF ELY
What was th' impediment that broke this off? 95

BISHOP OF CANTERBURY
The French ambassador upon that instant
Craved audience. And the hour, I think, is come
To give him hearing. Is it four o'clock?

BISHOP OF ELY   It is.

BISHOP OF CANTERBURY
Then go we in to know his embassy, 100
Which I could with a ready guess declare
Before the Frenchman speak a word of it.

BISHOP OF ELY
I'll wait upon you, and I long to hear it.

They exit.

⌜Scene 2⌝
Enter the King ⌜of England,⌝ Humphrey ⌜Duke of
Gloucester,⌝ Bedford, Clarence, Warwick, Westmoreland,
and Exeter, ⌜with other Attendants.⌝

KING HENRY
Where is my gracious Lord of Canterbury?

2. **presence:** i.e., the king's presence chamber or reception room

5. **We:** i.e., I (Henry uses the royal "we" through much of this scene.)

5–6. **resolved . . . of:** freed from doubt . . . about

7. **task:** fully occupy

9. **become:** grace, adorn

12. **unfold:** disclose

13. **law Salic:** This **law** will be described by Canterbury in lines 39–56.

14. **Or:** i.e., either; **our claim:** i.e., my **claim** to the French crown

16. **bow:** bend, force

18. **nicely charge:** subtly (and unwisely) burden

19. **With opening:** by declaring; **titles miscreate:** unfounded claims

20. **Suits not in native colors:** i.e., does not match

22. **approbation:** proof, support

23. **your Reverence:** i.e., you (a respectful form of address)

24. **impawn:** pledge

26. **charge:** command

29. **woe:** curse; **sore:** grievous

30. **wrongs:** wrongdoings

30–32. **gives . . . makes:** i.e., give . . . make

EXETER
  Not here in presence.
KING HENRY   Send for him, good uncle.
WESTMORELAND
  Shall we call in th' Ambassador, my liege?
KING HENRY
  Not yet, my cousin. We would be resolved,   5
  Before we hear him, of some things of weight
  That task our thoughts concerning us and France.

  Enter ⌐*the*⌐ *two Bishops* ⌐*of Canterbury and Ely.*⌐

BISHOP OF CANTERBURY
  God and his angels guard your sacred throne
  And make you long become it.
KING HENRY   Sure we thank you.   10
  My learnèd lord, we pray you to proceed
  And justly and religiously unfold
  Why the law Salic that they have in France
  Or should or should not bar us in our claim.
  And God forbid, my dear and faithful lord,   15
  That you should fashion, wrest, or bow your
    reading,
  Or nicely charge your understanding soul
  With opening titles miscreate, whose right
  Suits not in native colors with the truth;   20
  For God doth know how many now in health
  Shall drop their blood in approbation
  Of what your Reverence shall incite us to.
  Therefore take heed how you impawn our person,
  How you awake our sleeping sword of war.   25
  We charge you in the name of God, take heed,
  For never two such kingdoms did contend
  Without much fall of blood, whose guiltless drops
  Are every one a woe, a sore complaint
  'Gainst him whose wrongs gives edge unto the   30
    swords

32. **makes . . . waste:** cause . . . destruction; **mortality:** i.e., human lives

33. **conjuration:** solemn entreaty or request

36. **sin:** i.e., original **sin,** or corruption supposedly innate to all humans as a consequence of the Fall of Adam; **with:** by

39. **imperial:** magnificent; **There is no bar:** Canterbury's discussion of this bar addresses the fact that Henry's claim is through the female line.

41. **Pharamond:** a legendary Frankish king

43. **succeed:** i.e., inherit property or titles

44. **gloze:** gloss, explain

46. **this . . . bar:** i.e., this prohibition against women being heirs

49. **floods:** rivers

50. **Charles the Great:** i.e., Charlemagne (742–814 C.E.) See picture, page 22.

54. **dishonest:** unchaste

55. **to wit:** namely

62. **four . . . twenty:** Actually, the correct calculation is 379. (This error derives from Holinshed's *Chronicle,* a source for *Henry V.*)

63. **defunction:** i.e., the death

64. **Idly supposed:** i.e., claimed without grounds to be

65. **within . . . redemption:** *anno Domini* (A.D.), literally, in the year of the Lord, the Redeemer

That makes such waste in brief mortality.
Under this conjuration, speak, my lord,
For we will hear, note, and believe in heart
That what you speak is in your conscience washed   35
As pure as sin with baptism.

BISHOP OF CANTERBURY
    Then hear me, gracious sovereign, and you peers
That owe yourselves, your lives, and services
To this imperial throne. There is no bar
To make against your Highness' claim to France   40
But this, which they produce from Pharamond:
"In terram Salicam mulieres ne succedant"
(No woman shall succeed in Salic land),
Which Salic land the French unjustly gloze
To be the realm of France, and Pharamond   45
The founder of this law and female bar.
Yet their own authors faithfully affirm
That the land Salic is in Germany,
Between the floods of Sala and of Elbe,
Where Charles the Great, having subdued the   50
    Saxons,
There left behind and settled certain French,
Who, holding in disdain the German women
For some dishonest manners of their life,
Established then this law: to wit, no female   55
Should be inheritrix in Salic land,
Which "Salic," as I said, 'twixt Elbe and Sala
Is at this day in Germany called Meissen.
Then doth it well appear the Salic law
Was not devisèd for the realm of France,   60
Nor did the French possess the Salic land
Until four hundred one and twenty years
After defunction of King Pharamond,
Idly supposed the founder of this law,
Who died within the year of our redemption   65
Four hundred twenty-six; and Charles the Great

67. **seat:** settle

70–82. **Pepin . . . Tenth:** For the reigns of these kings, see longer note, page 239.

70. **which:** i.e., who

71. **heir general:** heir-at-law, one who succeeds another by right of blood relation

77. **find:** provide; **shows:** semblances

78. **naught:** worthless

79. **Conveyed . . . as:** i.e., declared **himself**

80. **Charlemagne:** in fact, Charles II, not Charlemagne (Again the error is found in Holinshed.)

82. **Tenth:** actually, Ninth (again as in Holinshed)

86. **fair:** beautiful

87. **lineal of:** directly descended from

93. **Lewis his:** i.e., Lewis's; **satisfaction:** See **satisfied,** line 85.

93–94. **appear / To:** i.e., obviously

94. **hold . . . of:** derive . . . from

96. **Howbeit:** i.e., however much; **would:** wish to

98. **them:** i.e., themselves; **net:** tangle (of contradictory rules for succession)

99. **imbar:** i.e., embar, bar

Charlemagne, or "Charles the Great." (1.2.50)
From H.C., *Abbrege de l'histoire Frâçoise . . .* (1596).

Subdued the Saxons and did seat the French
Beyond the river Sala in the year
Eight hundred five. Besides, their writers say,
King Pepin, which deposèd Childeric,   70
Did, as heir general, being descended
Of Blithild, which was daughter to King Clothair,
Make claim and title to the crown of France.
Hugh Capet also, who usurped the crown
Of Charles the Duke of Lorraine, sole heir male   75
Of the true line and stock of Charles the Great,
To find his title with some shows of truth,
Though in pure truth it was corrupt and naught,
Conveyed himself as th' heir to th' Lady Lingare,
Daughter to Charlemagne, who was the son   80
To Lewis the Emperor, and Lewis the son
Of Charles the Great. Also King Lewis the Tenth,
Who was sole heir to the usurper Capet,
Could not keep quiet in his conscience,
Wearing the crown of France, till satisfied   85
That fair Queen Isabel, his grandmother,
Was lineal of the Lady Ermengare,
Daughter to Charles the foresaid Duke of Lorraine:
By the which marriage the line of Charles the Great
Was reunited to the crown of France.   90
So that, as clear as is the summer's sun,
King Pepin's title and Hugh Capet's claim,
King Lewis his satisfaction, all appear
To hold in right and title of the female.
So do the kings of France unto this day,   95
Howbeit they would hold up this Salic law
To bar your Highness claiming from the female,
And rather choose to hide them in a net
Than amply to imbar their crooked titles
Usurped from you and your progenitors.   100
KING HENRY
    May I with right and conscience make this claim?

104–5. When . . . daughter: This is a partial version of Numbers 27.8, which reads in full: "If a man die, and have no son, then you shall turn his inheritance unto his daughter."

106. unwind: unfurl

107. into: i.e., to

108. great-grandsire: i.e., great-grandfather, Edward III (See note to 1.1.94, and pages 2 and, for his picture, 36.)

110. Edward the Black Prince: eldest son of Edward III

111. played a tragedy: an allusion to the Battle of Crécy in 1346

112. power: army

114. his lion's whelp: i.e., his son (The **lion** is traditionally associated with the monarch.)

115. Forage: glut himself

116. entertain: engage

119. for: i.e., for lack of

121. puissant: powerful

123. renownèd them: i.e., made **them renowned**

132. So hath your Highness: i.e., so, in fact, you *have*

The lion as monarch. (1.2.114)
From John Speed, *A prospect of the most famous parts of the world* (1631).

BISHOP OF CANTERBURY

  The sin upon my head, dread sovereign,
  For in the Book of Numbers is it writ:
  "When the man dies, let the inheritance
  Descend unto the daughter." Gracious lord,   105
  Stand for your own, unwind your bloody flag,
  Look back into your mighty ancestors.
  Go, my dread lord, to your great-grandsire's tomb,
  From whom you claim; invoke his warlike spirit
  And your great-uncle's, Edward the Black Prince,   110
  Who on the French ground played a tragedy,
  Making defeat on the full power of France
  Whiles his most mighty father on a hill
  Stood smiling to behold his lion's whelp
  Forage in blood of French nobility.   115
  O noble English, that could entertain
  With half their forces the full pride of France
  And let another half stand laughing by,
  All out of work and cold for action!

BISHOP OF ELY

  Awake remembrance of these valiant dead   120
  And with your puissant arm renew their feats.
  You are their heir, you sit upon their throne,
  The blood and courage that renownèd them
  Runs in your veins; and my thrice-puissant liege
  Is in the very May-morn of his youth,   125
  Ripe for exploits and mighty enterprises.

EXETER

  Your brother kings and monarchs of the Earth
  Do all expect that you should rouse yourself
  As did the former lions of your blood.

WESTMORELAND

  They know your Grace hath cause and means and   130
    might;
  So hath your Highness. Never king of England
  Had nobles richer, and more loyal subjects,

135. **pavilioned:** in (grand military) tents
138. **spiritualty:** clergy
143. **lay . . . proportions:** i.e., determine the proportion of our troops to be employed
144. **road:** i.e., raid
145. **With all advantages:** i.e., at every opportunity
146. **of those marches:** i.e., who live in the borderlands
148. **inland:** interior part of our country
149. **coursing snatchers:** i.e., thieving riders
150. **main intendment:** general (hostile) intention
151. **still:** always; **giddy:** inconstant, flighty
154. **unfurnished:** unprovided, unprepared
157. **Galling:** chafing, irritating; **gleanèd:** i.e., reaped (stripped of its defenders); **assays:** attacks
158. **Girding:** encircling
160. **ill neighborhood:** evil relations between neighbors
161. **She:** i.e., England; **feared:** perhaps, frightened (though England's actions, which Canterbury goes on to describe, could have caused her to be **feared** in the usual sense)
163. **hear . . . herself:** i.e., only listen to how she herself provides an instance (or model)
164. **chivalry hath:** knights have

Whose hearts have left their bodies here in England
And lie pavilioned in the fields of France.   135

BISHOP OF CANTERBURY
   O, let their bodies follow, my dear liege,
   With ⌐blood⌐ and sword and fire to win your right,
   In aid whereof we of the spiritualty
   Will raise your Highness such a mighty sum
   As never did the clergy at one time   140
   Bring in to any of your ancestors.

KING HENRY
   We must not only arm t' invade the French,
   But lay down our proportions to defend
   Against the Scot, who will make road upon us
   With all advantages.   145

BISHOP OF CANTERBURY
   They of those marches, gracious sovereign,
   Shall be a wall sufficient to defend
   Our inland from the pilfering borderers.

KING HENRY
   We do not mean the coursing snatchers only,
   But fear the main intendment of the Scot,   150
   Who hath been still a giddy neighbor to us.
   For you shall read that my great-grandfather
   Never went with his forces into France
   But that the Scot on his unfurnished kingdom
   Came pouring like the tide into a breach   155
   With ample and brim fullness of his force,
   Galling the gleanèd land with hot assays,
   Girding with grievous siege castles and towns,
   That England, being empty of defense,
   Hath shook and trembled at th' ill neighborhood.   160

BISHOP OF CANTERBURY
   She hath been then more feared than harmed, my
      liege,
   For hear her but exampled by herself:
   When all her chivalry hath been in France

167. **impounded ... stray:** i.e., confined in a pen as if he were **a stray** animal

168. **King of Scots:** David II, captured at Neville's Cross in 1346, while Edward III was in France

171. **ooze and bottom:** i.e., oozy **bottom**

172. **sunken wrack:** wrecked ships; **sumless:** incalculable; **treasuries:** treasures

174. **If that:** i.e., **if**

176. **in prey:** i.e., away seeking **prey**

180. **'tame and havoc:** i.e., spoil **'tame:** attame, or pierce **havoc:** lay waste

182. **that ... crushed necessity:** i.e., Ely's conclusion that **the cat** (Henry) **must stay home** is forced, not logical

184. **pretty:** ingenious

185. **While that:** i.e., **while**

185–86. **hand ... head:** The state is here represented as a human body. **advisèd:** wary, cautious

187–90. **government ... Like music:** Cooperation among the social ranks who make up government is compared to a song sung in parts for **high, low, and lower** voices. **keep ... consent:** (1) agree as to a course of action; (2) sing in harmony **Congreeing:** agreeing **close:** (1) closing together, union; (2) conclusion of a segment of music

192. **state of man:** kingdom of human beings

194. **aim or butt:** target

196. **by a rule in nature:** (1) through the rulership that is natural to them; (2) by virtue of the natural law that controls them

197. **The act of order:** i.e., orderly action

And she a mourning widow of her nobles,   165
She hath herself not only well defended
But taken and impounded as a stray
The King of Scots, whom she did send to France
To fill King Edward's fame with prisoner kings
And make ⌜her⌝ chronicle as rich with praise   170
As is the ooze and bottom of the sea
With sunken wrack and sumless treasuries.

BISHOP OF ELY
But there's a saying very old and true:
   "If that you will France win,
      Then with Scotland first begin."   175
For once the eagle England being in prey,
To her unguarded nest the weasel Scot
Comes sneaking and so sucks her princely eggs,
Playing the mouse in absence of the cat,
To 'tame and havoc more than she can eat.   180

EXETER
It follows, then, the cat must stay at home.
Yet that is but a crushed necessity,
Since we have locks to safeguard necessaries
And pretty traps to catch the petty thieves.
While that the armèd hand doth fight abroad,   185
Th' advisèd head defends itself at home.
For government, though high and low and lower,
Put into parts, doth keep in one consent,
Congreeing in a full and natural close,
Like music.   190

BISHOP OF CANTERBURY
                    Therefore doth heaven divide
The state of man in divers functions,
Setting endeavor in continual motion,
To which is fixèd as an aim or butt
Obedience; for so work the honeybees,   195
Creatures that by a rule in nature teach
The act of order to a peopled kingdom.

198. **They have a king:** a widespread error deriving from the Greek philosopher Aristotle (384–322 B.C.E.); **officers of sorts:** various ranks of officers

199. **correct:** punish

202. **Make boot:** prey

205. **majesty:** royal dignity

207. **civil:** orderly, well-governed

208. **mechanic:** carrying out manual labor

210. **sad-eyed:** serious-looking

211. **executors:** executioners

213–14. **having full reference / To one consent:** i.e., in complete agreement about their purpose **consent:** agreement as to a course of action

214. **contrariously:** in opposition (paradox)

215. **As:** i.e., just as; **loosèd several ways:** i.e., shot from different places

216. **mark:** target; **ways:** roads

218. **close:** unite; **dial's:** sundial's (See picture, page 72.)

221. **defeat:** frustration

222. **happy:** fortunate

224. **withal:** nevertheless; **Gallia:** France

225. **powers:** armies

227. **worried:** (1) assailed; (2) bitten and shaken (as by dogs)

228. **The name of:** i.e., its reputation for; **hardiness:** resoluteness; **policy:** political prudence

229. **Dauphin:** heir to the throne of France

230. **are we well resolved:** i.e., I am (1) utterly determined; (2) fully convinced

They have a king and officers of sorts,
Where some like magistrates correct at home,
Others like merchants venture trade abroad,   200
Others like soldiers armèd in their stings
Make boot upon the summer's velvet buds,
Which pillage they with merry march bring home
To the tent royal of their emperor,
Who, busied in his ⌜majesty,⌝ surveys   205
The singing masons building roofs of gold,
The civil citizens kneading up the honey,
The poor mechanic porters crowding in
Their heavy burdens at his narrow gate,
The sad-eyed justice with his surly hum   210
Delivering o'er to executors pale
The lazy yawning drone. I this infer:
That many things, having full reference
To one consent, may work contrariously,
As many arrows loosèd several ways   215
Come to one mark, as many ways meet in one town,
As many fresh streams meet in one salt sea,
As many lines close in the dial's center,
So may a thousand actions, once afoot,
⌜End⌝ in one purpose and be all well borne   220
Without defeat. Therefore to France, my liege!
Divide your happy England into four,
Whereof take you one quarter into France,
And you withal shall make all Gallia shake.
If we, with thrice such powers left at home,   225
Cannot defend our own doors from the dog,
Let us be worried, and our nation lose
The name of hardiness and policy.

KING HENRY
Call in the messengers sent from the Dauphin.
                                        ⌜*Attendants exit.*⌝
Now are we well resolved, and by God's help   230
And yours, the noble sinews of our power,

232. **France being ours:** i.e., since **France** is mine; **awe:** power to inspire fear

233. **Or there we'll sit:** i.e., either I'll sit there

234. **empery:** absolute dominion or authority

236. **urn:** grave

237. **remembrance:** memorial inscription

238. **with full mouth:** with the utmost force

239. **freely:** abundantly, profusely

240. **Turkish mute:** perhaps, a tongueless slave in a sultan's palace

241. **Not worshiped . . . epitaph:** i.e., not honored by an inscription carved even in perishable wax

243. **cousin:** For Henry's blood relationship to the French royal family, see page xvi.

246. **what we have in charge:** i.e., **what we have** been commanded to say

247. **sparingly:** with reserve; **far off:** at many removes

248. **embassy:** i.e., message

250. **grace:** (1) graciousness; (2) virtue

251. **is:** i.e., are

252. **uncurbèd:** unrestrained

254. **in few:** i.e., briefly

259. **savor:** taste

260. **advised:** warned

261. **galliard:** lively dance

263. **meeter:** more fitting

France being ours, we'll bend it to our awe
Or break it all to pieces. Or there we'll sit,
Ruling in large and ample empery
O'er France and all her almost kingly dukedoms,   235
Or lay these bones in an unworthy urn,
Tombless, with no remembrance over them.
Either our history shall with full mouth
Speak freely of our acts, or else our grave,
Like Turkish mute, shall have a tongueless mouth,   240
Not worshiped with a waxen epitaph.

Enter Ambassadors of France, ⌜*with Attendants.*⌝

Now are we well prepared to know the pleasure
Of our fair cousin Dauphin, for we hear
Your greeting is from him, not from the King.
AMBASSADOR
May 't please your Majesty to give us leave   245
Freely to render what we have in charge,
Or shall we sparingly show you far off
The Dauphin's meaning and our embassy?
KING HENRY
We are no tyrant, but a Christian king,
Unto whose grace our passion is as subject   250
As is our wretches fettered in our prisons.
Therefore with frank and with uncurbèd plainness
Tell us the Dauphin's mind.
AMBASSADOR   Thus, then, in few:
Your Highness, lately sending into France,   255
Did claim some certain dukedoms in the right
Of your great predecessor, King Edward the Third;
In answer of which claim, the Prince our master
Says that you savor too much of your youth
And bids you be advised there's naught in France   260
That can be with a nimble galliard won;
You cannot revel into dukedoms there.
He therefore sends you, meeter for your spirit,

264. **tun:** barrel, chest; **in lieu of:** in return for

265. **you let:** (1) that **you let;** (2) **you** to **let**

270. **pleasant:** jocular

272. **our rackets:** Here begins an extended comparison of Henry's proposed invasion of France and a game (**set**) of royal tennis, which was played inside a walled court.

274. **hazard:** hole in the wall of a royal tennis court

276. **wrangler:** debater (especially in a court of law)

277. **courts:** (1) royal **courts;** (2) tennis **courts**

278. **chases:** (1) winning strokes in tennis; (2) routs of enemies in battles

279. **comes o'er ... with:** i.e., demeans me by citing; **our wilder days:** See note to 1.1.26.

281. **seat:** (1) throne; (2) place of habitation

283. **barbarous license:** i.e., wildly excessive liberty

284. **merriest:** most self-indulgent; **from:** i.e., away from

285–89. **I will keep ... days:** Henry declares that he will appear all the more as a glorious king on the French throne because he has before seemed so unglamorous and unkingly. **keep my state:** observe the pomp and ceremony of kingship **rouse me:** raise myself up **For that: for that** purpose **for:** i.e., ready for

293. **pleasant:** joking

294. **gun-stones:** cannonballs; or, bullets

295. **stand sore chargèd:** be grievously burdened; **wasteful:** destructive; **vengeance:** i.e., Henry's revenge against the Dauphin for sending the tennis balls

This tun of treasure and, in lieu of this,
Desires you let the dukedoms that you claim   265
Hear no more of you. This the Dauphin speaks.
KING HENRY
What treasure, uncle?
EXETER   Tennis balls,
     my liege.
KING HENRY
We are glad the Dauphin is so pleasant with us.   270
His present and your pains we thank you for.
When we have matched our rackets to these balls,
We will in France, by God's grace, play a set
Shall strike his father's crown into the hazard.
Tell him he hath made a match with such a   275
     wrangler
That all the courts of France will be disturbed
With chases. And we understand him well,
How he comes o'er us with our wilder days,
Not measuring what use we made of them.   280
We never valued this poor seat of England,
And therefore, living hence, did give ourself
To barbarous license, as 'tis ever common
That men are merriest when they are from home.
But tell the Dauphin I will keep my state,   285
Be like a king, and show my sail of greatness
When I do rouse me in my throne of France,
For that I have laid by my majesty
And plodded like a man for working days;
But I will rise there with so full a glory   290
That I will dazzle all the eyes of France,
Yea, strike the Dauphin blind to look on us.
And tell the pleasant prince this mock of his
Hath turned his balls to gun-stones, and his soul
Shall stand sore chargèd for the wasteful vengeance   295
That shall fly with them; for many a thousand
     widows
Shall this his mock mock out of their dear husbands,

300. **ungotten:** unbegotten, not conceived
305. **venge:** avenge
306. **well-hallowed:** thoroughly sanctified
313. **happy:** favorable, fortunate
316. **Save those to:** except for those thoughts of; **run before:** keep ahead of, have priority over
317. **proportions:** See lines 222–23, where it is suggested that a proportion of one-quarter of England's troops invade France.
320. **God before:** under God's guidance
323. **fair:** honorable, excellent

King Edward III holding "a sword . . .
with crowns imperial." (2.Chor.9–10)
From John Taylor, *All the workes of . . .* (1630).

Mock mothers from their sons, mock castles down;
And some are yet ungotten and unborn   300
That shall have cause to curse the Dauphin's scorn.
But this lies all within the will of God,
To whom I do appeal, and in whose name
Tell you the Dauphin I am coming on,
To venge me as I may and to put forth   305
My rightful hand in a well-hallowed cause.
So get you hence in peace. And tell the Dauphin
His jest will savor but of shallow wit
When thousands weep more than did laugh at it.—
Convey them with safe conduct.—Fare you well.   310
          Ambassadors exit, ⌜with Attendants.⌝
EXETER   This was a merry message.
KING HENRY
We hope to make the sender blush at it.
Therefore, my lords, omit no happy hour
That may give furth'rance to our expedition;
For we have now no thought in us but France,   315
Save those to God, that run before our business.
Therefore let our proportions for these wars
Be soon collected, and all things thought upon
That may with reasonable swiftness add
More feathers to our wings. For, God before,   320
We'll chide this Dauphin at his father's door.
Therefore let every man now task his thought,
That this fair action may on foot be brought.
                  Flourish. They exit.

The Life of

HENRY V

ACT 2

2.Chorus The Chorus announces the enthusiastic support of English youth for Henry's French campaign, but also advises that the French have bribed three noblemen to attempt Henry's assassination.

---

2. **dalliance:** trivial activities, and the clothes worn for them

3. **honor's thought:** i.e., the intention to win honor (in war)

5. **horse:** i.e., great warhorse

6. **mirror:** paragon

7. **Mercurys:** Mercury is the messenger of the gods in Roman mythology, depicted with wings at the heels of his sandals and on his hat. (See picture, page 52.)

9. **hilts:** crosspiece on the sword handle (See picture, page 36.) **unto:** i.e., up to

10. **crowns imperial:** emperors' **crowns**

12. **advised:** warned; **intelligence:** information

14. **pale:** i.e., cowardly; **policy:** cunning tricks

16. **England:** i.e., the little island itself; **model to:** replica of

18. **would:** i.e., would have

19. **kind:** naturally filial or devoted to you

20. **fault:** flaw, crack; moral failing

21. **hollow:** (1) false; (2) empty; **bosoms:** (1) seats of loyalty; (2) places in clothes for the concealment of money

22. **crowns:** coins

⌜*ACT 2*⌝

Enter Chorus.

⌜CHORUS⌝
Now all the youth of England are on fire,
And silken dalliance in the wardrobe lies;
Now thrive the armorers, and honor's thought
Reigns solely in the breast of every man.
They sell the pasture now to buy the horse,   5
Following the mirror of all Christian kings
With wingèd heels, as English Mercurys.
For now sits Expectation in the air
And hides a sword, from hilts unto the point,
With crowns imperial, crowns, and coronets   10
Promised to Harry and his followers.
The French, advised by good intelligence
Of this most dreadful preparation,
Shake in their fear, and with pale policy
Seek to divert the English purposes.   15
O England, model to thy inward greatness,
Like little body with a mighty heart,
What might'st thou do, that honor would thee do,
Were all thy children kind and natural!
But see, thy fault France hath in thee found out,   20
A nest of hollow bosoms, which he fills
With treacherous crowns, and three corrupted men—
One, Richard, Earl of Cambridge, and the second,

41

26. **gilt:** i.e., gold
28. **this grace of kings:** i.e., the most honorable **of kings**
29. **hold:** keep
30. **Ere:** before
31. **Linger . . . on:** i.e., be patient and stay with us; **digest:** i.e., put up with, endure, brook, stomach
32. **Th' abuse of distance:** perhaps, the way spatial distance is portrayed onstage
34. **is set:** i.e., has **set** out
37. **safe:** i.e., safely
38. **charming:** i.e., putting a magic charm on; **narrow seas:** i.e., English Channel
39. **pass:** passage
40. **not . . . stomach:** (1) not make anybody seasick; (2) not do anything in bad taste
41–42. **But . . . scene:** Despite the promise in lines 34–35, the scene does not shift to Southampton until scene 2. See longer note, page 240.

2.1 King Henry's former tavern companion Bardolph prevents Pistol and Nym from fighting over Hostess Quickly, Pistol's wife. They are interrupted by the news that Sir John Falstaff, once Henry's intimate friend, is gravely ill.

———————

0 SD. **Nym:** To "nim" is to steal.
1, 2, 3. **Corporal, Lieutenant, Ancient:** These military titles seem not to have the precision they might in a modern army. Bardolph, for example, is later called "corporal." An **ancient** was a standard-bearer, or ensign.

(continued)

42

Henry, Lord Scroop of Masham, and the third,
Sir Thomas Grey, knight, of Northumberland—   25
Have, for the gilt of France (O guilt indeed!),
Confirmed conspiracy with fearful France,
And by their hands this grace of kings must die,
If hell and treason hold their promises,
Ere he take ship for France, and in Southampton.   30
Linger your patience on, and we'll digest
Th' abuse of distance, force a play.
The sum is paid, the traitors are agreed,
The King is set from London, and the scene
Is now transported, gentles, to Southampton.   35
There is the playhouse now, there must you sit,
And thence to France shall we convey you safe
And bring you back, charming the narrow seas
To give you gentle pass; for, if we may,
We'll not offend one stomach with our play.   40
But, till the King come forth, and not till then,
Unto Southampton do we shift our scene.

                                 He exits.

⌜Scene 1⌝
Enter Corporal Nym and Lieutenant Bardolph.

BARDOLPH Well met, Corporal Nym.
NYM Good morrow, Lieutenant Bardolph.
BARDOLPH What, are Ancient Pistol and you friends
    yet?
NYM For my part, I care not. I say little, but when time   5
    shall serve, there shall be smiles; but that shall be as
    it may. I dare not fight, but I will wink and hold out
    mine iron. It is a simple one, but what though? It
    will toast cheese, and it will endure cold as another
    man's sword will, and there's an end.   10
BARDOLPH I will bestow a breakfast to make you

7. **wink:** i.e., shut my eyes

8. **iron:** i.e., sword; **what though:** i.e., what of that (Nym is given language that is odd and often unidiomatic.)

12–13. **to France:** i.e., when we leave for **France**

14. **Faith:** i.e., by my **faith** (a mild oath)

16. **my rest:** the last of my stake (in the game of primero)

17. **rendezvous:** last resort

18. **he:** i.e., Pistol

20. **troth-plight:** betrothed, engaged

28. **patient:** calm

28–29. **How . . . Pistol:** See longer note, page 240.

30. **tyke:** mongrel cur

35. **honestly:** (1) respectably; (2) chastely; **by . . . needles:** i.e., as seamstresses

36. **thought we . . . straight:** i.e., immediately **thought** that **we**

37. **well-a-day:** exclamation of sorrow; **Lady:** i.e., by our **Lady** (the Virgin Mary)

37–38. **If . . . committed:** The humor of many of Hostess Quickly's speeches arises from their utter lack of logic combined with her misuse of particular words.

39–40. **offer . . . here:** i.e., do not fight

41. **Pish:** expression of disgust or contempt

42. **Iceland dog:** a small, hairy, quarrelsome breed of dog; **prick-eared:** with erect ears

friends, and we'll be all three sworn brothers to
France. Let 't be so, good Corporal Nym.

NYM   Faith, I will live so long as I may, that's the
certain of it; and when I cannot live any longer, I   15
will do as I may. That is my rest, that is the
rendezvous of it.

BARDOLPH   It is certain, corporal, that he is married to
Nell Quickly, and certainly she did you wrong, for
you were troth-plight to her.   20

NYM   I cannot tell. Things must be as they may. Men
may sleep, and they may have their throats about
them at that time, and some say knives have edges.
It must be as it may. Though patience be a tired
⌈mare,⌉ yet she will plod. There must be conclu-   25
sions. Well, I cannot tell.

              Enter Pistol and ⌈*Hostess*⌉ *Quickly.*

BARDOLPH   Here comes Ancient Pistol and his wife.
Good corporal, be patient here.—How now, mine
host Pistol?

PISTOL   Base tyke, call'st thou me host? Now, by this   30
hand, I swear I scorn the term, nor shall my Nell
keep lodgers.

HOSTESS   No, by my troth, not long; for we cannot
lodge and board a dozen or fourteen gentlewomen
that live honestly by the prick of their needles but it   35
will be thought we keep a bawdy house straight.
              ⌈*Nym and Pistol draw their swords.*⌉
O well-a-day, Lady! If he be not hewn now, we shall
see willful adultery and murder committed.

BARDOLPH   Good lieutenant, good corporal, offer nothing here.   40

NYM   Pish!

PISTOL   Pish for thee, Iceland dog, thou prick-eared
cur of Iceland!

46. **shog off:** go away

47. **solus:** alone (Latin)

48. **O viper vile:** Pistol's speech is characterized by scraps of poetry, archaic language, and echoes of ranting speeches (sometimes from other plays).

51. **maw:** stomach; **perdy:** i.e., by God (French, *par Dieu*)

53. **take:** strike; **take** fire (as a pistol)

53–54. **Pistol's cock . . . follow:** i.e., my hammer is cocked and ready to fire (**Cock** may also mean "penis" or "pizzle," a pronunciation of **Pistol.**)

55. **Barbason:** a name for a devil; **conjure:** Nym responds as if Pistol were reciting the *conjuratio,* or conjuring part of the ceremony of exorcism.

56. **humor:** inclination, fancy

56–58. **If . . . rapier:** i.e., (1) **if you,** a pistol, become fouled, I'll clean your barrel **with my** ramrod; (2) **if you** speak foully, I'll stab **you with my rapier**

60. **that's the humor of it:** i.e., that's the way it is (See longer note, page 240.)

61. **wight:** creature

63. **exhale:** i.e., evaporate; breathe out (your last breath)

67. **mickle:** much (Like much of Pistol's bombastic language, this word was already archaic in Shakespeare's time.)

68. **spirits:** courage, vital powers

69. **tall:** bold, brave

72. **Couple à gorge:** corrupt French for "cut the throat"; **word:** motto

73. **hound of Crete:** a breed of hunting dog

(continued)

HOSTESS   Good Corporal Nym, show thy valor, and put
   up your sword.   45
NYM   Will you shog off? ⌜*To Pistol.*⌝ I would have you
   solus.
PISTOL   "*Solus,*" egregious dog? O viper vile, the *solus*
   in thy most marvelous face, the *solus* in thy teeth
   and in thy throat and in thy hateful lungs, yea, in thy   50
   maw, perdy, and, which is worse, within thy nasty
   mouth! I do retort the *solus* in thy bowels, for I can
   take, and Pistol's cock is up, and flashing fire will
   follow.
NYM   I am not Barbason, you cannot conjure me. I   55
   have an humor to knock you indifferently well. If
   you grow foul with me, Pistol, I will scour you with
   my rapier, as I may, in fair terms. If you would walk
   off, I would prick your guts a little in good terms, as
   I may, and that's the humor of it.   60
PISTOL
   O braggart vile and damnèd furious wight,
   The grave doth gape, and doting death is near.
   Therefore exhale.
BARDOLPH   Hear me, hear me what I say: he that strikes
   the first stroke, I'll run him up to the hilts, as I am a   65
   soldier.   ⌜*He draws.*⌝
PISTOL   An oath of mickle might, and fury shall abate.
                    ⌜*Pistol and Nym and then Bardolph*
                              sheathe their swords.⌝
   Give me thy fist, thy forefoot to me give. Thy spirits
   are most tall.
NYM, ⌜*to Pistol*⌝   I will cut thy throat one time or other   70
   in fair terms, that is the humor of it.
PISTOL   *Couple à gorge,* that is the word. I defy thee
   again. O hound of Crete, think'st thou my spouse to
   get? No, to the spital go, and from the powd'ring tub
   of infamy fetch forth the lazar kite of Cressid's kind,   75
   Doll Tearsheet she by name, and her espouse. I

74. **spital:** hospital; **powd'ring tub:** a sweating tub for the treatment of venereal disease

75. **lazar:** leprous (Leprosy was associated with venereal disease.) **kite:** bird of prey; carrion bird; **Cressid's kind:** i.e., like Cressida (a leprous prostitute) (See longer note, page 240.)

76. **Doll Tearsheet:** a prostitute who appears in *Henry IV, Part 2*

77. **quondam:** former (**Quickly** is the maiden name of Pistol's wife.)

78. **pauca:** from *pauca verba*, Latin for "few words"; **Go to:** an expression of angry impatience

79. **my master:** i.e., Sir John Falstaff

80. **would:** i.e., wishes to go

81. **thy face:** In 3.6.104–6 (as in Shakespeare's *Henry IV* plays), Bardolph's face is described as inflamed with boils and pimples.

82. **do the office:** perform the function

85. **yield the crow a pudding:** i.e., make a meal for scavengers

86. **The King . . . heart:** In *Henry IV, Part 2*, as soon as Henry V succeeds to the throne, he banishes Falstaff.

87. **presently:** immediately

95. **That:** i.e., the money I am owed

96. **manhood:** courage; **compound:** i.e., settle the matter; **Push home:** an invitation to fight

102. **an:** i.e., if

104. **put up:** i.e., **put** away your sword

105. **noble:** a coin worth somewhat less than the eight shillings Nym has demanded

105–6. **present pay:** immediate payment

have, and I will hold, the quondam Quickly for the
only she: and *pauca*, there's enough too! Go to.

Enter the Boy.

BOY Mine host Pistol, you must come to my master,
and your hostess. He is very sick and would to   80
bed.—Good Bardolph, put thy face between his
sheets, and do the office of a warming-pan. Faith,
he's very ill.

BARDOLPH Away, you rogue!

HOSTESS By my troth, he'll yield the crow a pudding   85
one of these days. The King has killed his heart.
Good husband, come home presently.
                    She exits ⌜*with the Boy.*⌝

BARDOLPH Come, shall I make you two friends? We
must to France together. Why the devil should we
keep knives to cut one another's throats?   90

PISTOL
Let floods o'erswell and fiends for food howl on!

NYM You'll pay me the eight shillings I won of you at
betting?

PISTOL Base is the slave that pays.

NYM That now I will have, that's the humor of it.   95

PISTOL As manhood shall compound. Push home.
                    ⌜*They*⌝ *draw.*

BARDOLPH, ⌜*drawing his sword*⌝ By this sword, he that
makes the first thrust, I'll kill him. By this sword, I
will.

PISTOL, ⌜*sheathing his sword*⌝ "Sword" is an oath, and   100
oaths must have their course.

BARDOLPH Corporal Nym, an thou wilt be friends, be
friends; an thou wilt not, why then be enemies with
me too. Prithee, put up.

PISTOL, ⌜*to Nym*⌝ A noble shalt thou have, and present   105
pay, and liquor likewise will I give to thee, and

109. **sutler:** seller of provisions

114. **come of:** were born of

115–16. **shaked . . . quotidian-tertian:** i.e., shaking with a fever   **quotidian:** a fever recurring every day   **tertian:** a fever recurring every other day

118. **run . . . knight:** perhaps, mistreated **the knight**

119. **even:** plain truth

120. **right:** truth

121. **fracted:** broken; **corroborate:** strengthened (Pistol seems self-contradictory here, though it has been argued that he may be using theological language, in which a heart, in repentance, may be humbled [**fracted**] and then strengthened.)

123. **careers:** gallops; courses of action

124. **condole:** i.e., **condole** with

2.2 Henry, informed of the treachery of three of his friends, confronts them with their crimes. They throw themselves on his mercy, but, having just denied mercy to another, they are themselves denied. As they leave, now welcoming their execution as deserved, Henry looks toward his French war.

———————

2. **by and by:** soon

3. **smooth and even:** i.e., calmly

friendship shall combine, and brotherhood. I'll live
by Nym, and Nym shall live by me. Is not this just?
For I shall sutler be unto the camp, and profits will
accrue. Give me thy hand.   110
NYM   I shall have my noble?
PISTOL   In cash, most justly paid.
NYM   Well, then, ⌐that's⌐ the humor of 't.
                    ⌐*Nym and Bardolph sheathe their swords.*⌐

                    Enter Hostess.

HOSTESS   As ever you come of women, come in quickly
    to Sir John. Ah, poor heart, he is so shaked of a   115
    burning quotidian-tertian that it is most lamenta-
    ble to behold. Sweet men, come to him.
NYM   The King hath run bad humors on the knight,
    that's the even of it.
PISTOL   Nym, thou hast spoke the right. His heart is   120
    fracted and corroborate.
NYM   The King is a good king, but it must be as it may;
    he passes some humors and careers.
PISTOL   Let us condole the knight, for, lambkins, we
    will live.   125
                                        They exit.

                    ⌐Scene 2⌐
        Enter Exeter, Bedford, and Westmoreland.

BEDFORD
    'Fore God, his Grace is bold to trust these traitors.
EXETER
    They shall be apprehended by and by.
WESTMORELAND
    How smooth and even they do bear themselves,
    As if allegiance in their bosoms sat
    Crownèd with faith and constant loyalty.   5

6. **note:** information
9. **Whom . . . cloyed:** i.e., whose appetite he has gratified beyond desire so as to take off its sharp edge
11. **a foreign purse:** i.e., **foreign** money
13. **sits . . . fair:** i.e., blows . . . in the direction we need
17. **powers:** armies
19. **Doing . . . act:** i.e., executing **the act**
20. **in head:** as an armed force
22. **we are:** i.e., I am (the royal "we")
24. **grows . . . consent:** i.e., does not agree
25. **Nor leave not:** i.e., **nor leave**
26. **attend on:** accompany
27. **better:** i.e., more

"Wingèd heels, as English Mercurys." (2.Chor.7)
From Innocenzio Ringhiere,
Cento giuochi liberali . . . (1580).

BEDFORD
The King hath note of all that they intend,
By interception which they dream not of.

EXETER
Nay, but the man that was his bedfellow,
Whom he hath dulled and cloyed with gracious
  favors—   10
That he should, for a foreign purse, so sell
His sovereign's life to death and treachery!

    Sound Trumpets. Enter the King ⌜of England,⌝
    Scroop, Cambridge, and Grey, ⌜with Attendants.⌝

KING HENRY
Now sits the wind fair, and we will aboard.—
My Lord of Cambridge, and my kind Lord of
  Masham,   15
And you, my gentle knight, give me your thoughts.
Think you not that the powers we bear with us
Will cut their passage through the force of France,
Doing the execution and the act
For which we have in head assembled them?   20

SCROOP
No doubt, my liege, if each man do his best.

KING HENRY
I doubt not that, since we are well persuaded
We carry not a heart with us from hence
That grows not in a fair consent with ours,
Nor leave not one behind that doth not wish   25
Success and conquest to attend on us.

CAMBRIDGE
Never was monarch better feared and loved
Than is your Majesty. There's not, I think, a subject
That sits in heart-grief and uneasiness
Under the sweet shade of your government.   30

⌜GREY⌝
True. Those that were your father's enemies

32. **galls:** bitterness
33. **create:** i.e., created
35. **office:** function
36. **quittance:** recompense, repayment
37. **According to:** in accord with
42. **Enlarge:** set at large, set free; **committed:** sent to prison
45. **on ... advice:** i.e., now that he has thought more about it
46. **security:** carelessness, overconfidence
48. **his sufferance:** toleration of him
50. **So ... Highness:** i.e., you may be merciful
52. **correction:** corporal punishment, flogging
53. **too much:** excess
54. **heavy orisons:** oppressive or severe speeches **orisons:** literally, prayers
55. **proceeding on distemper:** i.e., caused by drunkenness
56. **winked at:** overlooked; **stretch:** i.e., open wide
57. **capital:** (1) very serious; (2) punishable by death
59. **yet:** nevertheless

A casque (Pro.14).
From Louis de Gaya, *Traité des armes,
des machines de guerre* ... (1678).

Have steeped their galls in honey, and do serve you
With hearts create of duty and of zeal.

KING HENRY
We therefore have great cause of thankfulness,
And shall forget the office of our hand   35
Sooner than quittance of desert and merit
According to the weight and worthiness.

SCROOP
So service shall with steelèd sinews toil,
And labor shall refresh itself with hope
To do your Grace incessant services.   40

KING HENRY
We judge no less.—Uncle of Exeter,
Enlarge the man committed yesterday
That railed against our person. We consider
It was excess of wine that set him on,
And on his more advice we pardon him.   45

SCROOP
That's mercy, but too much security.
Let him be punished, sovereign, lest example
Breed, by his sufferance, more of such a kind.

KING HENRY   O, let us yet be merciful.

CAMBRIDGE
So may your Highness, and yet punish too.   50

GREY
Sir, you show great mercy if you give him life
After the taste of much correction.

KING HENRY
Alas, your too much love and care of me
Are heavy orisons 'gainst this poor wretch.
If little faults proceeding on distemper   55
Shall not be winked at, how shall we stretch our eye
When capital crimes, chewed, swallowed, and
    digested,
Appear before us? We'll yet enlarge that man,

64. **causes:** matters
65. **late commissioners:** i.e., newly created officers
67. **it:** i.e., the commission
78. **complexion:** color (from your face); **change:**
i.e., grow pale
79. **paper:** i.e., the pale color of **paper**
80. **cowarded:** i.e., made cowardly
81. **appearance:** i.e., sight
85. **quick:** alive; **late:** recently
88. **reasons:** perhaps, **your reasons** why I should
show justice rather than mercy
89. **worrying:** tearing at, biting
90. **See you:** i.e., watch
93. **apt:** ready; **accord:** consent, agree

"An hourglass." (Pro.33; 2.4.146–47)
From August Casimir Redel,
Apophtegmata symbolica . . . (n.d.).

Though Cambridge, Scroop, and Grey, in their dear   60
  care
And tender preservation of our person,
Would have him punished. And now to our French
  causes.
Who are the late commissioners?   65
CAMBRIDGE   I one, my lord.
  Your Highness bade me ask for it today.
SCROOP   So did you me, my liege.
GREY   And I, my royal sovereign.
KING HENRY, ⌜*giving them papers*⌝
  Then Richard, Earl of Cambridge, there is yours—   70
  There yours, Lord Scroop of Masham.—And, sir
    knight,
  Grey of Northumberland, this same is yours.—
  Read them, and know I know your worthiness.—
  My Lord of Westmoreland and uncle Exeter,   75
  We will aboard tonight.—Why how now, gentlemen?
  What see you in those papers, that you lose
  So much complexion?—Look you, how they change.
  Their cheeks are paper.—Why, what read you there
  That have so cowarded and chased your blood   80
  Out of appearance?
CAMBRIDGE   I do confess my fault,
  And do submit me to your Highness' mercy.
GREY/SCROOP   To which we all appeal.
KING HENRY
  The mercy that was quick in us but late   85
  By your own counsel is suppressed and killed.
  You must not dare, for shame, to talk of mercy,
  For your own reasons turn into your bosoms
  As dogs upon their masters, worrying you.—
  See you, my princes and my noble peers,   90
  These English monsters. My Lord of Cambridge
    here,
  You know how apt our love was to accord

94–95. **all . . . Belonging:** i.e., everything appropriate or appertaining

96. **lightly:** easily, readily; wantonly

97. **practices:** schemes, intrigues; **France:** i.e., the king of **France**

99. **This knight:** i.e., Grey

105. **coined . . . gold:** i.e., turned **me into** coin

106. **Wouldst . . . me:** i.e., if you had taken advantage of me; **use:** interest; profit

109. **annoy:** harm, injure

110. **off:** i.e., out; **gross:** evidently, obviously

112–17. **Treason . . . murder:** i.e., **murder and treason** have always kept company, and so their union has been no cause for astonishment, but your attempted murder and treason are matters for amazement **yoke-devils:** i.e., devils yoked together **either's:** each other's **grossly:** monstrously, unnaturally **natural:** i.e., **natural** for devils, who are, by nature, monstrous **'gainst . . . proportion:** i.e., in violation of all harmony **Wonder:** amazement

119. **wrought:** worked; **preposterously:** unnaturally

120. **the voice:** fame

121–24. **All . . . piety:** i.e., **all the other devils** who tempt people into treason clumsily disguise the damnable crime in a patched but glittering costume of holiness **forms:** shapes

125–27. **But . . . traitor:** The devil's temptation of Scroop is compared to the ceremony in which a monarch calls forth a man to dub him knight. **tempered:** persuaded; i.e., tempted **instance:** motive

128. **gulled:** deceived, fooled

(continued)

To furnish ⌈him⌉ with all appurtenants
Belonging to his honor, and this man   95
Hath, for a few light crowns, lightly conspired
And sworn unto the practices of France
To kill us here in Hampton; to the which
This knight, no less for bounty bound to us
Than Cambridge is, hath likewise sworn.—But O,   100
What shall I say to thee, Lord Scroop, thou cruel,
Ingrateful, savage, and inhuman creature?
Thou that didst bear the key of all my counsels,
That knew'st the very bottom of my soul,
That almost mightst have coined me into gold,   105
Wouldst thou have practiced on me for thy use—
May it be possible that foreign hire
Could out of thee extract one spark of evil
That might annoy my finger? 'Tis so strange
That, though the truth of it stands off as gross   110
As black and white, my eye will scarcely see it.
Treason and murder ever kept together,
As two yoke-devils sworn to either's purpose,
Working so grossly in ⌈a⌉ natural cause
That admiration did not whoop at them.   115
But thou, 'gainst all proportion, didst bring in
Wonder to wait on treason and on murder,
And whatsoever cunning fiend it was
That wrought upon thee so preposterously
Hath got the voice in hell for excellence.   120
⌈All⌉ other devils that suggest by treasons
Do botch and bungle up damnation
With patches, colors, and with forms being fetched
From glist'ring semblances of piety;
But he that tempered thee bade thee stand up,   125
Gave thee no instance why thou shouldst do treason,
Unless to dub thee with the name of traitor.
If that same demon that hath gulled thee thus
Should with his lion gait walk the whole world,

129. **lion gait:** i.e., lionlike stride (1 Peter 5.8: "Be sober and watch, for your adversary the devil, as a roaring lion, walketh about seeking whom he may devour.")

130. **return . . . back:** i.e., go **back to** hell **Tartar:** Tartarus, the place of punishment in the classical underworld

131. **legions:** i.e., devils (See Mark 5.9 and picture, page 62.)

133. **jealousy:** suspicion

134. **affiance:** faith in a person; **Show men:** i.e., do **men** appear to be

138. **spare in diet:** i.e., moderate in their appetites

139. **or . . . or:** either . . . or

140. **blood:** passions

141. **Garnished . . . complement:** i.e., complete in modesty **complement:** that which makes something complete and perfect

142. **Not . . . ear:** i.e., not depending only on what is seen

143. **And but in purgèd:** i.e., rather, instead, in purified or clarified

144. **bolted:** sifted (See picture, page 150.)

145. **fall:** yielding to sin, **fall** from virtue

146. **the full . . . endued:** i.e., even **the man** fully endowed with the **best** qualities **full-fraught:** fully laden (as a ship with cargo)

148. **revolt:** renouncing of allegiance

149. **fall of man:** the sin committed by Adam and Eve in Eden; **open:** obvious

151. **acquit:** forgive; **of:** i.e., for

(continued)

He might return to vasty Tartar back   130
And tell the legions "I can never win
A soul so easy as that Englishman's."
O, how hast thou with jealousy infected
The sweetness of affiance! Show men dutiful?
Why, so didst thou. Seem they grave and learnèd?   135
Why, so didst thou. Come they of noble family?
Why, so didst thou. Seem they religious?
Why, so didst thou. Or are they spare in diet,
Free from gross passion or of mirth or anger,
Constant in spirit, not swerving with the blood,   140
Garnished and decked in modest complement,
Not working with the eye without the ear,
And but in purgèd judgment trusting neither?
Such and so finely bolted didst thou seem.
And thus thy fall hath left a kind of blot   145
To ⌜mark the⌝ full-fraught man and best endued
With some suspicion. I will weep for thee,
For this revolt of thine methinks is like
Another fall of man.—Their faults are open.
Arrest them to the answer of the law,   150
And God acquit them of their practices.
EXETER   I arrest thee of high treason, by the name of
        Richard, Earl of Cambridge.—
        I arrest thee of high treason, by the name of
        ⌜Henry,⌝ Lord Scroop of Masham.—   155
        I arrest thee of high treason, by the name of
        Thomas Grey, knight, of Northumberland.
SCROOP
    Our purposes God justly hath discovered,
    And I repent my fault more than my death,
    Which I beseech your Highness to forgive,   160
    Although my body pay the price of it.
CAMBRIDGE
    For me, the gold of France did not seduce,
    Although I did admit it as a motive
    The sooner to effect what I intended;

158. **discovered:** revealed
159. **more than my death:** i.e., **more than** I regret **my death**
160. **Which:** i.e., **my fault**
162–64. **For . . . intended:** Cambridge's motivation, according to historians, was to advance the Earl of March's claim to the English throne. **admit it as a motive:** i.e., allow it to motivate me
166. **sufferance:** suffering the penalty
173. **quit:** acquit, forgive
177. **earnest:** a small payment that promises a larger reward to come
183. **Touching:** concerning
184. **tender:** regard; take care of
190. **dear:** dire, grievous; **Bear:** i.e., conduct
191. **enterprise whereof:** i.e., the bold undertaking of whose conquest
192. **like:** equally
193. **fair:** favorable

"That same demon . . . might . . . tell the legions."
(2.2.128–31)
From Olaus Magnus, *Historia de gentibus . . .* (1555).

But God be thankèd for prevention,   165
Which ⌈I⌉ in sufferance heartily will rejoice,
Beseeching God and you to pardon me.

GREY
Never did faithful subject more rejoice
At the discovery of most dangerous treason
Than I do at this hour joy o'er myself,   170
Prevented from a damnèd enterprise.
My fault, but not my body, pardon, sovereign.

KING HENRY
God quit you in His mercy. Hear your sentence:
You have conspired against our royal person,
Joined with an enemy proclaimed, and from his   175
    coffers
Received the golden earnest of our death,
Wherein you would have sold your king to
    slaughter,
His princes and his peers to servitude,   180
His subjects to oppression and contempt,
And his whole kingdom into desolation.
Touching our person, seek we no revenge,
But we our kingdom's safety must so tender,
Whose ruin you ⌈have⌉ sought, that to her laws   185
We do deliver you. Get you therefore hence,
Poor miserable wretches, to your death,
The taste whereof God of His mercy give
You patience to endure, and true repentance
Of all your dear offenses.—Bear them hence.   190
                    ⌈*They*⌉ *exit* ⌈*under guard.*⌉
Now, lords, for France, the enterprise whereof
Shall be to you as us, like glorious.
We doubt not of a fair and lucky war,
Since God so graciously hath brought to light
This dangerous treason lurking in our way   195
To hinder our beginnings. We doubt not now

197. **rub:** obstacle—a term from the game of bowls, where a **rub** is an obstruction that hinders or deflects the course of the bowl (See picture, page 194.)

199. **puissance:** power, army

200. **straight:** immediately; **in expedition:** in motion

201. **Cheerly:** cheerily (i.e., let's go cheerfully or with a will); **The signs ... advance:** i.e., **advance** the insignia, standards, banners

2.3 The tavern crew—Bardolph, Pistol, Nym, and the Boy—join the Hostess in mourning the dead Falstaff and, saying good-bye to the Hostess, leave for France.

---

1. **bring:** accompany

2. **Staines:** a town twenty miles from London on the way to Southampton

3. **earn:** grieve

4. **rouse:** stir up; **vaunting:** bragging

7. **wheresome'er:** i.e., wheresoever, wherever

9–10. **Arthur's bosom:** the Hostess's mistake for "Abraham's bosom" (See longer note, page 241.)

11. **an it:** i.e., as if he

12. **christom:** i.e., chrisom, an infant in its baptismal robe (See picture, page 196.) **parted:** i.e., departed; **ev'n just:** exactly

16. **but:** only

17. **talked:** Here the Folio reads "Table." Editors since Theobald in 1733 have substituted "babbled"— perhaps the most famous emendation in Shake-

(continued)

64

But every rub is smooth**è**d on our way.
Then forth, dear countrymen. Let us deliver
Our puissance into the hand of God,
Putting it straight in expedition.   200
Cheerly to sea. The signs of war advance.
No king of England if not king of France.
                              Flourish. ⌐*They exit.*⌐

⌐Scene 3⌐
Enter Pistol, Nym, Bardolph, Boy, and Hostess.

HOSTESS Prithee, honey-sweet husband, let me bring
thee to Staines.
PISTOL No; for my manly heart doth earn.—Bardolph,
be blithe.—Nym, rouse thy vaunting veins.—Boy,
bristle thy courage up. For Falstaff, he is dead, and   5
we must earn therefore.
BARDOLPH Would I were with him, wheresome'er he
is, either in heaven or in hell.
HOSTESS Nay, sure, he's not in hell! He's in Arthur's
bosom, if ever man went to Arthur's bosom. He   10
made a finer end, and went away an it had been any
christom child. He parted ev'n just between twelve
and one, ev'n at the turning o' th' tide; for after I saw
him fumble with the sheets and play with flowers
and smile upon his finger's end, I knew there was   15
but one way, for his nose was as sharp as a pen and
he ⌐talked⌐ of green fields. "How now, Sir John?"
quoth I. "What, man, be o' good cheer!" So he cried
out "God, God, God!" three or four times. Now I, to
comfort him, bid him he should not think of God; I   20
hoped there was no need to trouble himself with
any such thoughts yet. So he bade me lay more
clothes on his feet. I put my hand into the bed and
felt them, and they were as cold as any stone. Then I

speare editing. (See longer note, page 241.) **green fields:** perhaps, an echo of Psalm 23's "green pasture"

27. **of sack:** i.e., against sherry

31–32. **incarnate:** embodied in flesh

33. **carnation:** the color light pink

35. **about:** i.e., because of

37. **handle:** discuss

38–39. **rheumatic . . . Whore of Babylon:** The Hostess's swerve from **rheumatic** to the **Whore of Babylon** has been explained by the resemblance in sound between **rheum-** and "Rome"; Protestants often attacked the Roman Catholic Church by calling it **Whore of Babylon,** a figure described in the last book of the New Testament, Revelation 17.4–5.

41. **Bardolph's nose:** See 3.6.104–8 for a detailed description of Bardolph's drink-inflamed face.

43. **fuel:** i.e., liquor

44. **riches:** perhaps a comparison of his red nose to such jewels as rubies and carbuncles. (Compare *Henry IV, Part 1* 3.3.83–85.)

45. **shog:** go

48. **chattels . . . movables: Chattels** are movable possessions.

49. **Let senses rule:** perhaps, keep alert; or, perhaps, use common sense; **Pitch and pay:** cash only, no credit

50–51. **oaths . . . wafer-cakes:** proverbial **wafer-cakes:** easily broken pastry

51. **Holdfast . . . dog:** Proverbial: "Hold fast when you have it." **Holdfast:** a hook, clamp, or bolt **duck:** dear

52. **Caveto:** beware

53. **crystals:** i.e., eyes

(continued)

felt to his knees, and so ⌜upward⌝ and upward, and   25
all was as cold as any stone.

NYM   They say he cried out of sack.

HOSTESS   Ay, that he did.

BARDOLPH   And of women.

HOSTESS   Nay, that he did not.   30

BOY   Yes, that he did, and said they were devils incarnate.

HOSTESS   He could never abide carnation. 'Twas a
color he never liked.

BOY   He said once, the devil would have him about   35
women.

HOSTESS   He did in some sort, indeed, handle women,
but then he was rheumatic and talked of the Whore
of Babylon.

BOY   Do you not remember he saw a flea stick upon   40
Bardolph's nose, and he said it was a black soul
burning in hell?

BARDOLPH   Well, the fuel is gone that maintained that
fire. That's all the riches I got in his service.

NYM   Shall we shog? The King will be gone from   45
Southampton.

PISTOL   Come, let's away.—My love, give me thy lips.
⌜*They kiss.*⌝ Look to my chattels and my movables.
Let senses rule. The ⌜word⌝ is "Pitch and pay." Trust
none, for oaths are straws, men's faiths are wafer-   50
cakes, and Holdfast is the only dog, my duck.
Therefore, *Caveto* be thy counselor. Go, clear thy
crystals.—Yoke-fellows in arms, let us to France,
like horse-leeches, my boys, to suck, to suck, the
very blood to suck.   55

BOY   And that's but unwholesome food, they say.

PISTOL   Touch her soft mouth, and march.

BARDOLPH, ⌜*kissing the Hostess*⌝ Farewell, hostess.

NYM   I cannot kiss, that is the humor of it. But adieu.

59. **adieu:** good-bye (in French)
60. **huswifery:** thrift
60–61. **Keep close:** i.e., perhaps, stay in the house **close:** hidden, secluded

2.4 The King of France and his court plan their defense against Henry's invasion. Exeter arrives to present the King with Henry's claim to the French throne, to threaten the French, and to return to the Dauphin the insulting defiance he sent to Henry.

———————

2.4 SD. **Constable:** commander in chief, in the absence of the king
1. **comes:** i.e., come
7. **line:** reinforce; **towns of war:** fortified places
8. **defendant:** defensive
9. **England:** i.e., Henry, King of **England**
10. **gulf:** whirlpool
11. **fits us:** is appropriate for us; **be as provident:** show such foresight
12. **late examples:** recent instances (namely, French defeats at Crécy [1346] and Poitiers [1356])
13. **fatal and neglected:** i.e., fatally underestimated or underrated
14. **fields:** battlefields
15. **redoubted:** dread, respected
16. **meet:** i.e., fitting that
19–20. **defenses . . . and collected:** i.e., **defenses maintained, musters assembled, and preparations collected**
21. **As . . . war:** i.e., **as if a war were**
24. **show:** appearance

PISTOL, ⌜*to the Hostess*⌝ Let huswifery appear. Keep   60
    close, I thee command.
HOSTESS   Farewell. Adieu.

                           They exit.

              ⌜Scene 4⌝
Flourish. Enter the French King, the Dauphin, the Dukes
   of Berri and Brittany, ⌜the Constable, and others.⌝

KING OF FRANCE
    Thus comes the English with full power upon us,
    And more than carefully it us concerns
    To answer royally in our defenses.
    Therefore the Dukes of Berri and of Brittany,
    Of Brabant and of Orléans, shall make forth,   5
    And you, Prince Dauphin, with all swift dispatch,
    To line and new-repair our towns of war
    With men of courage and with means defendant.
    For England his approaches makes as fierce
    As waters to the sucking of a gulf.   10
    It fits us then to be as provident
    As fear may teach us out of late examples
    Left by the fatal and neglected English
    Upon our fields.
DAUPHIN   My most redoubted father,   15
    It is most meet we arm us 'gainst the foe,
    For peace itself should not so dull a kingdom,
    Though war nor no known quarrel were in question
    But that defenses, musters, preparations
    Should be maintained, assembled, and collected   20
    As were a war in expectation.
    Therefore I say 'tis meet we all go forth
    To view the sick and feeble parts of France.
    And let us do it with no show of fear,
    No, with no more than if we heard that England   25

26. **Whitsun:** the festive May Sunday seven weeks after Easter; **morris-dance:** English folk dance that tells a story, performed by costumed figures

27. **she:** i.e., England; **idly:** ineffectively

28. **fantastically:** capriciously, strangely

29. **humorous:** whimsical

30. **fear . . . not:** i.e., no one fears England **attends:** waits upon

33. **Question . . . ambassadors:** i.e., let yourself (**your Grace**) **question** the messengers recently sent (to England)

34. **state:** ceremony; **embassy:** message

35. **councillors:** i.e., members of his council

36. **exception:** i.e., taking **exception,** disagreeing; **withal:** in addition

37. **terrible:** terrifying; **constant resolution:** fixed purpose

38–39. **his vanities . . . Brutus:** i.e., his previous frivolities were like Lucius Junius Brutus's feeblemindedness, which he feigned to deceive Tarquin, a tyrannical king of Rome in the sixth century B.C.E.

40. **discretion:** discernment, wisdom

41. **ordure:** dung

42. **spring:** grow

44. **though:** i.e., even if

45. **weigh:** consider

47–50. **So . . . cloth:** i.e., by overestimating the enemy's strength, we ensure that our **defense** is sufficient; if we underestimate the enemy and provide an inadequate **defense,** we are like the miser who ruins his coat by providing the tailor too **little cloth**

(continued)

70

Were busied with a Whitsun morris-dance.
For, my good liege, she is so idly kinged,
Her scepter so fantastically borne
By a vain, giddy, shallow, humorous youth,
That fear attends her not.　　　　　　　　　　30
CONSTABLE　　　　　　　　O peace, Prince Dauphin!
You are too much mistaken in this king.
Question your Grace the late ambassadors
With what great state he heard their embassy,
How well supplied with noble councillors,　　　35
How modest in exception, and withal
How terrible in constant resolution,
And you shall find his vanities forespent
Were but the outside of the Roman Brutus,
Covering discretion with a coat of folly,　　　40
As gardeners do with ordure hide those roots
That shall first spring and be most delicate.
DAUPHIN
Well, 'tis not so, my Lord High Constable.
But though we think it so, it is no matter.
In cases of defense, 'tis best to weigh　　　　45
The enemy more mighty than he seems.
So the proportions of defense are filled,
Which of a weak and niggardly projection
Doth, like a miser, spoil his coat with scanting
A little cloth.　　　　　　　　　　　　　50
KING OF FRANCE　　Think we King Harry strong,
And, princes, look you strongly arm to meet him.
The kindred of him hath been fleshed upon us,
And he is bred out of that bloody strain
That haunted us in our familiar paths.　　　55
Witness our too-much-memorable shame
When Cressy battle fatally was struck
And all our princes captived by the hand
Of that black name, Edward, Black Prince of
　　Wales,　　　　　　　　　　　　　60

53. **kindred of him:** e.g., Edward the Black Prince; **fleshed upon us:** initiated into bloodshed at our expense

54. **strain:** breed

57. **struck:** fought

61. **mountain sire:** Edward III, perhaps so called because he was born in the Welsh mountains

63. **seed:** i.e., son

64–66. **deface / The patterns . . . made:** i.e., kill twenty-year-old French fighters

67. **stock:** (1) tree; (2) progenitor of a family line

68. **native . . . him:** the might and destiny that are his by nature

71. **present:** immediate

73. **chase:** hunt

74. **Turn head: turn** at bay; i.e., stop and **turn** around (Like the French king, the Dauphin imagines the French as prey to English **dogs.**)

75. **Most spend their mouths:** i.e., bay loudest

78. **short:** sharply, abruptly

85. **apart:** aside

87. **law . . . nations:** laws implanted by **nature** in the human mind, and international law; **'longs:** i.e., belongs

A sundial (1.2.218).
From August Casimir Redel,
Apophtegmata symbolica . . . (n.d.).

Whiles that his mountain sire, on mountain standing
Up in the air, crowned with the golden sun,
Saw his heroical seed and smiled to see him
Mangle the work of nature and deface
The patterns that by God and by French fathers   65
Had twenty years been made. This is a stem
Of that victorious stock, and let us fear
The native mightiness and fate of him.

Enter a Messenger.

MESSENGER
Ambassadors from Harry King of England
Do crave admittance to your Majesty.   70

KING OF FRANCE
We'll give them present audience. Go, and bring
    them.   ⌜*Messenger exits.*⌝
You see this chase is hotly followed, friends.

DAUPHIN
Turn head and stop pursuit, for coward dogs
Most spend their mouths when what they seem to   75
    threaten
Runs far before them. Good my sovereign,
Take up the English short, and let them know
Of what a monarchy you are the head.
Self-love, my liege, is not so vile a sin   80
As self-neglecting.

Enter Exeter, ⌜*with Lords and Attendants.*⌝

KING OF FRANCE   From our brother of England?

EXETER
From him, and thus he greets your Majesty:
He wills you, in the name of God almighty,
That you divest yourself and lay apart   85
The borrowed glories that, by gift of heaven,
By law of nature and of nations, 'longs
To him and to his heirs—namely, the crown

89. **wide-stretchèd:** far-ranging
90. **ordinance of times:** tradition
92. **sinister:** dishonest; erroneous; **awkward:** perverse; oblique
95. **line: line** of descent, family tree
96. **truly demonstrative:** i.e., providing evidence of the truth
97. **Willing you overlook:** i.e., desiring that you look over
98. **evenly:** directly, justly, accurately
101. **indirectly:** wrongfully; **held:** kept
102. **native:** entitled by birth; **challenger:** claimant
104. **constraint:** force
106–7. **tempest . . . earthquake:** Compare Isaiah 29.6: "Thou shalt be visited of the Lord of hosts, with thunder, earthquake, and with a great noise, with storm and tempest." (Bishops' Bible, 1568)
107. **Jove:** in Roman mythology, king of the gods and wielder of thunderbolts (See picture, page 154.)
108. **requiring:** demanding
109. **bowels:** the seat of mercy (See Philippians 1.8: "in the bowels of Jesus Christ." Bishops' Bible, 1568)
112. **his:** its
114. **privèd:** i.e., deprived (of **betrothèd lovers** [line 116], just as **widows** and **orphans** [line 113] are deprived of **husbands** and **fathers** [line 116] respectively)
121. **us:** i.e., me (the royal "we")

And all wide-stretchèd honors that pertain
By custom and the ordinance of times   90
Unto the crown of France. That you may know
'Tis no sinister nor no awkward claim
Picked from the wormholes of long-vanished days
Nor from the dust of old oblivion raked,
He sends you this most memorable line,   95
                                     ⌜*He offers a paper.*⌝
In every branch truly demonstrative,
Willing you overlook this pedigree,
And when you find him evenly derived
From his most famed of famous ancestors,
Edward the Third, he bids you then resign   100
Your crown and kingdom, indirectly held
From him, the native and true challenger.
KING OF FRANCE   Or else what follows?
EXETER
Bloody constraint, for if you hide the crown
Even in your hearts, there will he rake for it.   105
Therefore in fierce tempest is he coming,
In thunder and in earthquake like a Jove,
That, if requiring fail, he will compel,
And bids you, in the bowels of the Lord,
Deliver up the crown and to take mercy   110
On the poor souls for whom this hungry war
Opens his vasty jaws, and on your head
Turning the widows' tears, the orphans' cries,
The dead men's blood, the ⌜privèd⌝ maidens'
    groans,   115
For husbands, fathers, and betrothèd lovers
That shall be swallowed in this controversy.
This is his claim, his threat'ning, and my message—
Unless the Dauphin be in presence here,
To whom expressly I bring greeting too.   120
KING OF FRANCE
For us, we will consider of this further.

125. **England:** i.e., Henry

127. **misbecome:** be inappropriate for

129. **an if:** i.e., **if**

130. **in grant . . . at large:** i.e., in acceding completely to all our demands

133. **womby vaultages:** womblike vaulted places (perhaps, caverns)

135. **second accent:** echo; **ordinance:** i.e., ordnance or cannon

136. **fair return:** i.e., pleasing or courteous reply

138. **odds:** conflict

139. **matching to:** fitting for; **vanity:** worthlessness

140. **Paris balls:** tennis **balls**

141. **Louvre:** royal palace (with a pun on "lover" that continues in the reference to **mistress court** in line 142)

142. **mistress:** i.e., greatest; **court:** (1) royal **court;** (2) tennis **court**

145. **greener:** i.e., younger

146. **masters:** possesses

146–47. **Now . . . grain:** a reference to an hourglass, with which time is measured by grains of sand dropping from the upper to the lower half through a narrow passage (See picture, page 56.)

Tomorrow shall you bear our full intent
Back to our brother of England.
DAUPHIN, ⌐*to Exeter*¬   For the Dauphin,
I stand here for him. What to him from England?   125
EXETER
Scorn and defiance, slight regard, contempt,
And anything that may not misbecome
The mighty sender, doth he prize you at.
Thus says my king: an if your father's Highness
Do not, in grant of all demands at large,   130
Sweeten the bitter mock you sent his Majesty,
He'll call you to so hot an answer of it
That caves and womby vaultages of France
Shall chide your trespass and return your mock
In second accent of his ordinance.   135
DAUPHIN
Say, if my father render fair return,
It is against my will, for I desire
Nothing but odds with England. To that end,
As matching to his youth and vanity,
I did present him with the Paris balls.   140
EXETER
He'll make your Paris ⌐Louvre¬ shake for it,
Were it the mistress court of mighty Europe.
And be assured you'll find a difference,
As we his subjects have in wonder found,
Between the promise of his greener days   145
And these he masters now. Now he weighs time
Even to the utmost grain. That you shall read
In your own losses, if he stay in France.
KING OF FRANCE
Tomorrow shall you know our mind at full.
                                        Flourish.
EXETER
Dispatch us with all speed, lest that our king   150

152. **footed . . . already:** i.e., **already** in France
153. **fair conditions:** For the French king's reply
to Henry's demands, see 3.Chorus.31–33.
   154. **breath:** i.e., breathing space

"I did present him with the Paris balls." (2.4.140)
From Guillaume de la Perrière,
Le théâtre des bons engins [1539?].

Come here himself to question our delay,
For he is footed in this land already.

KING OF FRANCE
You shall be soon dispatched with fair conditions.
A night is but small breath and little pause
To answer matters of this consequence.   155

Flourish. They exit.

The Life of

HENRY V

ACT 3

3.Chorus: The Chorus describes the embarkation of Henry's fleet for France, Henry's preparations to besiege the town of Harfleur, and the breakdown of talks between the French (who have offered Henry some land, and their princess in marriage) and the English, who now begin the siege.

---

1. **scene:** play
2. **celerity:** speed
4. **well-appointed:** well-equipped; **Dover:** In Act 2, Henry's army was said to be departing from Southampton; often plays of this period contain such discrepancies.
5. **Embark . . . royalty:** i.e., take ship; **brave:** splendid
6. **young Phoebus:** i.e., the morning sun **Phoebus:** Greco-Roman god of the sun
8. **fancies:** imaginations
9. **hempen tackle:** ropes, rigging
11. **threaden sails:** i.e., **sails** made of thread
12. **Borne:** carried forward
13. **bottoms:** ships' hulls
15. **rivage:** shore
18. **Harfleur:** French port at the mouth of the Seine River
19. **Grapple . . . navy:** i.e., hook your imaginations to the sterns of the ships
20. **as . . . still:** i.e., **as** quiet as if it were **midnight** (proverbial)
22. **pith and puissance:** i.e., strength

ACT ⌐3⌐

Enter Chorus.

⌐CHORUS⌐
Thus with imagined wing our swift scene flies
In motion of no less celerity
Than that of thought. Suppose that you have seen
The well-appointed king at Dover pier
Embark his royalty, and his brave fleet   5
With silken streamers the young Phoebus
   ⌐fanning.⌐
Play with your fancies and in them behold,
Upon the hempen tackle, shipboys climbing.
Hear the shrill whistle, which doth order give   10
To sounds confused. Behold the threaden sails,
Borne with th' invisible and creeping wind,
Draw the huge bottoms through the furrowed sea,
Breasting the lofty surge. O, do but think
You stand upon the rivage and behold   15
A city on th' inconstant billows dancing,
For so appears this fleet majestical,
Holding due course to Harfleur. Follow, follow!
Grapple your minds to sternage of this navy,
And leave your England, as dead midnight still,   20
Guarded with grandsires, babies, and old women,
Either past or not arrived to pith and puissance,
For who is he whose chin is but enriched
With one appearing hair that will not follow

83

25. **culled and choice-drawn:** selected (synonymous words); **cavaliers:** mounted knights

27. **carriages:** wheeled supports on which cannon are mounted

28. **girded:** i.e., perhaps, walled; perhaps, besieged (See pictures, pages 118 and 128.)

29. **Ambassador:** i.e., Exeter

32. **to:** i.e., as

34. **likes:** pleases

35. **linstock:** the cleft stick holding the match used to fire the cannon (See picture, page 124.)

35 SD. **Alarum:** call to arms; **chambers:** small cannon without carriages (fired offstage)

37. **eke out:** supplement

3.1 Henry delivers an oration to inspire his troops to take Harfleur.

---

1. **breach:** gap made by cannon in fortified walls (See picture, page 94.)

6. **blast of war:** trumpet sounding the **alarum** (0 SD)

9. **fair:** attractive; **hard-favored:** ill-favored, ugly

10. **terrible aspect:** terrifying look or glance

11. **portage:** ports, or portholes

12. **o'erwhelm:** overhang

13. **fearfully:** frighteningly; **gallèd:** i.e., projecting (literally, swollen)

These culled and choice-drawn cavaliers to France?   25
Work, work your thoughts, and therein see a siege;
Behold the ordnance on their carriages,
With fatal mouths gaping on girded Harfleur.
Suppose th' Ambassador from the French comes
    back,   30
Tells Harry that the King doth offer him
Katherine his daughter and with her, to dowry,
Some petty and unprofitable dukedoms.
The offer likes not, and the nimble gunner
With linstock now the devilish cannon touches,   35
              Alarum, and chambers go off.
And down goes all before them. Still be kind,
And eke out our performance with your mind.
                              He exits.

⌜Scene 1⌝
Enter the King ⌜of England,⌝ Exeter, Bedford, and
Gloucester. Alarum. ⌜Enter Soldiers with⌝ scaling
ladders at Harfleur.

KING HENRY
Once more unto the breach, dear friends, once
    more,
Or close the wall up with our English dead!
In peace there's nothing so becomes a man
As modest stillness and humility,   5
But when the blast of war blows in our ears,
Then imitate the action of the tiger:
Stiffen the sinews, ⌜summon⌝ up the blood,
Disguise fair nature with hard-favored rage,
Then lend the eye a terrible aspect,   10
Let it pry through the portage of the head
Like the brass cannon, let the brow o'erwhelm it
As fearfully as doth a gallèd rock

14. **jutty . . . base:** jut out beyond its demolished base

15. **Swilled:** drenched; **wasteful:** desolate

17. **bend up:** i.e., stretch (an image from archery)

18. **his:** its

19. **fet:** fetched; **war-proof:** (courage) tested by war

20. **Alexanders:** See note to 1.1.49.

21. **even:** evening

22. **argument:** subject for debate; i.e., enemy soldiers

25. **copy:** example; **grosser blood:** i.e., lower rank (in contrast to the highest social rank, the **noblest English,** line 18)

27. **yeomen:** commoners (below the rank of "gentleman") who cultivate their own land

29. **mettle . . . pasture:** i.e., spirit instilled in your breeding **pasture:** nourishment, sustenance (with wordplay on **pasture** as yeomen's land)

30. **worth:** i.e., worthy of; **breeding:** parentage; upbringing, education

32. **so mean and base:** i.e., of such low class

33. **That hath not:** i.e., but you have some

34. **in the slips:** i.e., leashed

35. **The game's afoot:** i.e., the quarry in the hunt has been roused and can be pursued (See picture, page 200.)

36. **upon . . . charge:** i.e., as you charge

37. **Saint George:** England's patron saint

3.2 Bardolph, Pistol, Nym, and the Boy withdraw from the assault on Harfleur. They are driven back

(continued)

O'erhang and jutty his confounded base
Swilled with the wild and wasteful ocean.   15
Now set the teeth, and stretch the nostril wide,
Hold hard the breath, and bend up every spirit
To his full height. On, on, you ⌜noblest⌝ English,
Whose blood is fet from fathers of war-proof,
Fathers that, like so many Alexanders,   20
Have in these parts from morn till even fought,
And sheathed their swords for lack of argument.
Dishonor not your mothers. Now attest
That those whom you called fathers did beget you.
Be copy now to ⌜men⌝ of grosser blood   25
And teach them how to war. And you, good yeomen,
Whose limbs were made in England, show us here
The mettle of your pasture. Let us swear
That you are worth your breeding, which I doubt
    not,   30
For there is none of you so mean and base
That hath not noble luster in your eyes.
I see you stand like greyhounds in the slips,
⌜Straining⌝ upon the start. The game's afoot.
Follow your spirit, and upon this charge   35
Cry "God for Harry, England, and Saint George!"
                    Alarum, and chambers go off.
                                        ⌜*They exit.*⌝

⌜Scene 2⌝
Enter Nym, Bardolph, Pistol, and Boy.

BARDOLPH   On, on, on, on, on! To the breach, to the
    breach!
NYM   Pray thee, corporal, stay. The knocks are too hot,
    and, for mine own part, I have not a case of lives.
    The humor of it is too hot; that is the very plainsong   5
    of it.

to it by Captain Fluellen. The Boy tells us of his masters' cowardice. Fluellen then discusses military tactics with Captain Gower, Captain Jamy, and Captain Macmorris.

———————

3. **knocks . . . hot:** i.e., perhaps, resistance is too fierce
4. **case:** set
5. **humor:** See longer note to 2.1.60, page 240. **plainsong:** i.e., plain truth (literally, early church music)
9. **vassals:** humble servants
13. **Would:** i.e., I wish
18. **hie:** hurry
19. **duly:** properly, right
20. **truly:** loyally, honestly
22. **Avaunt:** begone; **cullions:** term of contempt (literally, testicles)
23. **men of mold:** i.e., mortal **men** (literally, **men** of clay, the substance from which, according to the book of Genesis, God made Adam)
25. **bawcock:** good fellow (French *beau coq*, "fine bird"); **lenity:** gentleness
26. **chuck:** like **bawcock,** a term of endearment
30. **swashers:** swaggerers, braggarts; **boy:** (1) servant; (2) boy as opposed to man (line 32)
32, 33. **man:** (1) man of courage; (2) manservant
32. **antics:** buffoons, clowns
33. **for:** i.e., as for; **white-livered:** cowardly
34. **faces it out:** looks defiant
36–37. **breaks words:** (1) **breaks** his word; (2) mangles language

PISTOL   "The plainsong" is most just, for humors do
   abound.
   Knocks go and come. God's vassals drop and die,
      ⌜*Sings*⌝ And sword and shield,   10
         In bloody field,
      Doth win immortal fame.
BOY   Would I were in an alehouse in London! I would
   give all my fame for a pot of ale, and safety.
PISTOL   And I.   15
   ⌜*Sings*⌝   If wishes would prevail with me,
         My purpose should not fail with me,
         But thither would I hie.
BOY ⌜*sings*⌝   As duly,
            But not as truly,   20
         As bird doth sing on bough.

               Enter Fluellen.

FLUELLEN
   Up to the breach, you dogs! Avaunt, you cullions!
PISTOL   Be merciful, great duke, to men of mold. Abate
   thy rage, abate thy manly rage, abate thy rage, great
   duke. Good bawcock, 'bate thy rage. Use lenity,   25
   sweet chuck.
NYM, ⌜*to Fluellen*⌝   These be good humors. Your Honor
   wins bad humors.
               ⌜*All but the Boy*⌝ *exit.*
BOY   As young as I am, I have observed these three
   swashers. I am boy to them all three, but all they   30
   three, though they would serve me, could not be
   man to me. For indeed three such antics do not
   amount to a man: for Bardolph, he is white-livered
   and red-faced, by the means whereof he faces it out
   but fights not; for Pistol, he hath a killing tongue   35
   and a quiet sword, by the means whereof he breaks
   words and keeps whole weapons; for Nym, he hath
   heard that men of few words are the best men, and

37. **keeps whole weapons:** i.e., does not damage his **weapons** by using them

41. **broke:** cut

44. **purchase:** plunder; **lute:** stringed musical instrument; **bore:** carried

45. **leagues:** A league is approximately three miles.

46. **filching:** stealing

47. **fire shovel:** coal **shovel**

48. **carry coals:** i.e., suffer humiliation patiently

50–51. **makes ... against:** i.e., is contrary to

53. **pocketing ... wrongs:** (1) taking up stolen goods; (2) tolerating insults

54. **better service:** i.e., **service** with **better** masters

54–55. **Their villainy ... up:** i.e., (1) I have no tolerance (**stomach**) for **their villainy,** and will stop serving them; (2) **their villainy** makes me sick, and **I must** throw **up**

55 SD. **He exits:** See longer note, page 241.

56. **presently:** immediately

57. **mines:** In the practices of ancient warfare (which Fluellen prefers), mines were excavations of the foundations of walls to cause them to fall; in modern warfare following the introduction of gunpowder (as in *Henry V*), mines were tunnels dug under walls in which charges were laid to bring down the walls. **would:** wishes to

59. **Tell you:** i.e., **tell** (Fluellen, who represents Welsh speakers in this play, is made to speak broken and heavily accented English, as are Captain Jamy, the Scot, and Captain Macmorris, the Irishman.)

(continued)

therefore he scorns to say his prayers, lest he should
be thought a coward, but his few bad words are   40
matched with as few good deeds, for he never broke
any man's head but his own, and that was against a
post when he was drunk. They will steal anything
and call it purchase. Bardolph stole a lute case, bore
it twelve leagues, and sold it for three halfpence.   45
Nym and Bardolph are sworn brothers in filching,
and in Calais they stole a fire shovel. I knew by that
piece of service the men would carry coals. They
would have me as familiar with men's pockets as
their gloves or their handkerchers, which makes   50
much against my manhood, if I should take from
another's pocket to put into mine, for it is plain
pocketing up of wrongs. I must leave them and seek
some better service. Their villainy goes against my
weak stomach, and therefore I must cast it up.   55

He exits.

Enter ⌜*Fluellen and*⌝ *Gower.*

GOWER   Captain Fluellen, you must come presently to
the mines; the Duke of Gloucester would speak
with you.

FLUELLEN   To the mines? Tell you the Duke it is not so
good to come to the mines, for, look you, the mines   60
is not according to the disciplines of the war. The
concavities of it is not sufficient, for, look you, th'
athversary, you may discuss unto the Duke, look
you, is digt himself four yard under the countermines. By Cheshu, I think he will plow up all if   65
there is not better directions.

GOWER   The Duke of Gloucester, to whom the order of
the siege is given, is altogether directed by an
Irishman, a very valiant gentleman, i' faith.

FLUELLEN   It is Captain Macmorris, is it not?   70

GOWER   I think it be.

61. **disciplines of the war:** i.e., scholarly (usually classical) authorities who wrote about warfare

61–65. **The . . . countermines:** According to Fluellen, the French are threatening the English tunnels by digging **countermines** four yards beneath them, from which the French can blow up the English mines. **concavities:** i.e., depth

65. **Cheshu:** i.e., Jesu; **plow:** i.e., blow (Often Fluellen is made to use *p* for *b* and *f* for *v.*)

66. **directions:** military orders, commands

67. **order:** command

72. **an ass . . . world:** perhaps, as great **an ass as** there is **in the world**

73. **verify:** affirm to be true; **in his beard:** i.e., to his face

79. **expedition:** readiness in the refutation of arguments (a term from rhetoric)

80. **aunchient:** i.e., ancient

83. **pristine:** original, ancient

86. **Godden:** good evening, or good afternoon

89. **pioners:** soldiers who excavate trenches and mines; **given o'er:** stopped

94. **hour:** i.e., **hour** more

97. **voutsafe:** i.e., vouchsafe, grant

FLUELLEN By Cheshu, he is an ass, as in the world. I
will verify as much in his beard. He has no more
directions in the true disciplines of the wars, look
you, of the Roman disciplines, than is a puppy dog.   75

Enter ⌐Captain⌐ Macmorris, and Captain Jamy.

GOWER Here he comes, and the Scots captain, Captain
Jamy, with him.
FLUELLEN Captain Jamy is a marvelous falorous gentleman, that is certain, and of great expedition and
knowledge in th' aunchient wars, upon my particu-   80
lar knowledge of his directions. By Cheshu, he will
maintain his argument as well as any military man
in the world in the disciplines of the pristine wars
of the Romans.
JAMY I say gudday, Captain Fluellen.   85
FLUELLEN Godden to your Worship, good Captain
James.
GOWER How now, Captain Macmorris, have you quit
the mines? Have the pioners given o'er?
MACMORRIS By Chrish, la, 'tish ill done. The work ish   90
give over. The trompet sound the retreat. By my
hand I swear, and my father's soul, the work ish ill
done. It ish give over. I would have blowed up the
town, so Chrish save me, la, in an hour. O, 'tish ill
done, 'tish ill done, by my hand, 'tish ill done.   95
FLUELLEN Captain Macmorris, I beseech you now,
will you voutsafe me, look you, a few disputations
with you as partly touching or concerning the
disciplines of the war, the Roman wars? In the way
of argument, look you, and friendly communica-   100
tion, partly to satisfy my opinion, and partly for the
satisfaction, look you, of my mind, as touching the
direction of the military discipline, that is the point.
JAMY It sall be vary gud, gud feith, gud captens bath,

105. **quit . . . leve:** i.e., answer, if you permit me

106. **marry:** indeed (originally an oath on the name of the Virgin Mary)

110. **beseeched:** i.e., besieged; **An:** i.e., if

116. **Mess:** i.e., Mass

120. **breff . . . long:** i.e., short **and the long** (of it)

120–21. **wad . . . tway:** i.e., would very gladly have **heard some** topic debated between **you** two **fain:** gladly

125–27. **Of my nation . . . nation:** perhaps an expression of outrage that Fluellen may be about to slur the Irish

129. **peradventure:** perhaps

130. **use:** treat

131. **in discretion:** exercising good judgment

137. **will mistake:** i.e., are determined to misunderstand, or always misunderstand

138 SD. **parley:** trumpet signal for a conference between leaders of opposing sides

Cannons creating breaches in fortifications. (3.1.1)
From Niccolò Machiavelli, *The arte of warre* . . . (1588).

and I sall quit you with gud leve, as I may pick 105
occasion, that sall I, marry.
MACMORRIS It is no time to discourse, so Chrish save
me. The day is hot, and the weather, and the wars,
and the King, and the dukes. It is no time to
discourse. The town is beseeched. An the trumpet 110
call us to the breach and we talk and, be Chrish, do
nothing, 'tis shame for us all. So God sa' me, 'tis
shame to stand still. It is shame, by my hand. And
there is throats to be cut, and works to be done,
and there ish nothing done, so Christ sa' me, la. 115
JAMY By the Mess, ere theise eyes of mine take themselves to slomber, ay'll de gud service, or I'll lig i'
th' grund for it, ay, or go to death. And I'll pay 't as
valorously as I may, that sall I suerly do, that is the
breff and the long. Marry, I wad full fain heard 120
some question 'tween you tway.
FLUELLEN Captain Macmorris, I think, look you, under your correction, there is not many of your
nation—
MACMORRIS Of my nation? What ish my nation? Ish a 125
villain and a basterd and a knave and a rascal. What
ish my nation? Who talks of my nation?
FLUELLEN Look you, if you take the matter otherwise
than is meant, Captain Macmorris, peradventure I
shall think you do not use me with that affability as, 130
in discretion, you ought to use me, look you, being
as good a man as yourself, both in the disciplines of
war and in the derivation of my birth, and in other
particularities.
MACMORRIS I do not know you so good a man as 135
myself. So Chrish save me, I will cut off your head.
GOWER Gentlemen both, you will mistake each other.
JAMY Ah, that's a foul fault.
                                        A parley ⌈sounds.⌉
GOWER The town sounds a parley.

3.3 Henry threatens the men of Harfleur with the destruction of the town and its population if they do not yield to him. The Governor then surrenders the town to Henry, who spares its people.

---

1. **resolves:** determines, decides
2. **latest parle:** i.e., last conference; **admit:** grant, allow
4. **like to:** i.e., **like; proud of destruction:** i.e., elated by the possibility **of destruction**
7. **batt'ry:** i.e., bombardment
8. **half-achieved:** half-conquered
11. **fleshed soldier: soldier** who has tasted blood
12. **In liberty . . . hand:** i.e., completely free to be violent; **range:** roam
13. **wide as hell:** i.e., allowing every atrocity
15. **impious:** wicked
16. **prince of fiends:** i.e., Lucifer, the archangel whose name means "lightbearing," and who, after leading the revolt against God, was the prince of devils
17. **smirched:** blackened (by gunpowder); **fell:** fierce, savage
18. **Enlinked to:** joined in company with; **waste:** destruction
23. **he . . . his:** it . . . its; **career:** gallop at full speed
24. **bootless:** futilely; **vain:** useless

FLUELLEN Captain Macmorris, when there is more   140
   better opportunity to be required, look you, I will
   be so bold as to tell you I know the disciplines of
   war, and there is an end.
                                    ⌜*They*⌝ *exit.*

⌜Scene 3⌝
Enter the King ⌜*of England*⌝ *and all his train*
before the gates.

KING HENRY, ⌜*to the men of Harfleur*⌝
   How yet resolves the Governor of the town?
   This is the latest parle we will admit.
   Therefore to our best mercy give yourselves
   Or, like to men proud of destruction,
   Defy us to our worst. For, as I am a soldier,   5
   A name that in my thoughts becomes me best,
   If I begin the batt'ry once again,
   I will not leave the half-achieved Harfleur
   Till in her ashes she lie burièd.
   The gates of mercy shall be all shut up,   10
   And the fleshed soldier, rough and hard of heart,
   In liberty of bloody hand, shall range
   With conscience wide as hell, mowing like grass
   Your fresh fair virgins and your flow'ring infants.
   What is it then to me if impious war,   15
   Arrayed in flames like to the prince of fiends,
   Do with his smirched complexion all fell feats
   Enlinked to waste and desolation?
   What is 't to me, when you yourselves are cause,
   If your pure maidens fall into the hand   20
   Of hot and forcing violation?
   What rein can hold licentious wickedness
   When down the hill he holds his fierce career?
   We may as bootless spend our vain command

25. **spoil:** looting and plundering

26. **precepts:** written summons; **Leviathan:** a monstrous sea creature mentioned in the Bible

28. **pity of . . . of:** i.e., **pity** on . . . on

30. **grace:** mercy

31. **O'erblows:** disperses; **contagious: Clouds** and mists were thought to carry disease.

32. **heady:** headstrong, violent

33. **look:** expect

34. **blind and bloody:** indiscriminately butchering

35. **Desire:** See longer note, page 242.

38. **spitted:** impaled

40–41. **wives . . . slaughtermen:** Herod's "slaughter of the innocents" in his effort to kill the child Jesus is narrated in Matthew 2.16–18. (See picture, page 176.)

43. **guilty in defense:** i.e., **guilty** by reason of having defended yourselves (See longer note, page 242.)

45. **succors:** help

46. **Returns us:** replies; **powers:** armies

47. **raise:** put an end to

50. **defensible:** capable of defending ourselves (See longer note to line 43, page 242.)

55. **Use mercy to them all:** In history, Henry's troops plundered and looted Harfleur and, according to some commentators, drove citizens from the town. (Since Pope's edition of the play [1725], some editors have put a period after **all** and a comma after **uncle.**)

Upon th' enragèd soldiers in their spoil   25
As send precepts to the Leviathan
To come ashore. Therefore, you men of Harfleur,
Take pity of your town and of your people
Whiles yet my soldiers are in my command,
Whiles yet the cool and temperate wind of grace   30
O'erblows the filthy and contagious clouds
Of ⌐heady⌐ murder, spoil, and villainy.
If not, why, in a moment look to see
The blind and bloody soldier with foul hand
Desire the locks of your shrill-shrieking daughters,   35
Your fathers taken by the silver beards
And their most reverend heads dashed to the walls,
Your naked infants spitted upon pikes
Whiles the mad mothers with their howls confused
Do break the clouds, as did the wives of Jewry   40
At Herod's bloody-hunting slaughtermen.
What say you? Will you yield and this avoid
Or, guilty in defense, be thus destroyed?

                    Enter Governor.

GOVERNOR
Our expectation hath this day an end.
The Dauphin, whom of succors we entreated,   45
Returns us that his powers are yet not ready
To raise so great a siege. Therefore, great king,
We yield our town and lives to thy soft mercy.
Enter our gates, dispose of us and ours,
For we no longer are defensible.   50
KING HENRY
Open your gates.   ⌐*Governor exits.*⌐
                    Come, uncle Exeter,
Go you and enter Harfleur. There remain,
And fortify it strongly 'gainst the French.
Use mercy to them all for us, dear uncle.   55

56–57. **growing / Upon:** i.e., increasing among
59. **addressed:** prepared

3.4 An old gentlewoman, Alice, begins to teach English to Katherine, Princess of France.

KATHERINE   Alice, you were in England, and you speak the language well.
ALICE   A little, madam.
KATHERINE   I beg you, teach me. I must learn to speak. What do you call *la main* in English?   5
ALICE   *La main?* It is called "de hand."
KATHERINE   De hand. And *les doigts?*
ALICE   *Les doigts?* My faith, I forget *les doigts;* but I will remember. *Les doigts?* I think they are called "de fingres"; yes, de fingres.   10
KATHERINE   *La main,* de hand. *Les doigts,* le fingres. I think I am a good student. I have quickly mastered two words of English. What do you call *les ongles?*   15
ALICE   *Les ongles?* We call them "de nailes."
KATHERINE   De nailes. Listen. Tell me if I speak well: de hand, de fingres, and de nailes.
ALICE   That's well said, madam. It is very good English.
KATHERINE   Tell me the English for *le bras.*   20
ALICE   "De arme," madam.
KATHERINE   And *le coude?*
ALICE   "D' elbow."
KATHERINE   D' elbow. I will repeat all the words that you have taught me so far.   25
ALICE   It is too difficult, madam, I think.

100

The winter coming on and sickness growing
Upon our soldiers, we will retire to Calais.
Tonight in Harfleur will we be your guest.
Tomorrow for the march are we addressed.

Flourish, and enter the town.

⌈Scene 4⌉

Enter Katherine and ⌈*Alice,*⌉ *an old Gentlewoman.*

KATHERINE *Alice, tu as été en Angleterre, et tu parles
bien le langage.*
ALICE *Un peu, madame.*
KATHERINE *Je te prie, m'enseignez. Il faut que j'ap-
prenne à parler. Comment appelez-vous "la main" en   5
anglais?*
ALICE *La main? Elle est appelée "de hand."*
KATHERINE De hand. *Et "les doigts"?*
⌈ALICE⌉ *Les doigts? Ma foi, j'oublie les doigts; mais je
me souviendrai. Les doigts? Je pense qu'ils sont   10
appelés "de fingres"; oui,* de fingres.
⌈KATHERINE⌉ *La main,* de hand. *Les doigts,* le fingres.
*Je pense que je suis le bon écolier. J'ai gagné deux
mots d'anglais vitement. Comment appelez-vous "les
ongles"?*   15
ALICE *Les ongles? Nous les appelons "de nailes."*
KATHERINE De nailes. *Écoutez. Dites-moi si je parle
bien:* de hand, de fingres, *et* de nailes.
ALICE *C'est bien dit, madame. Il est fort bon anglais.*
KATHERINE *Dites-moi l'anglais pour "le bras."*   20
ALICE *"De arme," madame.*
KATHERINE *Et "le coude"?*
ALICE *"D' elbow."*
KATHERINE D' elbow. *Je m'en fais la répétition de tous
les mots que vous m'avez appris dès à présent.*   25
ALICE *Il est trop difficile, madame, comme je pense.*

KATHERINE Excuse me, Alice. Listen: d' hand, de fingre, de nailes, d' arma, de bilbow.

ALICE D' elbow, madam.

KATHERINE O Lord God! I forget it: d' elbow. What do you call *le col?* 30

ALICE "De nick," madam.

KATHERINE De nick. And *le menton?*

ALICE "De chin."

KATHERINE De sin. *Le col,* de nick; *le menton,* de sin. 35

ALICE Yes. Saving your honor [i.e., with all due respect], in truth you pronounce the words as correctly as the natives of England.

KATHERINE I have no doubt about learning it, by the grace of God, and in little time.

ALICE Haven't you already forgotten what I have taught you? 40

KATHERINE No. I will recite promptly to you: d' hand, de fingre, de mailes—

ALICE De nailes, madam.

KATHERINE De nailes, de arme, de ilbow— 45

ALICE With all due respect, d' elbow.

KATHERINE That's what I say: d' elbow, de nick, and de sin. What do you call *le pied* and *la robe?*

ALICE "Le foot," madam, and "le count" [i.e., the gown].

KATHERINE Le foot, and le count. O Lord 50 God! They are ill-sounding words, corrupt, foul, and lewd, and not for ladies of honor to use. [See longer note, page 242.] I would not pronounce these words in front of the lords of France for the

(continued)

KATHERINE *Excusez-moi, Alice. Écoutez:* d' hand, de
fingre, de nailes, d' arma, de bilbow.
ALICE D' elbow, *madame.*
KATHERINE *Ô Seigneur Dieu! Je m'en oublie;* d' elbow.   30
Comment appelez-vous "le col"?
ALICE "De nick," *madame.*
KATHERINE De nick. *Et "le menton"?*
ALICE "De chin."
KATHERINE De sin. *Le col,* de nick; *le menton,* de sin.   35
ALICE *Oui. Sauf votre honneur, en vérité vous pro-
noncez les mots aussi droit que les natifs d'Angleterre.*
KATHERINE *Je ne doute point d'apprendre, par la grâce
de Dieu, et en peu de temps.*
ALICE *N'avez-vous pas déjà oublié ce que je vous ai*   40
enseigné?
KATHERINE *Non. Je réciterai à vous promptement:* d'
hand, de fingre, de mailes—
ALICE De nailes, *madame.*
KATHERINE De nailes, de arme, de ilbow—   45
ALICE *Sauf votre honneur,* d' elbow.
KATHERINE *Ainsi dis-je:* d' elbow, de nick, *et* de sin.
Comment appelez-vous "le pied" et "la robe"?
ALICE "Le foot," *madame, et* "le count."
KATHERINE Le foot, *et* le count. *Ô Seigneur Dieu! Ils*   50
*sont les mots de son mauvais, corruptible, gros, et
impudique, et non pour les dames d'honneur d'user.
Je ne voudrais prononcer ces mots devant les seign-
eurs de France, pour tout le monde. Foh!* Le foot *et* le
count! *Néanmoins, je réciterai une autre fois ma*   55
leçon ensemble: d' hand, de fingre, de nailes, d'
arme, d' elbow, de nick, de sin, de foot, le count.
ALICE *Excellent, madame.*
KATHERINE *C'est assez pour une fois. Allons-nous à*
dîner.   60
                                    ⌜*They*⌝ *exit.*

whole world. Foh! Le foot and le count! Nevertheless, I will recite one more time the whole of 55
my lesson: d' hand, de fingre, de nailes, d' arme, d'
elbow, de nick, de sin, de foot, le count.

    ALICE   Excellent, madam.

    KATHERINE   That is enough for one time. Let's
go to dinner. 60

3.5 The French nobles speak of their shame at
the success of Henry's invasion. The French King
plans to block Henry's march to Calais and orders
the royal herald Montjoy sent to Henry to learn how
much ransom Henry will pay for his release from
certain capture by the French.

---

  1. **he:** i.e., Henry
  2. **withal:** with
  3. **quit all:** renounce everything
  5. **Ô Dieu vivant:** O living God; **sprays:** shoots,
twigs (The Dauphin continues the gardening image
in lines 7–9, referring to the English as French
scions, or slips grafted to the **stock,** or stem, of a
wild plant [i.e., the Saxons], where they did sprout
[**spurt**] to such a height that they now look down
with contempt on [i.e., **overlook**] the plants from
which they were originally taken [**their grafters**].)
See picture, page 198.
  6. **The . . . luxury:** i.e., the dregs of our ancestors'
lust
  10. **Normans:** natives of Normandy, home of William the Conqueror, who invaded Saxon England in
1066

(continued)

⌜Scene 5⌝

Enter the King of France, the Dauphin, ⌜the Duke of Brittany,⌝ the Constable of France, and others.

KING OF FRANCE
'Tis certain he hath passed the river Somme.

CONSTABLE
An if he be not fought withal, my lord,
Let us not live in France. Let us quit all,
And give our vineyards to a barbarous people.

DAUPHIN
Ô Dieu vivant, shall a few sprays of us,   5
The emptying of our fathers' luxury,
Our scions, put in wild and savage stock,
Spurt up so suddenly into the clouds
And overlook their grafters?

BRITTANY
Normans, but bastard Normans, Norman bastards!   10
Mort de ma vie, if they march along
Unfought withal, but I will sell my dukedom
To buy a slobb'ry and a dirty farm
In that nook-shotten isle of Albion.

CONSTABLE
Dieu de batailles, where have they this mettle?   15
Is not their climate foggy, raw, and dull,
On whom, as in despite, the sun looks pale,
Killing their fruit with frowns? Can sodden water,
A drench for sur-reined jades, their barley broth,
Decoct their cold blood to such valiant heat?   20
And shall our quick blood, spirited with wine,
Seem frosty? O, for honor of our land,
Let us not hang like roping icicles
Upon our houses' thatch, whiles a more frosty
    people   25
Sweat drops of gallant youth in our rich fields!
"Poor" we ⌜may⌝ call them in their native lords.

11. **Mort de ma vie:** death of my life; i.e., may I die
12. **but I will:** i.e., if I do not
13. **slobb'ry:** wet and slimy
14. **nook-shotten:** running into corners or angles (coastal inlets); **Albion:** Great Britain
15. **Dieu de batailles:** god of battles; **where have they:** i.e., from **where** do **they** have
17. **as in despite:** i.e., **as** if **in** contempt
18. **sodden:** boiled (in the making of beer or ale)
19. **drench . . . jades:** a medicinal drink for over-worked broken-down horses; **barley broth:** ale
20. **Decoct:** cook, or warm up
21. **quick:** lively
23. **roping:** i.e., ropelike
24. **thatch:** i.e., roof
26. **drops . . . youth:** i.e., the blood of their brave young
27. **them:** i.e., our rich fields; **in . . . lords:** i.e., because **their lords** are so cowardly
29. **madams:** wives, ladies
30. **bred out:** exhausted
32. **new-store:** freshly supply
33. **bid us to:** tell **us** to go **to**
34. **lavoltas:** dances with leaping steps; **corantos:** dances with running steps
35. **grace:** attractiveness; excellence; **in our heels:** (1) in running from battle; (2) in dancing
36. **lofty runaways:** i.e., (1) high leaping and running dancers; (2) aristocratic cowards
37. **Montjoy:** Although in the play this is the herald's proper name, in history it was a title of the royal herald.
49. **For . . . seats:** in return **for your great** positions; **quit you:** rid yourselves

(continued)

DAUPHIN   By faith and honor,
Our madams mock at us and plainly say
Our mettle is bred out, and they will give   30
Their bodies to the lust of English youth
To new-store France with bastard warriors.
BRITTANY
They bid us to the English dancing-schools,
And teach lavoltas high, and swift corantos,
Saying our grace is only in our heels   35
And that we are most lofty runaways.
KING OF FRANCE
Where is Montjoy the herald? Speed him hence.
Let him greet England with our sharp defiance.
Up, princes, and, with spirit of honor edged
More sharper than your swords, hie to the field: 40
Charles Delabreth, High Constable of France;
You Dukes of Orléans, Bourbon, and of Berri,
Alençon, Brabant, Bar, and Burgundy;
Jacques Chatillon, Rambures, ⌜Vaudemont,⌝
Beaumont, Grandpré, Roussi, and Faulconbridge,   45
⌜Foix,⌝ Lestrale, Bouciqualt, and Charolois;
High dukes, great princes, barons, lords, and
  ⌜knights,⌝
For your great seats now quit you of great shames.
Bar Harry England, that sweeps through our land   50
With pennons painted in the blood of Harfleur.
Rush on his host, as doth the melted snow
Upon the valleys, whose low vassal seat
The Alps doth spit and void his rheum upon.
Go down upon him—you have power enough—   55
And in a captive chariot into Rouen
Bring him our prisoner.
CONSTABLE   This becomes the great!
Sorry am I his numbers are so few,
His soldiers sick and famished in their march,   60
For, I am sure, when he shall see our army,

51. **pennons:** streamers on heads of lances (See picture, page 174.)

52. **host:** army

53. **low . . . seat:** place of a humble servant

54. **rheum:** (1) water; (2) mucus

55. **power enough:** a great **enough** army

56. **captive chariot:** i.e., **chariot** drawing him as a **captive** (as in a Roman triumphal procession)

58. **This . . . great:** i.e., the capture of Henry is a task suitable for great men

62. **sink:** pit

63. **for achievement:** i.e., instead of winning his planned victory; **ransom:** See longer note, page 242.

64. **haste on Montjoy:** i.e., make **Montjoy** hurry

66. **willing:** voluntary

67–69. **Prince . . . us:** In the 1623 Folio text the Dauphin joins the fight; in the much shorter 1600 quarto, as in history, he does not.

3.6 Captains Fluellen and Gower meet Pistol, who pleads for Bardolph, sentenced to die for robbery. Fluellen refuses to intervene and Pistol insults him and leaves. Henry enters and learns about Bardolph's sentence of death, which he upholds. Montjoy enters to urge that Henry propose a ransom. Henry offers only his body as ransom.

---

0 SD. **Captains, English and Welsh:** The **English** captain is Gower, the **Welsh** Fluellen.

(continued)

He'll drop his heart into the sink of fear
And for achievement offer us his ransom.

KING OF FRANCE
Therefore, Lord Constable, haste on Montjoy,
And let him say to England that we send   65
To know what willing ransom he will give.—
Prince Dauphin, you shall stay with us in Rouen.

DAUPHIN
Not so, I do beseech your Majesty.

KING
Be patient, for you shall remain with us.—
Now forth, Lord Constable and princes all,   70
And quickly bring us word of England's fall.

They exit.

⌜Scene 6⌝
Enter Captains, English and Welsh, Gower and Fluellen.

GOWER   How now, Captain Fluellen? Come you from
the bridge?

FLUELLEN   I assure you there is very excellent services
committed at the bridge.

GOWER   Is the Duke of Exeter safe?   5

FLUELLEN   The Duke of Exeter is as magnanimous as
Agamemnon, and a man that I love and honor with
my soul and my heart and my duty and my life and
my living and my uttermost power. He is not, God
be praised and blessed, any hurt in the world, but   10
keeps the bridge most valiantly, with excellent
discipline. There is an aunchient lieutenant there at
the pridge; I think in my very conscience he is as
valiant a man as Mark Antony, and he is a man of no
estimation in the world, but I did see him do as   15
gallant service.

GOWER   What do you call him?

2. **bridge:** i.e., perhaps **the bridge** over the Ternoise River, essential to the English march from Harfleur to Calais

3. **services:** military operations

6. **magnanimous:** courageous, nobly ambitious

7. **Agamemnon:** the general of the Greek army in the Trojan War (See picture, page 140.)

14. **Mark Antony:** famous Roman military leader (See Shakespeare's *Julius Caesar* and *Antony and Cleopatra.*)

14–15. **no . . . world:** no reputation or standing

18. **Aunchient:** i.e., ancient, or standard-bearer

26. **buxom:** lively

27. **Fortune:** In lines 29–36 Fluellen provides a detailed explanation of contemporary depictions of the goddess Fortune. (See picture, page 166.) **furious:** menacing

30. **muffler:** blindfold

34. **mutability and variation:** i.e., changeable and variable

35. **fixed:** placed firmly

38. **moral:** symbolic figure

39. **Fortune . . . him:** Pistol echoes a line from a well-known contemporary ballad: "**Fortune** my **foe,** why dost thou frown on me?"

40. **pax:** metal tablet (often of gold or silver) usually bearing a representation of the Crucifixion

41. **gallows . . . dog:** Animals were sometimes hung for offenses.

42. **hemp:** i.e., the hangman's rope

43. **doom:** judgment

44. **price:** value

(continued)

FLUELLEN He is called Aunchient Pistol.
GOWER I know him not.

Enter Pistol.

FLUELLEN Here is the man.   20
PISTOL Captain, I thee beseech to do me favors. The
     Duke of Exeter doth love thee well.
FLUELLEN Ay, I praise God, and I have merited some
     love at his hands.
PISTOL Bardolph, a soldier firm and sound of heart and   25
     of buxom valor, hath, by cruel Fate and giddy
     Fortune's furious fickle wheel, that goddess blind,
     that stands upon the rolling restless stone—
FLUELLEN By your patience, Aunchient Pistol, Fortune
     is painted blind, with a muffler afore ⌜her⌝ eyes, to   30
     signify to you that Fortune is blind; and she is
     painted also with a wheel to signify to you, which is
     the moral of it, that she is turning and inconstant,
     and mutability and variation; and her foot, look you,
     is fixed upon a spherical stone, which rolls and rolls   35
     and rolls. In good truth, the poet makes a most
     excellent description of it. Fortune is an excellent
     moral.
PISTOL Fortune is Bardolph's foe and frowns on him,
     for he hath stolen a pax and hangèd must he be. A   40
     damnèd death! Let gallows gape for dog, let man go
     free, and let not hemp his windpipe suffocate. But
     Exeter hath given the doom of death for pax of little
     price. Therefore go speak; the Duke will hear thy
     voice, and let not Bardolph's vital thread be cut   45
     with edge of penny cord and vile reproach. Speak,
     captain, for his life, and I will thee requite.
FLUELLEN Aunchient Pistol, I do partly understand
     your meaning.
PISTOL Why then, rejoice therefore.   50
FLUELLEN Certainly, aunchient, it is not a thing to

45. **vital thread:** i.e., the thread woven by the three Fates—Clotho, Lachesis, and Atropos—who weave one's life and cut the **vital thread** at death. (See picture, page 208.) Pistol changes the myth to make their knife's **edge** the **penny cord** (i.e., rope) **and vile reproach** of hanging.

47. **requite:** reward

56. **figo:** like **the fig of Spain** (line 58), a contemptuous gesture that consisted in thrusting the thumb between two clenched fingers or into the mouth

60. **arrant:** notorious

61. **cutpurse:** pickpocket

65. **is serve:** i.e., serves, or provides opportunity

66. **gull:** simpleton

67. **grace:** honor

69. **are perfect in:** i.e., have memorized

70. **learn ... rote:** i.e., teach you from what they have memorized

70–71. **where ... done:** i.e., **where** military operations **were** conducted

71. **sconce:** small fort or earthwork

72. **convoy:** protective escort; **came off:** acquited himself

74. **stood:** insisted; **con:** memorize

75. **phrase of:** language peculiar to; **trick up:** adorn

75–76. **new-tuned:** fashionable

77. **horrid ... camp:** rough battle dress

80. **slanders ... age:** people who bring down disgrace on the time in which we live

80–81. **marvelously mistook:** greatly mistaken

84. **If ... coat:** Proverbial: **if I** can get the upper hand over him

rejoice at, for if, look you, he were my brother, I would desire the Duke to use his good pleasure and put him to execution, for discipline ought to be used.   55

PISTOL   Die and be damned, and *figo* for thy friendship!
FLUELLEN   It is well.
PISTOL   The fig of Spain!   *He exits.*
FLUELLEN   Very good.
GOWER   Why, this is an arrant counterfeit rascal. I   60
remember him now, a bawd, a cutpurse.
FLUELLEN   I'll assure you he uttered as prave words at the pridge as you shall see in a summer's day. But it is very well; what he has spoke to me, that is well, I warrant you, when time is serve.   65
GOWER   Why, 'tis a gull, a fool, a rogue, that now and then goes to the wars to grace himself at his return into London under the form of a soldier; and such fellows are perfect in the great commanders' names, and they will learn you by rote where   70
services were done—at such and such a sconce, at such a breach, at such a convoy; who came off bravely, who was shot, who disgraced, what terms the enemy stood on; and this they con perfectly in the phrase of war, which they trick up with new-   75
tuned oaths; and what a beard of the general's cut and a horrid suit of the camp will do among foaming bottles and ale-washed wits is wonderful to be thought on. But you must learn to know such slanders of the age, or else you may be marvelously   80
mistook.
FLUELLEN   I tell you what, Captain Gower. I do perceive he is not the man that he would gladly make show to the world he is. If I find a hole in his coat, I will tell him my mind.   85

85 SD. **poor:** unhealthy (See 3.3.56–57.)

86–87. **speak . . . pridge:** i.e., inform him of what happened at the bridge

94. **passages:** fights

100. **perdition:** losses

103. **like:** i.e., likely

105–6. **bubukles and whelks . . . fire:** i.e., inflamed **bubukles:** confusion of "bubo" (inflamed swelling) and "carbuncle" (inflammatory tumor) **whelks:** pimples **knobs:** pustules

106. **lips . . . nose:** i.e., as if **his lips** were a bellows blowing on **his nose like a coal**

108. **his fire's:** i.e., its fire's

110. **charge:** command

111. **compelled:** taken by force

113. **upbraided:** reproached

115. **gamester:** gambler

116 SD. **Tucket:** trumpet signal

Mars (Pro.6).
From Vincenzo Cartari, *Le imagini de i dei de gli antichi* . . . (1587).

*Drum and Colors. Enter the King ⌐of England¬ and his
poor Soldiers, ⌐and Gloucester.¬*

Hark you, the King is coming, and I must speak
with him from the pridge.—God pless your
Majesty.

KING HENRY How now, Fluellen, cam'st thou from the
bridge?   90

FLUELLEN Ay, so please your Majesty. The Duke of
Exeter has very gallantly maintained the pridge.
The French is gone off, look you, and there is gallant
and most prave passages. Marry, th' athversary was
have possession of the pridge, but he is enforced   95
to retire, and the Duke of Exeter is master of the
pridge. I can tell your Majesty, the Duke is a prave
man.

KING HENRY What men have you lost, Fluellen?

FLUELLEN The perdition of th' athversary hath been   100
very great, reasonable great. Marry, for my part, I
think the Duke hath lost never a man but one that is
like to be executed for robbing a church, one
Bardolph, if your Majesty know the man. His face is
all bubukles and whelks and knobs and flames o'   105
fire; and his lips blows at his nose, and it is like a
coal of fire, sometimes plue and sometimes red, but
his nose is executed, and his fire's out.

KING HENRY We would have all such offenders so cut
off; and we give express charge that in our marches   110
through the country there be nothing compelled
from the villages, nothing taken but paid for,
none of the French upbraided or abused in dis-
dainful language; for when ⌐lenity¬ and cruelty play
for a kingdom, the gentler gamester is the soonest   115
winner.

Tucket. Enter Montjoy.

117. **habit:** clothing (i.e., the herald's sleeveless tabard, with the coat of arms of his master emblazoned on it)

121. **Unfold:** disclose, reveal

124. **Advantage:** superior position

125. **rebuked him:** forced him back; **but:** except

126. **injury:** perhaps, a boil or pustule

129. **sufferance:** forbearance

130. **ransom:** See longer note to 3.5.63, page 242.

130–31. **proportion:** i.e., be equivalent to

132. **digested:** borne without resistance, endured

132–33. **which . . . under:** i.e., which he is insufficient to recompense **his pettiness:** a mocking parody of "his Majesty"

134. **For:** i.e., to recompense; **exchequer:** treasury

135. **effusion . . . blood:** i.e., for our dead (literally, for the blood he has caused to be shed); **muster:** assembly, collection

136. **faint:** i.e., small

140. **whose . . . pronounced:** i.e., whom we have condemned to death

141. **office:** duty (as a herald)

142. **quality:** rank; ability

144. **fairly:** properly

146. **could:** i.e., would

147. **impeachment:** obstruction; **sooth:** truth

148. **confess:** reveal

149. **craft:** skill; **vantage:** advantage, superiority

MONTJOY   You know me by my habit.
KING HENRY   Well then, I know thee. What shall I know
    of thee?
MONTJOY   My master's mind.   120
KING HENRY   Unfold it.
MONTJOY   Thus says my king: "Say thou to Harry of
    England, though we seemed dead, we did but sleep.
    Advantage is a better soldier than rashness. Tell him
    we could have rebuked him at Harfleur, but that we   125
    thought not good to bruise an injury till it were full
    ripe. Now we speak upon our cue, and our voice is
    imperial. England shall repent his folly, see his
    weakness, and admire our sufferance. Bid him
    therefore consider of his ransom, which must pro-   130
    portion the losses we have borne, the subjects we
    have lost, the disgrace we have digested, which, in
    weight to reanswer, his pettiness would bow under.
    For our losses, his exchequer is too poor; for th'
    effusion of our blood, the muster of his kingdom   135
    too faint a number; and for our disgrace, his own
    person kneeling at our feet but a weak and worth-
    less satisfaction. To this, add defiance, and tell him,
    for conclusion, he hath betrayed his followers,
    whose condemnation is pronounced." So far my   140
    king and master; so much my office.
KING HENRY
    What is thy name? I know thy quality.
MONTJOY   Montjoy.
KING HENRY
    Thou dost thy office fairly. Turn thee back,
    And tell thy king I do not seek him now   145
    But could be willing to march on to Calais
    Without impeachment, for, to say the sooth,
    Though 'tis no wisdom to confess so much
    Unto an enemy of craft and vantage,
    My people are with sickness much enfeebled,   150

153. **Who:** i.e., **those few I have** (the remaining English soldiers)

157. **blown:** (1) aroused; (2) inflated; (3) magnified

159. **trunk:** i.e., body

160. **guard:** i.e., small body of soldiers assigned to escort or sentry duty

161. **God before:** i.e., **God** as my witness

164. **well advise himself:** consider carefully

175. **It . . . night:** i.e., **night draws** near

176. **encamp ourselves:** i.e., make our camp

177. **them:** i.e., the English army

A siege with cannons and bows and arrows.
(3.Chor.28, 3.1, 3.2, 3.3)
From [John Lydgate], *The hystorye sege and dystruccyon of Troye* [1513].

My numbers lessened, and those few I have
Almost no better than so many French,
Who when they were in health, I tell thee, herald,
I thought upon one pair of English legs
Did march three Frenchmen. Yet forgive me, God,   155
That I do brag thus. This your air of France
Hath blown that vice in me. I must repent.
Go therefore, tell thy master: here I am.
My ransom is this frail and worthless trunk,
My army but a weak and sickly guard,   160
Yet, God before, tell him we will come on
Though France himself and such another neighbor
Stand in our way. There's for thy labor, Montjoy.
                              ⌜*Gives money.*⌝
Go bid thy master well advise himself:
If we may pass, we will; if we be hindered,   165
We shall your tawny ground with your red blood
Discolor. And so, Montjoy, fare you well.
The sum of all our answer is but this:
We would not seek a battle as we are,
Nor, as we are, we say we will not shun it.   170
So tell your master.

MONTJOY
I shall deliver so. Thanks to your Highness.
                              ⌜*He exits.*⌝

GLOUCESTER
I hope they will not come upon us now.

KING HENRY
We are in God's hand, brother, not in theirs.
March to the bridge. It now draws toward night.   175
Beyond the river we'll encamp ourselves,
And on tomorrow bid them march away.
                              They exit.

3.7 On the eve of battle, the French nobles, confident of their army's superiority, engage in verbal competition.

---

1. **armor:** suit of **armor; of:** i.e., in
11–12. **change . . . with:** i.e., exchange . . . for
12–13. **pasterns:** A pastern is the part of a horse's foot between the fetlock and the hoof.
13. **Çà:** here (an interjection)
13–14. **as if . . . hairs:** i.e., **as if** he **were** a tennis ball, which was filled with hair
14. **le cheval volant:** the flying horse; **the Pegasus:** mythological winged horse (See picture, page 138, and longer note, page 243.)
14–15. **qui . . . feu:** which has nostrils of fire
17. **horn:** (1) part of the hoof; (2) wind instrument
18. **Hermes:** in Greek mythology, the god who was, among other things, patron of music (See also longer note to line 14, page 243.)
21. **Perseus:** This Greek mythological hero rode Pegasus when he rescued Andromeda from the dragon.
23. **patient:** calm
24. **jades:** horses of poor quality
26. **absolute:** perfect
28. **palfreys:** literally, saddle horses (as opposed to warhorses), especially small ones ridden by ladies (It is odd that the Dauphin is made to refer to his horse this way, especially since, at line 46, he calls it a **courser,** i.e., warhorse.)

⌜Scene 7⌝
Enter the Constable of France, the Lord Rambures,
Orléans, Dauphin, with others.

CONSTABLE　Tut, I have the best armor of the world.
Would it were day!
ORLÉANS　You have an excellent armor, but let my
horse have his due.
CONSTABLE　It is the best horse of Europe.　　　　5
ORLÉANS　Will it never be morning?
DAUPHIN　My Lord of Orléans and my Lord High Constable, you talk of horse and armor?
ORLÉANS　You are as well provided of both as any
prince in the world.　　　　　　　　　　　　10
DAUPHIN　What a long night is this! I will not change
my horse with any that treads but on four ⌜pas-
terns.⌝ *Çà*, ha! He bounds from the earth, as if his
entrails were hairs, *le cheval volant,* the Pegasus, ⌜*qui*
a⌝ *les narines de feu.* When I bestride him, I soar; I　15
am a hawk; he trots the air. The earth sings when he
touches it. The basest horn of his hoof is more
musical than the pipe of Hermes.
ORLÉANS　He's of the color of the nutmeg.
DAUPHIN　And of the heat of the ginger. It is a beast for　20
Perseus. He is pure air and fire, and the dull
elements of earth and water never appear in him,
but only in patient stillness while his rider mounts
him. He is indeed a horse, and all other jades you
may call beasts.　　　　　　　　　　　　　25
CONSTABLE　Indeed, my lord, it is a most absolute and
excellent horse.
DAUPHIN　It is the prince of palfreys; his neigh is like
the bidding of a monarch, and his countenance
enforces homage.　　　　　　　　　　　　30
ORLÉANS　No more, cousin.
DAUPHIN　Nay, the man hath no wit that cannot, from

33. **the rising ... lamb:** all day long   **lodging:** i.e., lying down

34. **vary:** deliver variations of; **on:** i.e., concerning

35. **fluent:** flowing abundantly

36. **argument:** subject matter

37. **subject:** (1) theme; (2) one ruled by, or subject to, a sovereign (The Dauphin plays not only with the **subject/sovereign** combination, but also with the phrase "sovereign reason.") **reason:** talk, discourse

38–39. **world ... unknown:** i.e., the people from the parts of the world that we know, and those from parts still **unknown** to us

39. **apart:** aside

40. **functions:** activities

46. **my horse ... mistress:** This line begins a series of comparisons between horseback-riding and sexual relations with a mistress that extends through line 65, involving such terms as "bears," "shook your back," "ride," and "foul bogs."

48. **Me well:** i.e., **bears me well; prescript:** prescribed

49. **particular:** belonging to one alone

51. **shrewdly:** shrewishly; severely

54. **belike:** likely

55. **kern:** foot soldier (See picture, page 186.) **French hose:** wide breeches

56. **in ... strossers:** in tight trousers (with the suggestion of "bare-legged")

61. **lief:** gladly; **jade:** (1) horse of poor quality; (2) shrew, hag

65. **to:** i.e., for

(continued)

the rising of the lark to the lodging of the lamb,
vary deserved praise on my palfrey. It is a theme as
fluent as the sea. Turn the sands into eloquent   35
tongues, and my horse is argument for them all. 'Tis
a subject for a sovereign to reason on, and for a
sovereign's sovereign to ride on, and for the world,
familiar to us and unknown, to lay apart their
particular functions and wonder at him. I once writ   40
a sonnet in his praise and began thus: "Wonder of
nature—"

ORLÉANS I have heard a sonnet begin so to one's
mistress.

DAUPHIN Then did they imitate that which I composed   45
to my courser, for my horse is my mistress.

ORLÉANS Your mistress bears well.

DAUPHIN Me well—which is the prescript praise and
perfection of a good and particular mistress.

CONSTABLE Nay, for methought yesterday your mistress   50
shrewdly shook your back.

DAUPHIN So perhaps did yours.

CONSTABLE Mine was not bridled.

DAUPHIN O, then belike she was old and gentle, and
you rode like a kern of Ireland, your French hose   55
off, and in your strait strossers.

CONSTABLE You have good judgment in horsemanship.

DAUPHIN Be warned by me, then: they that ride so, and
ride not warily, fall into foul bogs. I had rather have
my horse to my mistress.   60

CONSTABLE I had as lief have my mistress a jade.

DAUPHIN I tell thee, constable, my mistress wears his
own hair.

CONSTABLE I could make as true a boast as that if I had
a sow to my mistress.   65

DAUPHIN *"Le chien est retourné à son propre vomisse-*
ment, et la truie lavée au bourbier." Thou mak'st use
of anything.

66–67. **Le chien . . . bourbier:** Proverb: "The dog is returning to his own vomit, and the sow that was washed, to the wallowing in the mire" (quoted in 2 Peter 2.22).

70. **kin:** i.e., relative, relevant

75. **want:** lack

76. **a many:** i.e., **many**

77. **'twere . . . away:** i.e., it would be a greater **honor** to you if you had fewer stars

80. **dismounted:** taken down from its back

82. **desert:** what he (i.e., it) deserves

84. **faced:** bullied

86. **fain:** gladly

87. **go to hazard:** bet, gamble

89. **go . . . ere:** put yourself in danger before

94. **he . . . kills:** i.e., **he will** kill no one

101. **still:** always

102. **did harm:** i.e., gave offense

103. **do none:** i.e., injure no one in battle

"With linstock . . . the . . . cannon touches." (3.Chor.35)
From Edward Webbe, *The rare and most wonderful things . . .* (1590, facsimile reprint 1868–72).

CONSTABLE Yet do I not use my horse for my mistress,
or any such proverb so little kin to the purpose. 70

RAMBURES My Lord Constable, the armor that I saw in
your tent tonight, are those stars or suns upon it?

CONSTABLE Stars, my lord.

DAUPHIN Some of them will fall tomorrow, I hope.

CONSTABLE And yet my sky shall not want. 75

DAUPHIN That may be, for you bear a many superflu-
ously, and 'twere more honor some were away.

CONSTABLE Ev'n as your horse bears your praises—
who would trot as well were some of your brags
dismounted. 80

DAUPHIN Would I were able to load him with his
desert! Will it never be day? I will trot tomorrow a
mile, and my way shall be paved with English faces.

CONSTABLE I will not say so for fear I should be faced
out of my way. But I would it were morning, for I 85
would fain be about the ears of the English.

RAMBURES Who will go to hazard with me for twenty
prisoners?

CONSTABLE You must first go yourself to hazard ere you
have them. 90

DAUPHIN 'Tis midnight. I'll go arm myself. *He exits.*

ORLÉANS The Dauphin longs for morning.

RAMBURES He longs to eat the English.

CONSTABLE I think he will eat all he kills.

ORLÉANS By the white hand of my lady, he's a gallant 95
prince.

CONSTABLE Swear by her foot, that she may tread out
the oath.

ORLÉANS He is simply the most active gentleman of
France. 100

CONSTABLE Doing is activity, and he will still be doing.

ORLÉANS He never did harm, that I heard of.

CONSTABLE Nor will do none tomorrow. He will keep
that good name still.

111. **needs not:** i.e., need not have told you; or, need not care

112–13. **never . . . lackey:** i.e., the Dauphin's only show of valor has been to beat his servant

113–14. **'Tis . . . bate:** i.e., his courage is hidden, and, when it is revealed, it will abate, or decrease (Hoods were put on the heads of hunting falcons to stop them from beating their wings. See picture, page 142.)   **bate:** (1) beat its wings; (2) abate, decrease

115. **Ill . . . well:** With this proverb begins a contest in which the speakers attempt to best each other's proverbs.

120. **your friend:** i.e., the Dauphin

121. **Have at:** i.e., I will attack

122. **pox:** plague; **of:** i.e., on

123. **how much:** i.e., as much as

124. **bolt:** short, blunt arrow

125. **shot over:** overshot, missed (the target)

126. **overshot:** i.e., outshot, defeated

134. **peevish:** obstinate

135. **mope:** move without the guidance of thought

137. **apprehension:** (1) conscious perception (of their plight); (2) fear

ORLÉANS I know him to be valiant.   105
CONSTABLE I was told that by one that knows him
better than you.
ORLÉANS What's he?
CONSTABLE Marry, he told me so himself, and he said
he cared not who knew it.   110
ORLÉANS He needs not. It is no hidden virtue in him.
CONSTABLE By my faith, sir, but it is; never anybody
saw it but his lackey. 'Tis a hooded valor, and when
it appears, it will bate.
ORLÉANS Ill will never said well.   115
CONSTABLE I will cap that proverb with "There is
flattery in friendship."
ORLÉANS And I will take up that with "Give the devil
his due."
CONSTABLE Well placed; there stands your friend for   120
the devil. Have at the very eye of that proverb with
"A pox of the devil."
ORLÉANS You are the better at proverbs, by how much
"A fool's bolt is soon shot."
CONSTABLE You have shot over.   125
ORLÉANS 'Tis not the first time you were overshot.

Enter a Messenger.

MESSENGER My Lord High Constable, the English lie
within fifteen hundred paces of your tents.
CONSTABLE Who hath measured the ground?
MESSENGER The Lord Grandpré.   130
CONSTABLE A valiant and most expert gentleman.—
Would it were day! Alas, poor Harry of England! He
longs not for the dawning as we do.
ORLÉANS What a wretched and peevish fellow is this
King of England to mope with his fat-brained   135
followers so far out of his knowledge.
CONSTABLE If the English had any apprehension, they
would run away.

140. **intellectual armor:** i.e., brains

143–47. **Their mastiffs . . . apples:** an allusion to the bloodsport of bearbaiting, in which **mastiffs** attacked **a bear** chained to a post (See picture, page 188.) **winking:** with their eyes closed

150. **Just:** exactly; **sympathize with:** resemble

151. **robustious:** violent; **coming on:** attacking

155. **shrewdly:** grievously

158. **stomachs:** appetites

The siege of a city, using scaling ladders.
(3.Chor.28, 3.1, 3.2, 3.3)
From [John Lydgate,] *The hystorye sege and dystruccyon of Troye* [1513].

ORLÉANS That they lack; for if their heads had any intellectual armor, they could never wear such 140 heavy headpieces.

RAMBURES That island of England breeds very valiant creatures. Their mastiffs are of unmatchable courage.

ORLÉANS Foolish curs, that run winking into the 145 mouth of a Russian bear and have their heads crushed like rotten apples. You may as well say that's a valiant flea that dare eat his breakfast on the lip of a lion.

CONSTABLE Just, just; and the men do sympathize with 150 the mastiffs in robustious and rough coming on, leaving their wits with their wives. And then give them great meals of beef and iron and steel, they will eat like wolves and fight like devils.

ORLÉANS Ay, but these English are shrewdly out of 155 beef.

CONSTABLE Then shall we find tomorrow they have only stomachs to eat and none to fight. Now is it time to arm. Come, shall we about it?

ORLÉANS
It is now two o'clock. But, let me see, by ten 160
We shall have each a hundred Englishmen.

                                          They exit.

The Life of

HENRY V

ACT 4

4. Chorus The Chorus describes the confident French and anxious English armies on the night before the battle of Agincourt, and portrays Henry as passing among his troops cheering them up. Again the Chorus laments that the stage and actors are so inadequate to the presentation of the battle to come.

---

1. **entertain conjecture of:** i.e., imagine
2. **poring:** eye-straining
3. **Fills:** i.e., fill
4. **womb:** abdomen
6. **stilly:** i.e., quietly
7. **That:** i.e., so that
8. **watch:** sentinels, guards
9. **paly:** pale
10. **Each battle:** i.e., each of the opposing armies; **umbered:** darkened
13. **accomplishing:** equipping (with armor)
15. **note:** (1) notice; (2) musical note
17. **the third . . . named:** i.e., **the third hour** having been **named,** or announced, by the cocks' crowing and the clocks' tolling
18. **secure:** free of anxiety
19. **overlusty:** overly cheerful, merry
20. **play at dice:** i.e., gamble on (perhaps, used as stakes in their gambling the ransoms they were confident of obtaining)
21. **tardy-gaited:** slow-moving
23. **condemnèd:** doomed

ACT ⌐4¬

⌐*Enter*¬ *Chorus.*

⌐CHORUS¬
Now entertain conjecture of a time
When creeping murmur and the poring dark
Fills the wide vessel of the universe.
From camp to camp, through the foul womb of
    night,   5
The hum of either army stilly sounds,
That the fixed sentinels almost receive
The secret whispers of each other's watch.
Fire answers fire, and through their paly flames
Each battle sees the other's umbered face;   10
Steed threatens steed in high and boastful neighs
Piercing the night's dull ear; and from the tents
The armorers, accomplishing the knights,
With busy hammers closing rivets up,
Give dreadful note of preparation.   15
The country cocks do crow, the clocks do toll,
And, the third hour of drowsy morning named,
Proud of their numbers and secure in soul,
The confident and overlusty French
Do the low-rated English play at dice   20
And chide the cripple, tardy-gaited night,
Who like a foul and ugly witch doth limp
So tediously away. The poor condemnèd English,

24. **sacrifices:** animals about to be sacrificed; **watchful fires:** i.e., sleepless **by their fires** (transferred epithet)

25. **inly:** i.e., inwardly

26. **gesture sad:** grave bearing

27. **Investing:** occupying; **lank-lean:** hollow

29. **So:** i.e., as so; **horrid:** frightening; **who:** i.e., whoever

31. **watch:** party of sentinels

33. **host:** army

36. **note:** sign

37. **enrounded:** surrounded

38–39. **Nor . . . night:** i.e., he is not a bit pale in spite of his weariness at not having slept all **night**

40. **overbears attaint:** overcomes fatigue; or, represses any stain on his freshness

41. **semblance:** appearance, look

44. **largesse:** bountifulness

46. **mean and gentle:** baseborn and noble

47. **as . . . define:** our inadequacy may present

51. **ragged:** rough-edged; **foils:** blunted fencing weapons

52. **Right:** completely; **ill-disposed:** i.e., inappropriate

54. **Minding . . . be:** i.e., bringing to mind what happened through seeing a ridiculously inadequate representation of it

Like sacrifices, by their watchful fires
Sit patiently and inly ruminate   25
The morning's danger; and their gesture sad,
Investing lank-lean cheeks and war-worn coats,
⌜Presenteth⌝ them unto the gazing moon
So many horrid ghosts. O now, who will behold
The royal captain of this ruined band   30
Walking from watch to watch, from tent to tent,
Let him cry, "Praise and glory on his head!"
For forth he goes and visits all his host,
Bids them good morrow with a modest smile,
And calls them brothers, friends, and countrymen.   35
Upon his royal face there is no note
How dread an army hath enrounded him,
Nor doth he dedicate one jot of color
Unto the weary and all-watchèd night,
But freshly looks and overbears attaint   40
With cheerful semblance and sweet majesty,
That every wretch, pining and pale before,
Beholding him, plucks comfort from his looks.
A largesse universal, like the sun,
His liberal eye doth give to everyone,   45
Thawing cold fear, that mean and gentle all
Behold, as may unworthiness define,
A little touch of Harry in the night.
And so our scene must to the battle fly,
Where, O for pity, we shall much disgrace,   50
With four or five most vile and ragged foils
Right ill-disposed in brawl ridiculous,
The name of Agincourt. Yet sit and see,
Minding true things by what their mock'ries be.

                                       He exits.

4.1 Henry borrows Erpingham's cloak and, in this disguise, passes through his camp, meeting Pistol, overhearing a conversation between Fluellen and Gower, and getting into an argument with one of his soldiers, Michael Williams, about the King's responsibility for the spiritual fate of those of his soldiers who die in battle. Henry (in disguise) and Williams postpone their disagreement until after the battle, exchanging gloves as pledges to fight with each other later. Alone, Henry laments the care that accompanies his crown and then prays that God will not avenge upon him, in the upcoming battle, his father's usurpation of Richard II's throne and instigation of Richard's death.

---

4. **soul:** element, principle
5. **observingly:** i.e., observantly
7. **husbandry:** management
8. **they:** i.e., the French
10. **dress us fairly:** i.e., properly prepare
12. **moral:** symbolic figure; or, moral lesson
15. **churlish:** boorish (i.e., inhospitable)
16. **lodging:** i.e., place to lie down; **likes:** pleases
18–19. **to . . . example:** i.e., to be given an **example** of how to take pleasure in present discomfort
20. **quickened:** i.e., enlivened; **out of doubt:** i.e., without **doubt**
23. **With casted slough:** i.e., like a snake that has cast off its old skin; **legerity:** nimbleness

⌜Scene 1⌝

Enter the King ⌜of England,⌝ Bedford, and Gloucester.

KING HENRY
Gloucester, 'tis true that we are in great danger.
The greater therefore should our courage be.—
Good morrow, brother Bedford. God almighty,
There is some soul of goodness in things evil,
Would men observingly distill it out.   5
For our bad neighbor makes us early stirrers,
Which is both healthful and good husbandry.
Besides, they are our outward consciences
And preachers to us all, admonishing
That we should dress us fairly for our end.   10
Thus may we gather honey from the weed
And make a moral of the devil himself.

Enter Erpingham.

Good morrow, old Sir Thomas Erpingham.
A good soft pillow for that good white head
Were better than a churlish turf of France.   15
ERPINGHAM
Not so, my liege, this lodging likes me better,
Since I may say "Now lie I like a king."
KING HENRY
'Tis good for men to love their present pains
Upon example. So the spirit is eased;
And when the mind is quickened, out of doubt,   20
The organs, though defunct and dead before,
Break up their drowsy grave and newly move
With casted slough and fresh legerity.
Lend me thy cloak, Sir Thomas.
                    ⌜*He puts on Erpingham's cloak.*⌝
                              Brothers both,   25
Commend me to the princes in our camp,

27. **Do:** i.e., say; **anon:** soon
28. **Desire:** invite
33. **bosom:** thoughts and feelings
34. **would:** i.e., would have
37. **Qui vous là:** bad French for "Qui va là?" or "Who goes there?"
40. **base . . . popular:** synonymous terms
41. **gentleman of a company:** a rank between **common** soldier and **officer**
42. **Trail'st . . . pike?:** i.e., are you infantry? **puissant:** powerful
46. **bawcock:** See note to 3.2.25.
47. **imp:** child, lad
49. **bully:** fine fellow
50. **le Roy:** i.e., *le roi*, French for "the king"
51–52. **of Cornish crew:** from the **Cornish** force
56. **pate:** head
57. **Saint Davy's day:** March 1, the feast day of the patron saint of Wales, when Welshmen wear leeks in their caps

Pegasus. (3.7.14)
From August Casimir Redel,
Apophtegmata symbolica . . . (n.d.).

Do my good morrow to them, and anon
Desire them all to my pavilion.
GLOUCESTER   We shall, my liege.
ERPINGHAM   Shall I attend your Grace?   30
KING HENRY   No, my good knight.
Go with my brothers to my lords of England.
I and my bosom must debate awhile,
And then I would no other company.
ERPINGHAM
The Lord in heaven bless thee, noble Harry.   35
                                    ⌐*All but the King*⌐ *exit.*

KING HENRY
God-a-mercy, old heart, thou speak'st cheerfully.

                              Enter Pistol.

PISTOL   *Qui vous là?*
KING HENRY   A friend.
PISTOL   Discuss unto me: art thou officer or art thou
    base, common, and popular?   40
KING HENRY   I am a gentleman of a company.
PISTOL   Trail'st thou the puissant pike?
KING HENRY   Even so. What are you?
PISTOL   As good a gentleman as the Emperor.
KING HENRY   Then you are a better than the King.   45
PISTOL   The King's a bawcock and a heart of gold, a lad
    of life, an imp of fame, of parents good, of fist most
    valiant. I kiss his dirty shoe, and from heartstring I
    love the lovely bully. What is thy name?
KING HENRY   Harry le Roy.   50
PISTOL   Le Roy? A Cornish name. Art thou of Cornish
    crew?
KING HENRY   No, I am a Welshman.
PISTOL   Know'st thou Fluellen?
KING HENRY   Yes.   55
PISTOL   Tell him I'll knock his leek about his pate upon
    Saint Davy's day.

62. See note to 3.6.56.

65. **sorts:** corresponds

67. **'So:** i.e., Godso, an oath; **speak fewer:** i.e., do not talk so much

68. **admiration:** wonder

69. **prerogatifes:** i.e., prerogatives, privileges (Probably Fluellen is made comically to use the wrong word. *Rules* would suit the sense of his speech.)

71–72. **Pompey the Great:** the elder Pompey, a great Roman military leader

80. **prating:** talkative, chattering

81. **coxcomb:** i.e., fool (literally, a fool's cap); **meet:** appropriate

Agamemnon. (3.6.7)
From Geoffrey Whitney,
A choice of emblemes . . . (1586).

KING HENRY   Do not you wear your dagger in your cap
   that day, lest he knock that about yours.
PISTOL   Art thou his friend?   60
KING HENRY   And his kinsman too.
PISTOL   The *figo* for thee then!
KING HENRY   I thank you. God be with you.
PISTOL   My name is Pistol called.   *He exits.*
KING HENRY   It sorts well with your fierceness.   65
                                    ⌐*He steps aside.*⌐

               Enter Fluellen and Gower.

GOWER   Captain Fluellen.
FLUELLEN   'So. In the name of Jesu Christ, speak fewer.
   It is the greatest admiration in the universal world
   when the true and aunchient prerogatifes and
   laws of the wars is not kept. If you would take the   70
   pains but to examine the wars of Pompey the
   Great, you shall find, I warrant you, that there is
   no tiddle taddle nor pibble babble in Pompey's
   camp. I warrant you, you shall find the ceremonies of the wars and the cares of it and the forms   75
   of it and the sobriety of it and the modesty of it to
   be otherwise.
GOWER   Why, the enemy is loud. You hear him all
   night.
FLUELLEN   If the enemy is an ass and a fool and a prating   80
   coxcomb, is it meet, think you, that we should also,
   look you, be an ass and a fool and a prating
   coxcomb, in your own conscience now?
GOWER   I will speak lower.
FLUELLEN   I pray you and beseech you that you will.   85
                          ⌐*Gower and Fluellen*⌐ *exit.*
KING HENRY
   Though it appear a little out of fashion,
   There is much care and valor in this Welshman.

100. **estate:** condition, situation

101. **wracked:** shipwrecked; **sand:** sandbank, shoal

107. **element:** sky

108. **have . . . conditions:** i.e., are only **human**

108–9. **His ceremonies:** formal acts or observances that express deference to and respect for him

110–12. **his affections . . . wing:** Here emotions or desires are compared to falcons that soar (**are mounted**) and plunge (**stoop**).   **like:** same

112. **of fears:** i.e., to fear

113. **relish:** taste

114. **possess him:** affect him strongly

115. **he:** i.e., the King; **it:** i.e., fear

118. **could wish:** i.e., wishes

119. **would:** wish

Falconer with hooded falcon. (3.7.113)
From Antonio Francesco Doni, *L'academia Peregrina* . . . (1552).

*Enter three Soldiers, John Bates, Alexander Court, and
Michael Williams.*

COURT   Brother John Bates, is not that the morning
which breaks yonder?

BATES   I think it be, but we have no great cause to desire   90
the approach of day.

WILLIAMS   We see yonder the beginning of the day, but
I think we shall never see the end of it.—Who goes
there?

KING HENRY   A friend.   95

WILLIAMS   Under what captain serve you?

KING HENRY   Under Sir ⌈Thomas⌉ Erpingham.

WILLIAMS   A good old commander and a most kind
gentleman. I pray you, what thinks he of our
estate?   100

KING HENRY   Even as men wracked upon a sand, that
look to be washed off the next tide.

BATES   He hath not told his thought to the King?

KING HENRY   No. Nor it is not meet he should, for,
though I speak it to you, I think the King is but a   105
man as I am. The violet smells to him as it doth to
me. The element shows to him as it doth to me. All
his senses have but human conditions. His ceremonies laid by, in his nakedness he appears but a man,
and though his affections are higher mounted than   110
ours, yet when they stoop, they stoop with the like
wing. Therefore, when he sees reason of fears as we
do, his fears, out of doubt, be of the same relish as
ours are. Yet, in reason, no man should possess him
with any appearance of fear, lest he, by showing it,   115
should dishearten his army.

BATES   He may show what outward courage he will,
but I believe, as cold a night as 'tis, he could wish
himself in Thames up to the neck; and so I would

120. **at all adventures:** i.e., whatever might happen

120–21. **so we were quit here:** i.e., **so** long as **we were** away from **here**

122. **my conscience:** i.e., what I believe

126. **ransomed:** See longer note on 3.5.63, page 242. **a many:** a great number of

129. **feel:** i.e., **feel** out, test

139. **heavy . . . make:** grievous account of his life to deliver

141. **join together:** i.e., be restored to whole bodies; **at the latter day:** on the last day of the world, when, according to Christian doctrine, bodies will rise from the grave and be brought to the Last Judgment

141–42. **cry all:** i.e., **all** the bodies shall **cry**

143. **upon:** i.e., about

145. **rawly left:** left at an immature age; **afeard:** afraid

146. **die well: die** in a state of grace

147. **blood:** perhaps, the taking of life

148. **argument:** perhaps, motive (for fighting)

150. **who:** i.e., whom

150–51. **against . . . subjection:** i.e., contrary to all relations of subjects to their king

153. **do sinfully miscarry:** dies outside a state of grace

154. **imputation of:** accusation for

he were, and I by him, at all adventures, so we were   120
   quit here.
KING HENRY   By my troth, I will speak my conscience
   of the King. I think he would not wish himself
   anywhere but where he is.
BATES   Then I would he were here alone; so should he   125
   be sure to be ransomed, and a many poor men's
   lives saved.
KING HENRY   I dare say you love him not so ill to wish
   him here alone, howsoever you speak this to feel
   other men's minds. Methinks I could not die any-   130
   where so contented as in the King's company, his
   cause being just and his quarrel honorable.
WILLIAMS   That's more than we know.
BATES   Ay, or more than we should seek after, for we
   know enough if we know we are the King's sub-   135
   jects. If his cause be wrong, our obedience to the
   King wipes the crime of it out of us.
WILLIAMS   But if the cause be not good, the King
   himself hath a heavy reckoning to make, when all
   those legs and arms and heads, chopped off in a   140
   battle, shall join together at the latter day, and cry
   all "We died at such a place," some swearing, some
   crying for a surgeon, some upon their wives left
   poor behind them, some upon the debts they owe,
   some upon their children rawly left. I am afeard   145
   there are few die well that die in a battle, for how
   can they charitably dispose of anything when blood
   is their argument? Now, if these men do not die
   well, it will be a black matter for the king that led
   them to it, who to disobey were against all propor-   150
   tion of subjection.
KING HENRY   So, if a son that is by his father sent about
   merchandise do sinfully miscarry upon the sea,
   the imputation of his wickedness, by your rule,
   should be imposed upon his father that sent him.   155

158. **irreconciled iniquities:** sins unforgiven and unatoned for

160–61. **bound . . . soldiers:** obliged to be accountable for the states in which **his** individual **soldiers** die

163. **purpose:** intend

165–66. **arbitrament of swords:** decision by combat

166. **try it out:** i.e., fight a war to achieve his cause; **unspotted:** sinless

167. **peradventure:** perhaps

169. **seals:** promises; **perjury:** false oaths

170. **bulwark:** safeguard

171. **before:** earlier (i.e., before going to war)

173. **native punishment:** perhaps, **punishment** at home

175. **beadle:** messenger of justice

176. **before-breach:** i.e., their earlier breaking

177–78. **Where . . . life away:** i.e., **where they feared** capital punishment, **they have** escaped with their lives

179. **would be:** wish to be; think they will be

179–80. **unprovided:** i.e., without Last Rites

182. **visited:** punished; caused to die

185. **mote:** speck

186–87. **death . . . advantage:** Philippians 1.21: "**death is to** me **advantage**" (Bishops' Bible 1568)

187. **lost:** spent (**lost . . . gained:** antithesis)

Or if a servant, under his master's command trans-
porting a sum of money, be assailed by robbers and
die in many irreconciled iniquities, you may call the
business of the master the author of the servant's
damnation. But this is not so. The King is not bound   160
to answer the particular endings of his soldiers, the
father of his son, nor the master of his servant, for
they purpose not their death when they purpose
their services. Besides, there is no king, be his cause
never so spotless, if it come to the arbitrament of   165
swords, can try it out with all unspotted soldiers.
Some, peradventure, have on them the guilt of
premeditated and contrived murder; some, of be-
guiling virgins with the broken seals of perjury;
some, making the wars their bulwark, that have   170
before gored the gentle bosom of peace with pillage
and robbery. Now, if these men have defeated the
law and outrun native punishment, though they can
outstrip men, they have no wings to fly from God.
War is His beadle, war is His vengeance, so that here   175
men are punished for before-breach of the King's
laws in now the King's quarrel. Where they feared
the death, they have borne life away; and where they
would be safe, they perish. Then, if they die unprovided, no more is the King guilty of their damnation   180
than he was before guilty of those impieties for the
which they are now visited. Every subject's duty is
the King's, but every subject's soul is his own.
Therefore should every soldier in the wars do as
every sick man in his bed: wash every mote out of   185
his conscience. And, dying so, death is to him
advantage; or not dying, the time was blessedly lost
wherein such preparation was gained. And in him
that escapes, it were not sin to think that, making
God so free an offer, He let him outlive that day to   190

193. **dies ill:** i.e., **dies** in sin; **the ill:** i.e., the sin
194. **answer:** i.e., **answer** for
196. **lustily:** vigorously
204. **pay:** avenge yourself on
205. **elder gun:** popgun or pea-shooter, made from a hollowed **elder** branch
205–6. **poor . . . displeasure:** i.e., the **displeasure** of a poor private subject
206–7. **go about:** attempt
207. **his face:** i.e., its **face**
210. **round:** harsh
211. **should:** i.e., would
216. **gage:** pledge
217. **bonnet:** brimless cap
225. **see it:** i.e., **see** the **glove**

An armorer. (2.Chor.3)
From Hartmann Schopper, *ΠΑΝΟΠΛΙΑ omnium . . .* (1568).

see His greatness and to teach others how they should prepare.

WILLIAMS 'Tis certain, every man that dies ill, the ill upon his own head; the King is not to answer it.

BATES I do not desire he should answer for me, and yet 195 I determine to fight lustily for him.

KING HENRY I myself heard the King say he would not be ransomed.

WILLIAMS Ay, he said so to make us fight cheerfully, but when our throats are cut, he may be ransomed 200 and we ne'er the wiser.

KING HENRY If I live to see it, I will never trust his word after.

WILLIAMS You pay him then. That's a perilous shot out of an elder gun, that a poor and a private displea- 205 sure can do against a monarch. You may as well go about to turn the sun to ice with fanning in his face with a peacock's feather. You'll "never trust his word after." Come, 'tis a foolish saying.

KING HENRY Your reproof is something too round. I 210 should be angry with you if the time were convenient.

WILLIAMS Let it be a quarrel between us, if you live.

KING HENRY I embrace it.

WILLIAMS How shall I know thee again? 215

KING HENRY Give me any gage of thine, and I will wear it in my bonnet. Then, if ever thou dar'st acknowledge it, I will make it my quarrel.

WILLIAMS Here's my glove. Give me another of thine.

KING HENRY There.   ⌜*They exchange gloves.*⌝ 220

WILLIAMS This will I also wear in my cap. If ever thou come to me and say, after tomorrow, "This is my glove," by this hand I will take thee a box on the ear.

KING HENRY If ever I live to see it, I will challenge it. 225

WILLIAMS Thou dar'st as well be hanged.

227. **take:** find
231–32. **could . . . reckon:** i.e., knew how to count
233. **lay:** bet
234. **crowns:** (1) gold coins; (2) heads
236. **treason . . . crowns:** It was a crime to clip gold from the edges of coins.
239. **careful:** i.e., worried (literally, full of cares)
242. **breath:** i.e., talk
244. **his own wringing:** what pinches him
245. **neglect:** disregard
246. **privates:** private subjects
247. **ceremony:** pomp, state, ceremonial rites
251. **rents, comings-in:** incomes
253. **What . . . adoration:** perhaps, "Why are you adored?"
254. **aught:** anything; **place:** position, office; **degree:** rank
261. **go out:** be quenched (i.e., cured)

"Finely bolted." (2.2.144)
From Geoffrey Whitney,
A choice of emblemes . . . (1586).

KING HENRY   Well, I will do it, though I take thee in the
King's company.

WILLIAMS   Keep thy word. Fare thee well.

BATES   Be friends, you English fools, be friends. We   230
have French quarrels enough, if you could tell how
to reckon.

KING HENRY   Indeed, the French may lay twenty
French crowns to one they will beat us, for they
bear them on their shoulders. But it is no English   235
treason to cut French crowns, and tomorrow the
King himself will be a clipper.
                                            Soldiers exit.
Upon the King! Let us our lives, our souls, our
debts, our careful wives, our children, and our sins,
lay on the King!   240
We must bear all. O hard condition,
Twin-born with greatness, subject to the breath
Of every fool whose sense no more can feel
But his own wringing. What infinite heart's ease
Must kings neglect that private men enjoy?   245
And what have kings that privates have not too,
Save ceremony, save general ceremony?
And what art thou, thou idol ceremony?
What kind of god art thou that suffer'st more
Of mortal griefs than do thy worshipers?   250
What are thy rents? What are thy comings-in?
O ceremony, show me but thy worth!
What is thy soul of adoration?
Art thou aught else but place, degree, and form,
Creating awe and fear in other men,   255
Wherein thou art less happy, being feared,
Than they in fearing?
What drink'st thou oft, instead of homage sweet,
But poisoned flattery? O, be sick, great greatness,
And bid thy ceremony give thee cure!   260
Think'st thou the fiery fever will go out

262. **With:** by; **adulation:** servile flattery
263. **it:** i.e., the fever; **flexure:** perhaps, kneeling; perhaps, bowing
264–65. **the beggar's knee:** i.e., the beggar to kneel
266. **it:** i.e., **the beggar's knee; thou proud dream:** i.e., ceremony
268. **find:** uncover
269–73. **balm . . . throne:** the material symbols of kingship **balm:** oil with which a monarch is anointed upon coronation **crown imperial:** emperor's crown **intertissued . . . pearl:** robe interwoven with **gold and pearl farcèd:** i.e., overly grand (literally, stuffed)
277. **wretched slave:** i.e., peasant
279. **distressful bread:** i.e., **bread** earned painfully
281. **lackey:** footman; **rise to set:** sunrise to sunset
282. **Phoebus:** Greco-Roman god of the sun
283. **Elysium:** i.e., bliss (as if in the Elysian Fields, where the heroes of classical mythology enjoyed eternity)
284. **Hyperion:** another name for the sun god
286. **profitable:** useful, beneficial
289. **Had:** i.e., would have; **forehand and vantage of:** i.e., the upper hand and the advantage over
290. **member of:** one who benefits from
291. **it:** i.e., the **peace; wots:** knows
292. **watch:** sleepless night
293. **Whose . . . advantages:** i.e., whose time does most good for **the peasant,** rather than for himself
294. **jealous of:** anxious at

With titles blown from adulation?
Will it give place to flexure and low bending?
Canst thou, when thou command'st the beggar's
    knee,   265
Command the health of it? No, thou proud dream,
That play'st so subtly with a king's repose.
I am a king that find thee, and I know
'Tis not the balm, the scepter, and the ball,
The sword, the mace, the crown imperial,   270
The intertissued robe of gold and pearl,
The farcèd title running 'fore the King,
The throne he sits on, nor the tide of pomp
That beats upon the high shore of this world;
No, not all these, thrice-gorgeous ceremony,   275
Not all these, laid in bed majestical,
Can sleep so soundly as the wretched slave
Who, with a body filled and vacant mind,
Gets him to rest, crammed with distressful bread;
Never sees horrid night, the child of hell,   280
But, like a lackey, from the rise to set
Sweats in the eye of Phoebus, and all night
Sleeps in Elysium; next day after dawn
Doth rise and help Hyperion to his horse,
And follows so the ever-running year   285
With profitable labor to his grave.
And, but for ceremony, such a wretch,
Winding up days with toil and nights with sleep,
Had the forehand and vantage of a king.
The slave, a member of the country's peace,   290
Enjoys it, but in gross brain little wots
What watch the King keeps to maintain the peace,
Whose hours the peasant best advantages.

Enter Erpingham.

ERPINGHAM
    My lord, your nobles, jealous of your absence,

298. **be:** i.e., be there

301. **Possess:** acquaint

302. **sense of reck'ning:** i.e., ability to calculate, count; **or:** before

303. **hearts:** i.e., courage

304–5. **the fault ... crown:** Henry Bolingbroke, father of Henry V, deposed Richard II and took his crown to become Henry IV. Richard was subsequently imprisoned and killed. **compassing:** seizing

306. **new:** anew

309–13. **Five ... soul:** See longer note, page 243.

311. **to pardon blood:** i.e., to pray for pardon for Richard's death

312. **chantries:** endowed chapels; **sad:** grave

313. **still:** continually

314–15. **all ... all:** i.e., **all** the good works **I can do** are worthless in meriting pardon, because, **after all** I have done and will do, I can only offer my repentance

"In thunder and in earthquake like a Jove." (2.4.107)
From Vincenzo Cartari, *Le vere e noue imagini* ... (1615).

Seek through your camp to find you.   295
KING HENRY   Good old knight,
Collect them all together at my tent.
I'll be before thee.
ERPINGHAM   I shall do 't, my lord.   *He exits.*
KING HENRY
O God of battles, steel my soldiers' hearts.   300
Possess them not with fear. Take from them now
The sense of reck'ning ⌜or⌝ th' opposèd numbers
Pluck their hearts from them. Not today, O Lord,
O, not today, think not upon the fault
My father made in compassing the crown.   305
I Richard's body have interrèd new
And on it have bestowed more contrite tears
Than from it issued forcèd drops of blood.
Five hundred poor I have in yearly pay
Who twice a day their withered hands hold up   310
Toward heaven to pardon blood. And I have built
Two chantries where the sad and solemn priests
Sing still for Richard's soul. More will I do—
Though all that I can do is nothing worth,
Since that my penitence comes after all,   315
Imploring pardon.

Enter Gloucester.

GLOUCESTER   My liege.
KING HENRY   My brother Gloucester's voice.—Ay,
I know thy errand. I will go with thee.
The day, my ⌜friends,⌝ and all things stay for me.   320
                                              They exit.

4.2 The French nobles, about to fight, lament that the English are so few and so weak.

---

1. **Up:** i.e., take horse
2. **Montez à cheval:** i.e., mount up; **varlet:** groom; rascal; **Lackey:** footman
4. **Via . . . terre:** by way of the waters and earth (a grandiose expression of where the horse will take him)
5. **Rien . . . feu:** Nothing after that? Air and fire? (i.e., certainly air and fire too, naming the other two elements besides water and earth)
6. **Cieux:** the heavens
8. **present service:** immediate action
9. **make incision:** i.e., with spurs
10. **spin:** stream, spurt
11. **dout them:** put them out; **superfluous courage:** overabundant vigor
14. **embattled:** drawn up in proper order for battle
17. **fair show:** beautiful display of military strength
18. **shales:** shells
21. **curtal ax:** cutlass

⌜Scene 2⌝

Enter the Dauphin, Orléans, Rambures, and Beaumont.

ORLÉANS
The sun doth gild our armor. Up, my lords.

DAUPHIN
Montez à cheval! My horse, varlet! Lackey! Ha!

ORLÉANS　O brave spirit!

DAUPHIN　*Via les eaux et terre.*

ORLÉANS　*Rien puis? L'air et feu?*　　　　　　　　　5

DAUPHIN　*Cieux,* cousin Orléans.

Enter Constable.

　Now, my Lord Constable?

CONSTABLE
Hark how our steeds for present service neigh.

DAUPHIN
Mount them, and make incision in their hides,
That their hot blood may spin in English eyes　　　10
And dout them with superfluous courage. Ha!

RAMBURES
What, will you have them weep our horses' blood?
How shall we then behold their natural tears?

Enter Messenger.

MESSENGER
The English are embattled, you French peers.

CONSTABLE
To horse, you gallant princes, straight to horse.　　15
Do but behold yond poor and starvèd band,
And your fair show shall suck away their souls,
Leaving them but the shales and husks of men.
There is not work enough for all our hands,
Scarce blood enough in all their sickly veins　　　20
To give each naked curtal ax a stain,
That our French gallants shall today draw out

26. **positive . . . exceptions:** i.e., certain
29. **squares of battle:** troops drawn up in square formations (See picture, page 190.)
30. **hilding:** good-for-nothing
31. **upon this mountain's basis:** i.e., on the base of this mountain; **by:** nearby
32. **speculation:** looking on
33. **our honors:** i.e., for our honor's sake, we
36. **tucket sonance:** signal to march
37. **dare:** dazzle
38. **England:** King Henry; **couch down:** cower
40–51. **Yond . . . motionless:** Grandpré compares the English soldiers to immobile corpses and skeletons, and emphasizes the raggedness of their insignia, the rottenness of their armor, and the thinness and sickness of their horses.
40. **carrions:** corpses
41. **Ill-favoredly become:** are unsuited in their ugliness to
42. **curtains:** flags, banners
43. **passing:** surpassingly, exceedingly
44. **beggared host:** i.e., army of beggars
45. **faintly:** timidly; feebly; **beaver:** front piece of the helmet in a suit of armor (See picture, page 178.)
46–47. **like . . . hand:** i.e., immobile, holding **torch staves** (staffs fitted with torches)
48. **Lob down:** droop
49. **gum down-roping . . . eyes:** i.e., matter discharged **from their eyes** trickling down like ropes
50. **gemeled bit:** a **bit** with either a hinge or a double ring

(continued)

158

And sheathe for lack of sport. Let us but blow on
    them,
The vapor of our valor will o'erturn them.   25
'Tis positive against all exceptions, lords,
That our superfluous lackeys and our peasants,
Who in unnecessary action swarm
About our squares of battle, were enough
To purge this field of such a hilding foe,   30
Though we upon this mountain's basis by
Took stand for idle speculation,
But that our honors must not. What's to say?
A very little little let us do,
And all is done. Then let the trumpets sound   35
The tucket sonance and the note to mount,
For our approach shall so much dare the field
That England shall couch down in fear and yield.

                    Enter Grandpré.

GRANDPRÉ
Why do you stay so long, my lords of France?
Yond island carrions, desperate of their bones,   40
Ill-favoredly become the morning field.
Their ragged curtains poorly are let loose,
And our air shakes them passing scornfully.
Big Mars seems bankrupt in their beggared host
And faintly through a rusty beaver peeps.   45
The horsemen sit like fixèd candlesticks
With torch staves in their hand, and their poor jades
Lob down their heads, ⌜drooping⌝ the hides and hips,
The gum down-roping from their pale dead eyes,
And in their pale dull mouths the gemeled bit   50
Lies foul with chawed grass, still and motionless.
And their executors, the knavish crows,
Fly o'er them all, impatient for their hour.
Description cannot suit itself in words
To demonstrate the life of such a battle   55
In life so lifeless, as it shows itself.

52. **executors:** those who dispose of what the dead leave behind (here, their bodies)

54. **suit . . . words:** (1) find suitable **words;** (2) clothe **itself in words**

55–56. **the life . . . itself:** in a lively way an army which **shows itself** to be **so lifeless**

60. **after:** i.e., then

61. **guard:** escort (which would perhaps be carrying his flag or banner)

62. **trumpet:** i.e., trumpeter

64. **outwear:** spend, waste

4.3 Henry delivers an oration to his troops urging them on to win glory in the battle. Montjoy again comes to establish the terms of Henry's ransom, and Henry again refuses to be ransomed should he be defeated and captured.

---

0 SD. **host:** army

2. **battle:** army

3. **full . . . thousand:** i.e., fully 60,000

6. **my charge:** i.e., the troops that I am to lead

10. **kinsman:** Westmoreland

CONSTABLE
They have said their prayers, and they stay for death.
DAUPHIN
Shall we go send them dinners and fresh suits,
And give their fasting horses provender,
And after fight with them?   60
CONSTABLE
I stay but for my guard. On, to the field!
I will the banner from a trumpet take
And use it for my haste. Come, come away.
The sun is high, and we outwear the day.
                                        They exit.

⌜Scene 3⌝
*Enter Gloucester, Bedford, Exeter, Erpingham with all
his host, Salisbury, and Westmoreland.*

GLOUCESTER   Where is the King?
BEDFORD
The King himself is rode to view their battle.
WESTMORELAND
Of fighting men they have full threescore thousand.
EXETER
There's five to one. Besides, they all are fresh.
SALISBURY
God's arm strike with us! 'Tis a fearful odds.   5
God be wi' you, princes all. I'll to my charge.
If we no more meet till we meet in heaven,
Then joyfully, my noble Lord of Bedford,
My dear Lord Gloucester, and my good Lord Exeter,
And my kind kinsman, warriors all, adieu.   10
BEDFORD
Farewell, good Salisbury, and good luck go with
    thee.

13–14. **And yet . . . valor:** i.e., I need not wish you **good luck,** since you have so much courage you do not need luck (Editors often move these lines to follow line 15, where they become part of Exeter's speech.) **mind thee of it:** bring it to your mind **framed:** built

19. **one ten thousand:** i.e., ten thousand

21. **What's:** who is

23. **marked:** destined

24. **if to live:** i.e., **if we are marked to live**

28. **doth feed . . . cost:** i.e., eats at my expense

29. **yearns:** grieves

33. **coz:** i.e., cousin (familiar form of address among members of the aristocracy); **from:** i.e., to come to us from

35. **share from me:** i.e., take **from me** by sharing (in the honor)

36. **For:** i.e., in exchange for; **best hope:** i.e., **hope** of salvation

38. **stomach to:** appetite for

39. **passport:** permit given to discharged soldiers, allowing them to travel

40. **crowns for convoy:** money for passage

42. **fears . . . us:** is afraid **to die with us**

43. **feast of Crispian:** October 25, actually the feast day of the Roman brothers Crispin and Crispinian, the patrons of shoemakers; see **Crispin Crispian** (line 59 below).

And yet I do thee wrong to mind thee of it,
For thou art framed of the firm truth of valor.

EXETER
Farewell, kind lord. Fight valiantly today.   15
      ⌜*Salisbury exits.*⌝

BEDFORD
He is as full of valor as of kindness,
Princely in both.

    Enter the King ⌜*of England.*⌝

WESTMORELAND O, that we now had here
But one ten thousand of those men in England
That do no work today.   20
KING HENRY What's he that wishes so?
My cousin Westmoreland? No, my fair cousin.
If we are marked to die, we are enough
To do our country loss; and if to live,
The fewer men, the greater share of honor. 25
God's will, I pray thee wish not one man more.
By Jove, I am not covetous for gold,
Nor care I who doth feed upon my cost;
It yearns me not if men my garments wear;
Such outward things dwell not in my desires. 30
But if it be a sin to covet honor,
I am the most offending soul alive.
No, 'faith, my coz, wish not a man from England.
God's peace, I would not lose so great an honor
As one man more, methinks, would share from me, 35
For the best hope I have. O, do not wish one more!
Rather proclaim it, Westmoreland, through my host,
That he which hath no stomach to this fight,
Let him depart. His passport shall be made,
And crowns for convoy put into his purse. 40
We would not die in that man's company
That fears his fellowship to die with us.
This day is called the feast of Crispian.

47. **live old age:** i.e., live to an **old age**

48. **vigil:** evening before

50. **scars:** Since Malone (1790), many editors have added here a line found only in the quarto of 1600: "And say 'These wounds I had on Crispin's day.'" The quarto line, although perhaps rhetorically strong, is not necessary to the sense of the speech.

51–52. **yet ... remember:** i.e., after the old man forgets everything else, he will still **remember**

52. **advantages:** enhancements

56. **Warwick and Talbot:** See longer note, p. 245.

57. **Be ... remembered:** i.e., be toasted **flowing:** overflowing

64. **vile:** lowly in birth

65. **gentle his condition:** ennoble his status

68. **hold:** regard

70. **bestow ... speed:** i.e., prepare speedily

71. **bravely ... set:** splendidly arrayed in their battalions

Hydra. (1.1.37)
From Jacob Typot, *Symbola diuina* ... (1652).

He that outlives this day and comes safe home
Will stand o' tiptoe when this day is named   45
And rouse him at the name of Crispian.
He that shall see this day, and live old age,
Will yearly on the vigil feast his neighbors
And say "Tomorrow is Saint Crispian."
Then will he strip his sleeve and show his scars.   50
Old men forget; yet all shall be forgot,
But he'll remember with advantages
What feats he did that day. Then shall our names,
Familiar in his mouth as household words,
Harry the King, Bedford and Exeter,   55
Warwick and Talbot, Salisbury and Gloucester,
Be in their flowing cups freshly remembered.
This story shall the good man teach his son,
And Crispin Crispian shall ne'er go by,
From this day to the ending of the world,   60
But we in it shall be rememberèd—
We few, we happy few, we band of brothers;
For he today that sheds his blood with me
Shall be my brother; be he ne'er so vile,
This day shall gentle his condition;   65
And gentlemen in England now abed
Shall think themselves accursed they were not here,
And hold their manhoods cheap whiles any speaks
That fought with us upon Saint Crispin's day.

Enter Salisbury.

SALISBURY
My sovereign lord, bestow yourself with speed.   70
The French are bravely in their battles set,
And will with all expedience charge on us.
KING HENRY
All things are ready if our minds be so.
WESTMORELAND
Perish the man whose mind is backward now!

76. **would:** i.e., I wish
79. **likes:** pleases
82. **compound:** come to terms
84. **gulf:** yawning chasm, abyss
85. **englutted:** swallowed up
86. **mind:** remind
88. **retire:** retreat
95. **achieve:** acquire
100. **A many:** i.e., many
101. **native graves: graves** in England

"Giddy Fortune." (3.6.26–27)
From [Robert Recorde,] *The castle of knowledge . . .* [1556].

KING HENRY
  Thou dost not wish more help from England, coz?   75
WESTMORELAND
  God's will, my liege, would you and I alone,
  Without more help, could fight this royal battle!
KING HENRY
  Why, now thou hast unwished five thousand men,
  Which likes me better than to wish us one.—
  You know your places. God be with you all.   80

          Tucket. Enter Montjoy.

MONTJOY
  Once more I come to know of thee, King Harry,
  If for thy ransom thou wilt now compound,
  Before thy most assurèd overthrow.
  For certainly thou art so near the gulf
  Thou needs must be englutted. Besides, in mercy,   85
  The Constable desires thee thou wilt mind
  Thy followers of repentance, that their souls
  May make a peaceful and a sweet retire
  From off these fields where, wretches, their poor
    bodies   90
  Must lie and fester.
KING HENRY   Who hath sent thee now?
MONTJOY   The Constable of France.
KING HENRY
  I pray thee bear my former answer back.
  Bid them achieve me and then sell my bones.   95
  Good God, why should they mock poor fellows
    thus?
  The man that once did sell the lion's skin
  While the beast lived was killed with hunting him.
  A many of our bodies shall no doubt   100
  Find native graves, upon the which, I trust,
  Shall witness live in brass of this day's work.

108. **clime:** region (i.e., France)

110. **Mark:** notice; **abounding valor:** abundant courage (with possible wordplay on "bounding")

111. **like . . . crazing:** i.e., like a ricocheting bullet

112. **Break . . . mischief:** i.e., kill again (by causing a plague) **mischief:** injury, evil

113. **Killing . . . mortality:** i.e., **killing** as they fall back in death **relapse:** falling back **mortality:** death (with wordplay on some of its other senses: namely, "deadliness" and "plague")

115. **but . . . day:** i.e., soldiers dressed for the workday (rather than the holiday)

116. **gayness:** dressiness; **gilt:** gilding

117. **rainy . . . field:** i.e., **painful marching in the rainy field** (transferred epithets)

119. **argument:** evidence; **fly:** i.e., run away

120. **slovenry:** an untidy appearance

121. **in the trim:** i.e., dressed in the latest fashion

123–25. **pluck . . . service:** i.e., treat **the French** soldiers as their servants whom they are dismissing, pulling the servants' livery off

127. **levied:** raised

129. **They:** i.e., the French

134–35. **I . . . ransom:** Editors often mark these lines as an aside, arguing that the assertion is an expression of Henry's fear of defeat, which he would not want his men to hear. However, the lines may be no more than a (perhaps jocular) contradiction of Montjoy that calls attention to his already evident persistence in seeking Henry's ransom.

And those that leave their valiant bones in France,
Dying like men, though buried in your dunghills,
They shall be famed; for there the sun shall greet   105
    them
And draw their honors reeking up to heaven,
Leaving their earthly parts to choke your clime,
The smell whereof shall breed a plague in France.
Mark, then, abounding valor in our English,   110
That being dead, like to the bullet's crazing,
Break out into a second course of mischief,
Killing in relapse of mortality.
Let me speak proudly: tell the Constable
We are but warriors for the working day;   115
Our gayness and our gilt are all besmirched
With rainy marching in the painful field.
There's not a piece of feather in our host—
Good argument, I hope, we will not fly—
And time hath worn us into slovenry.   120
But, by the Mass, our hearts are in the trim,
And my poor soldiers tell me, yet ere night
They'll be in fresher robes, or they will pluck
The gay new coats o'er the French soldiers' heads
And turn them out of service. If they do this,   125
As, if God please, they shall, my ransom then
Will soon be levied. Herald, save thou thy labor.
Come thou no more for ransom, gentle herald.
They shall have none, I swear, but these my joints,
Which, if they have, as I will leave 'em them,   130
Shall yield them little, tell the Constable.
MONTJOY
I shall, King Harry. And so fare thee well.
Thou never shalt hear herald anymore.
KING HENRY   I fear thou wilt once more come again
    for a ransom.   ⌜*Montjoy*⌝ *exits.*   135

                    Enter York.

137. **vaward:** vanguard, the foremost division of an army
140. **dispose the day:** assign victory

4.4 A French soldier surrenders to Pistol, who threatens him with death until the soldier promises to pay a ransom of two hundred gold coins.

---

0 SD. **Alarum:** call to arms; **Excursions:** i.e., movements of soldiers over the stage (literally, raids, sorties)
2–3. **Je . . . qualité:** I think you are a gentleman of high rank.
4. **Qualtitie . . . me:** nonsense as printed in the Folio, although editors have tried to emend it so that it echoes the refrain of an Irish ballad
6. **Ô . . . Dieu:** O Lord God
7–8. **Perpend:** consider
8. **mark:** take note
9. **fox:** a kind of sword
10. **egregious:** extraordinary
11–12. **Ô . . . moi:** O, have mercy! Have pity on me!
13. **Moy:** Pistol transforms the pronoun **moi** (me) into the name of an otherwise unknown coin or sum of money.
14. **rim:** belly, paunch
16–17. **Est-il . . . bras:** Is it impossible to escape the strength of your arm?
18. **luxurious:** lecherous
20. **Ô, pardonnez-moi:** O, pardon me.

YORK, ⌜*kneeling*⌝
    My lord, most humbly on my knee I beg
    The leading of the vaward.   .
KING HENRY
    Take it, brave York.   ⌜*York rises.*⌝
                Now, soldiers, march away,
    And how Thou pleasest, God, dispose the day.   140
                                        They exit.

                        ⌜Scene 4⌝
        Alarum. Excursions. Enter Pistol, French Soldier,
                        ⌜*and*⌝ *Boy.*

PISTOL   Yield, cur.
FRENCH ⌜SOLDIER⌝ *Je pense que vous êtes le gentil-*
    homme de bonne qualité.
PISTOL   *Qualtitie calmie custure me.* Art thou a gentle-
    man? What is thy name? Discuss.   5
FRENCH ⌜SOLDIER⌝ *Ô Seigneur Dieu!*
PISTOL   O, Seigneur Dew should be a gentleman. Per-
    pend my words, O Seigneur Dew, and mark: O
    Seigneur Dew, thou diest on point of fox, except, O
    Seigneur, thou do give to me egregious ransom.   10
FRENCH ⌜SOLDIER⌝ *Ô, prenez miséricorde! Ayez pitié de*
    moi!
PISTOL   *Moy* shall not serve. I will have forty *moys,* ⌜or⌝
    I will fetch thy rim out at thy throat in drops of
    crimson blood.   15
FRENCH ⌜SOLDIER⌝ *Est-il impossible d'échapper la force*
    de ton bras?
PISTOL   Brass, cur? Thou damned and luxurious
    mountain goat, offer'st me brass?
FRENCH ⌜SOLDIER⌝ *Ô, pardonnez-moi!*   20
PISTOL   Say'st thou me so? Is that a ton of *moys?*—

22. **Ask me:** i.e., **ask; slave:** rascal

24. **Écoutez ... appelé:** Listen. What is your name?

26. **Fer:** in French, **fer** means iron or steel

27. **firk:** beat, trounce; **ferret:** worry (i.e., tear, bite)

32. **Que ... monsieur:** What is he saying, sir?

33–35. **Il ... gorge:** He orders me to say to you that you are to make yourself ready, for this soldier here is disposed to cut your throat immediately.

36. **Owy ... permafoy:** broken French for "Yes, cut throat, by my faith"

37. **brave:** splendid

39–42. **Ô ... écus:** O, I beg you, for the love of God, to pardon me. I am a gentleman of a good house. Preserve my life, and I will give you two hundred crowns.   **maison:** house, i.e., family

49. **Petit ... il:** Little sir, what is he saying?

50–53. **Encore ... franchisement:** Once again that it is against his oath to pardon any prisoner; nevertheless, (in return) for the crowns that you have promised him, he is content to give you liberty, freedom.

54–57. **Sur ... Angleterre:** See lines 59–63 for the translation.

Come hither, boy. Ask me this slave in French what
is his name.

BOY *Écoutez. Comment êtes-vous appelé?*

FRENCH ⌜SOLDIER⌝ *Monsieur le Fer.*   25

BOY He says his name is Master Fer.

PISTOL Master Fer. I'll fer him, and firk him, and ferret
him. Discuss the same in French unto him.

BOY I do not know the French for "fer," and "ferret,"
and "firk."   30

PISTOL Bid him prepare, for I will cut his throat.

FRENCH ⌜SOLDIER, *to the Boy*⌝ *Que dit-il, monsieur?*

BOY *Il me commande à vous dire que vous faites vous
prêt, car ce soldat ici est disposé tout à cette heure de
couper votre gorge.*   35

PISTOL *Owy, cuppele gorge, permafoy,* peasant, unless
thou give me crowns, brave crowns, or mangled
shalt thou be by this my sword.

FRENCH ⌜SOLDIER⌝ *Ô, je vous supplie, pour l'amour de
Dieu, me pardonner. Je suis le gentilhomme de bonne*   40
*maison. Gardez ma vie, et je vous donnerai deux
cents écus.*

PISTOL What are his words?

BOY He prays you to save his life. He is a gentleman of a
good house, and for his ransom he will give you two   45
hundred crowns.

PISTOL Tell him my fury shall abate, and I the crowns
will take.

FRENCH ⌜SOLDIER, *to the Boy*⌝ *Petit monsieur, que dit-il?*

BOY *Encore qu'il est contre son jurement de pardonner*   50
*aucun prisonnier; néanmoins, pour les écus que vous
lui avez promis, il est content à vous donner la liberté,
le franchisement.*

⌜*French soldier kneels.*⌝

FRENCH ⌜SOLDIER⌝ *Sur mes genoux je vous donne mille
remercîments, et je m'estime heureux que j'ai tombé*   55

66. **Suivez ... capitaine:** Follow the great captain.
67. **empty:** i.e., cowardly
70. **this roaring devil:** i.e., this fellow who is nothing but the **roaring devil (i' th' old play)**
71–72. **that everyone ... dagger:** As in *Twelfth Night* 4.2.128–32, Shakespeare here alludes to the paring of a stage devil's **nails with a wooden dagger. that:** i.e., so that
74. **lackeys:** footmen
75. **might have a good prey of us:** i.e., might easily prey on us; **he:** i.e., the French

4.5 The French nobles, shamed in their defeat, decide to die fighting.

---

1. **Ô diable!:** O, the devil!
2. **Ô ... perdu:** O Lord! The day is lost, all is lost!
3. **Mort ... vie:** Death of my life; **confounded:** disordered, in confusion
5. **plumes:** the feathers adorning their helmets

Cavalry with pennon. (3.5.51)
From [Raimond ... baron de Fourquevaux,]
Instructions for the warres ... (1589).

entre les mains d'un chevalier, je pense, le plus brave,
vaillant, et très distingué seigneur d'Angleterre.
PISTOL Expound unto me, boy.
BOY He gives you upon his knees a thousand thanks,
and he esteems himself happy that he hath fall'n   60
into the hands of one, as he thinks, the most
brave, valorous, and thrice-worthy seigneur of
England.
PISTOL As I suck blood, I will some mercy show.
Follow me.   65
BOY *Suivez-vous le grand capitaine.*
⌜*The French Soldier stands up. He and Pistol exit.*⌝
I did never know so full a voice issue from so empty
a heart. But the saying is true: "The empty vessel
makes the greatest sound." Bardolph and Nym had
ten times more valor than this roaring devil i' th' old   70
play, that everyone may pare his nails with a wood-
en dagger, and they are both hanged, and so would
this be if he durst steal anything adventurously. I
must stay with the lackeys with the luggage of our
camp. The French might have a good prey of us if he   75
knew of it, for there is none to guard it but boys.
                                             He exits.

⌜Scene 5⌝
Enter Constable, Orléans, Bourbon, Dauphin, and
Rambures.

CONSTABLE *Ô dìable!*
ORLÉANS
   Ô Seigneur! Le jour est perdu, tout est perdu!
DAUPHIN
   Mort de ma vie, all is confounded, all!
   Reproach and everlasting shame
   Sits mocking in our plumes.   *A short Alarum.*   5

6. **Ô méchante Fortune!:** O evil Fortune!
9. **perdurable:** enduring
17. **gentler:** more noble by birth
18. **contaminate:** contaminated (i.e., raped)
19. **spoiled:** ruined; **friend:** befriend
20. **on:** i.e., in

4.6 Henry, in doubt about the outcome of the battle, hears of York's and Suffolk's deaths, and then, when a French call to arms is again sounded, orders his troops to kill their prisoners.

2. **Yet:** still

"Herod's bloody-hunting slaughtermen." (3.3.41)
From [Guillaume Guéroult,] *Figures de la Bible . . .* (1565–70).

                 Ô méchante Fortune!

Do not run away.

CONSTABLE   Why, all our ranks are broke.

DAUPHIN
  O perdurable shame! Let's stab ourselves.
  Be these the wretches that we played at dice for?   10

ORLÉANS
  Is this the king we sent to for his ransom?

BOURBON
  Shame, and eternal shame, nothing but shame!
  Let us die. In once more! Back again!
  And he that will not follow Bourbon now,
  Let him go hence, and with his cap in hand   15
  Like a base pander hold the chamber door,
  Whilst ⌐by a⌐ slave, no gentler than my dog,
  His fairest daughter is ⌐contaminate.⌐

CONSTABLE
  Disorder, that hath spoiled us, friend us now.
  Let us on heaps go offer up our lives.   20

ORLÉANS
  We are enough yet living in the field
  To smother up the English in our throngs,
  If any order might be thought upon.

BOURBON
  The devil take order now! I'll to the throng.
  Let life be short, else shame will be too long.   25
                         ⌐*They*⌐ *exit.*

⌐Scene 6⌐
Alarum. Enter the King ⌐*of England*⌐ *and his train,*
with prisoners.

KING HENRY
  Well have we done, thrice-valiant countrymen,
  But all's not done. Yet keep the French the field.

3. **commends him to:** greets
7. **array:** attire
8. **Larding:** i.e., covering with blood
9. **honor-owing:** i.e., honor-owning, honorable
11. **haggled:** hacked, mangled
12. **insteeped:** steeped, immersed
15. **He:** i.e., York
19. **chivalry:** bravery
20. **cheered him up:** encouraged him
21. **smiled . . . hand:** i.e., **smiled in** my **face** and reached out **his hand** to **me**
26–27. **espoused . . . testament:** i.e., married **to death,** he put his seal in **blood** upon a will
29. **waters:** i.e., tears
31. **all my mother:** According to the beliefs of the time, men inherited weak traits (like weeping) from their mothers.

A soldier peeping "through a . . . beaver." (4.2.45)
From Bonaventura Pistofilo, *Il torneo* . . . (1627).

⌜*Enter Exeter.*⌝

EXETER
  The Duke of York commends him to your Majesty.
KING HENRY
  Lives he, good uncle? Thrice within this hour
  I saw him down, thrice up again and fighting.   5
  From helmet to the spur, all blood he was.
EXETER
  In which array, brave soldier, doth he lie,
  Larding the plain, and by his bloody side,
  Yoke-fellow to his honor-owing wounds,
  The noble Earl of Suffolk also lies.   10
  Suffolk first died, and York, all haggled over,
  Comes to him where in gore he lay insteeped,
  And takes him by the beard, kisses the gashes
  That bloodily did yawn upon his face.
  He cries aloud "Tarry, my cousin Suffolk.   15
  My soul shall thine keep company to heaven.
  Tarry, sweet soul, for mine; then fly abreast,
  As in this glorious and well-foughten field
  We kept together in our chivalry."
  Upon these words I came and cheered him up.   20
  He smiled me in the face, raught me his hand,
  And with a feeble grip, says "Dear my lord,
  Commend my service to my sovereign."
  So did he turn, and over Suffolk's neck
  He threw his wounded arm and kissed his lips,   25
  And so, espoused to death, with blood he sealed
  A testament of noble-ending love.
  The pretty and sweet manner of it forced
  Those waters from me which I would have stopped,
  But I had not so much of man in me,   30
  And all my mother came into mine eyes
  And gave me up to tears.
KING HENRY   I blame you not,

34. **compound:** come to terms
35. **full:** i.e., tearful; **issue:** shed tears
39. **through:** i.e., throughout the army
39 SD. **They exit:** As the last line of this scene, the quarto prints "Pist. Couple gorge," a repetition of Pistol's line at 4.4.36. The quarto has Pistol enter at the beginning of 4.6 and stand silent, unheeded and idle, until he delivers this closing line.

4.7 Fluellen, in conversation with Gower, compares Henry to the classical world-conqueror Alexander the Great. Montjoy arrives to concede the French defeat. Williams appears with Henry's glove, which Henry does not acknowledge. Instead Henry sends Fluellen to challenge Williams, and then, to prevent the fight certain to ensue, sends Warwick and Gloucester after Fluellen.

---

2. **arrant:** notorious
3–4. **in your conscience:** i.e., according to your true belief
9. **wherefore:** i.e., for which reason
11. **gallant:** excellent
12. **Monmouth:** a town in Wales
15. **Alexander the Great:** See note to 1.1.49.
18. **magnanimous:** great in courage, nobly ambitious

For, hearing this, I must perforce compound
With ⌜my full⌝ eyes, or they will issue too.   *Alarum.*   35
But hark, what new alarum is this same?
The French have reinforced their scattered men.
Then every soldier kill his prisoners.
Give the word through.

⌜*They*⌝ *exit.*

⌜Scene 7⌝
Enter Fluellen and Gower.

FLUELLEN   Kill the poys and the luggage! 'Tis expressly
against the law of arms. 'Tis as arrant a piece of
knavery, mark you now, as can be offert, in your
conscience now, is it not?

GOWER   'Tis certain there's not a boy left alive, and   5
the cowardly rascals that ran from the battle ha'
done this slaughter. Besides, they have burned
and carried away all that was in the King's tent,
wherefore the King, most worthily, hath caused
every soldier to cut his prisoner's throat. O, 'tis a   10
gallant king!

FLUELLEN   Ay, he was porn at Monmouth, Captain
Gower. What call you the town's name where
Alexander the Pig was born?

GOWER   Alexander the Great.   15

FLUELLEN   Why, I pray you, is not "pig" great? The pig,
or the great, or the mighty, or the huge, or the
magnanimous, are all one reckonings, save the
phrase is a little variations.

GOWER   I think Alexander the Great was born in Mace-   20
don. His father was called Philip of Macedon, as I
take it.

FLUELLEN   I think it is in Macedon where Alexander is
porn. I tell you, captain, if you look in the maps of

31. **'tis all one:** i.e., it does not matter

32. **both:** i.e., both rivers

33–34. **is . . . well:** i.e., fits it quite closely

34. **figures:** comparisons (See line 45.)

37. **cholers:** anger

49–50. **great-belly doublet:** jacket stuffed to give its wearer the appearance of having a fat stomach (Falstaff is represented in Shakespeare's plays as fat.)

50. **gipes:** perhaps, jeers, scoffs

Gordian knot. (1.1.49)
From Claude Paradin, *Deuises heroiques . . .* (1557).

the 'orld, I warrant you sall find, in the compari-   25
sons between Macedon and Monmouth, that the
situations, look you, is both alike. There is a river in
Macedon, and there is also, moreover, a river at
Monmouth. It is called Wye at Monmouth, but it is
out of my prains what is the name of the other river.   30
But 'tis all one; 'tis alike as my fingers is to my
fingers, and there is salmons in both. If you mark
Alexander's life well, Harry of Monmouth's life is
come after it indifferent well, for there is figures in
all things. Alexander, God knows and you know, in   35
his rages and his furies and his wraths and his
cholers and his moods and his displeasures and his
indignations, and also being a little intoxicates in
his prains, did, in his ales and his angers, look you,
kill his best friend, Cleitus.   40

GOWER   Our king is not like him in that. He never
  killed any of his friends.

FLUELLEN   It is not well done, mark you now, to take
  the tales out of my mouth ere it is made and
  finished. I speak but in the figures and comparisons   45
  of it. As Alexander killed his friend Cleitus, being in
  his ales and his cups, so also Harry Monmouth,
  being in his right wits and his good judgments,
  turned away the fat knight with the great-belly
  doublet; he was full of jests and gipes and knaveries   50
  and mocks—I have forgot his name.

GOWER   Sir John Falstaff.

FLUELLEN   That is he. I'll tell you, there is good men
  porn at Monmouth.

GOWER   Here comes his Majesty.   55

Alarum. Enter King Harry, ⌐*Exeter, Warwick, Gloucester,*
Heralds⌐ *and Bourbon with* ⌐*other*⌐ *prisoners. Flourish.*

KING HENRY
  I was not angry since I came to France

57. **trumpet:** i.e., trumpeter
60. **Or:** i.e., or else; **void:** withdraw from
62. **skirr:** flee
63. **Enforcèd . . . slings:** Judith 9.7: "The Assyrians . . . trust in shield, and spear, and bow, and sling." **Enforcèd:** driven by force
71. **fined:** paid
74. **charitable license:** benevolent permission
76. **book:** record
79. **mercenary blood:** i.e., the **blood** of soldiers who were paid to fight
80. **vulgar:** common people
82. **Fret:** chafe
83. **Yerk:** lash; **armèd:** i.e., iron-shod

Soldiers plundering a village. (3.6.110–12)
From Raphael Holinshed, . . . *The chronicles of England . . .* (1577).

Until this instant. Take a trumpet, herald.
Ride thou unto the horsemen on yond hill.
If they will fight with us, bid them come down,
Or void the field. They do offend our sight.   60
If they'll do neither, we will come to them
And make them skirr away as swift as stones
Enforcèd from the old Assyrian slings.
Besides, we'll cut the throats of those we have,
And not a man of them that we shall take   65
Shall taste our mercy. Go and tell them so.

Enter Montjoy.

EXETER
Here comes the herald of the French, my liege.
GLOUCESTER
His eyes are humbler than they used to be.
KING HENRY
How now, what means this, herald? Know'st thou
   not   70
That I have fined these bones of mine for ransom?
Com'st thou again for ransom?
MONTJOY   No, great king.
I come to thee for charitable license,
That we may wander o'er this bloody field   75
To book our dead and then to bury them,
To sort our nobles from our common men,
For many of our princes—woe the while!—
Lie drowned and soaked in mercenary blood.
So do our vulgar drench their peasant limbs   80
In blood of princes, and ⌐the⌐ wounded steeds
Fret fetlock deep in gore, and with wild rage
Yerk out their armèd heels at their dead masters,
Killing them twice. O, give us leave, great king,
To view the field in safety and dispose   85
Of their dead bodies.
KING HENRY   I tell thee truly, herald,

88. **day:** i.e., victory

89. **peer:** come in sight, appear

93. **hard:** close

95. **field:** battle

97. **grandfather:** Edward III, actually Henry V's great-grandfather

105. **service:** military operations

106. **Monmouth caps:** round high-crowned caps without brims

107. **an honorable badge:** i.e., a **badge** worn in honor

A "kern of Ireland." (3.7.55)
From John Derricke, *The image of Irelande, with a discouerie of woodkarne . . .* (1581, facsimile rpt. 1883).

I know not if the day be ours or no,
For yet a many of your horsemen peer
And gallop o'er the field.   90
MONTJOY   The day is yours.
KING HENRY
Praised be God, and not our strength, for it!
What is this castle called that stands hard by?
MONTJOY They call it Agincourt.
KING HENRY
Then call we this the field of Agincourt,   95
Fought on the day of Crispin Crispianus.
FLUELLEN Your grandfather of famous memory, an 't
    please your Majesty, and your great-uncle Edward
    the Plack Prince of Wales, as I have read in the
    chronicles, fought a most prave pattle here in   100
    France.
KING HENRY They did, Fluellen.
FLUELLEN Your Majesty says very true. If your Majes-
    ties is remembered of it, the Welshmen did good
    service in a garden where leeks did grow, wearing   105
    leeks in their Monmouth caps, which, your Majesty
    know, to this hour is an honorable badge of the
    service. And I do believe your Majesty takes no
    scorn to wear the leek upon Saint Tavy's day.
KING HENRY
I wear it for a memorable honor,   110
For I am Welsh, you know, good countryman.
FLUELLEN All the water in Wye cannot wash your
    Majesty's Welsh plood out of your pody, I can tell
    you that. God pless it and preserve it as long as it
    pleases his Grace and his Majesty too.   115
KING HENRY Thanks, good my ⌜countryman.⌝
FLUELLEN By Jeshu, I am your Majesty's countryman,
    I care not who know it. I will confess it to all the
    'orld. I need not to be ashamed of your Majesty,

121. **honest:** noble
122. **him:** i.e., Montjoy
123. **just:** exact
129. **gage:** pledge
133. **swaggered:** quarreled
134. **take:** give
137. **soundly:** smartly, severely
138. **fit:** appropriate
143. **great sort:** high rank; **quite . . . degree:** i.e., far removed from the obligation to take up a challenge from someone of Williams's (low) social rank
144–45. **gentleman . . . himself:** Perhaps proverbial: "The Prince of Darkness is **a gentleman**" (*King Lear* 3.4.151). **Beelzebub:** Matthew 12.24: "**Beelzebub** the prince of devils."
147. **be perjured:** fail to keep his oath
148. **arrant:** notorious, **Jack Sauce:** i.e., saucy (insolent) fellow

Bearbaiting. (3.7.145–47)
From [William Lily,] *Antibossicon* (1521).

praised be God, so long as your Majesty is an   120
honest man.

KING HENRY
⌐God⌐ keep me so.—Our heralds, go with him.
Bring me just notice of the numbers dead
On both our parts.
                    ⌐*Montjoy, English Heralds, and Gower exit.*⌐

                    Enter Williams.

                    Call yonder fellow hither.   125
EXETER   Soldier, you must come to the King.
KING HENRY   Soldier, why wear'st thou that glove in thy
   cap?
WILLIAMS   An 't please your Majesty, 'tis the gage of
   one that I should fight withal, if he be alive.   130
KING HENRY   An Englishman?
WILLIAMS   An 't please your Majesty, a rascal that
   swaggered with me last night, who, if alive and ever
   dare to challenge this glove, I have sworn to take
   him a box o' th' ear, or if I can see my glove in his   135
   cap, which he swore, as he was a soldier, he would
   wear if alive, I will strike it out soundly.
KING HENRY   What think you, Captain Fluellen, is it fit
   this soldier keep his oath?
FLUELLEN   He is a craven and a villain else, an 't   140
   please your Majesty, in my conscience.
KING HENRY   It may be his enemy is a gentleman of
   great sort, quite from the answer of his degree.
FLUELLEN   Though he be as good a gentleman as the
   devil is, as Lucifer and Beelzebub himself, it is   145
   necessary, look your Grace, that he keep his vow
   and his oath. If he be perjured, see you now, his
   reputation is as arrant a villain and a Jack Sauce as
   ever his black shoe trod upon God's ground and His
   earth, in my conscience, la.   150

151. **sirrah:** term of address to a social inferior
154. **Who:** i.e., whom
156–57. **good knowledge and literatured:** i.e., knowledgeable and well read
161. **favor:** token
163. **helm:** helmet
165. **our person:** i.e., me
169. **fain:** gladly
171. **an:** i.e., if it
181. **haply:** perhaps

Fronte of the battel. Square of men.

144 Pikes.
48 Musk.
36 Musk.
76 Musk.
57 Musk.

361

A square of battle. (4.2.29)
From Gerrat Barry, *A discourse of military discipline* . . . (1634).

KING HENRY　Then keep thy vow, sirrah, when thou
　meet'st the fellow.
WILLIAMS　So I will, my liege, as I live.
KING HENRY　Who serv'st thou under?
WILLIAMS　Under Captain Gower, my liege.　　　　155
FLUELLEN　Gower is a good captain, and is good knowl-
　edge and literatured in the wars.
KING HENRY　Call him hither to me, soldier.
WILLIAMS　I will, my liege.　　　　　　　*He exits.*
KING HENRY, ⌜*giving Fluellen Williams's glove*⌝ Here,　160
　Fluellen, wear thou this favor for me, and stick it in
　thy cap. When Alençon and myself were down
　together, I plucked this glove from his helm. If any
　man challenge this, he is a friend to Alençon and an
　enemy to our person. If thou encounter any such,　165
　apprehend him, an thou dost me love.
FLUELLEN, ⌜*putting the glove in his cap*⌝ Your Grace
　does me as great honors as can be desired in the
　hearts of his subjects. I would fain see the man that
　has but two legs that shall find himself aggriefed at　170
　this glove, that is all; but I would fain see it once, an
　please God of His grace that I might see.
KING HENRY　Know'st thou Gower?
FLUELLEN　He is my dear friend, an please you.
KING HENRY　Pray thee, go seek him, and bring him to　175
　my tent.
FLUELLEN　I will fetch him.　　　　　　*He exits.*
KING HENRY
　My Lord of Warwick and my brother Gloucester,
　Follow Fluellen closely at the heels.
　The glove which I have given him for a favor　　　　180
　May haply purchase him a box o' th' ear.
　It is the soldier's. I by bargain should
　Wear it myself. Follow, good cousin Warwick.
　If that the soldier strike him, as I judge
　By his blunt bearing he will keep his word,　　　　185

186. **mischief:** harmful action

187–89. **Fluellen . . . injury:** Ignited by his anger (**choler**) because of an insult or hurt (**injury**), Fluellen's valor will explode in retaliation (**quickly will return an injury**), just as gunpowder in a cannon goes off when it is **touched** by the gunner's match.

4.8 Williams and Fluellen are prevented from fighting by Warwick and Gloucester. Henry arrives and accuses Williams of promising to strike him. Williams successfully excuses himself and is rewarded. Henry learns of the huge number of French casualties and the very few English. He declares the English victory to be God's own work, and he plans to return to England.

———

1. **I warrant:** i.e., I'll bet

4. **peradventure:** perhaps

8. **this:** i.e., the **glove** in Fluellen's cap

9. **'Sblood:** i.e., God's blood (a very strong oath)

12. **be forsworn:** i.e., break my vow

14. **his payment:** i.e., its **payment** (although possibly Fluellen's **treason** refers to Williams himself); **plows:** i.e., blows

16. **lie . . . throat:** infamous **lie**

Some sudden mischief may arise of it,
For I do know Fluellen valiant
And, touched with choler, hot as gunpowder,
And quickly will return an injury.
Follow, and see there be no harm between them.—   190
Go you with me, uncle of Exeter.

They exit.

⌜Scene 8⌝
Enter Gower and Williams.

WILLIAMS   I warrant it is to knight you, captain.

Enter Fluellen, ⌜wearing Williams's glove.⌝

FLUELLEN, ⌜*to Gower*⌝   God's will and His pleasure,
   captain, I beseech you now, come apace to the
   King. There is more good toward you peradventure
   than is in your knowledge to dream of.   5
WILLIAMS, ⌜*to Fluellen, pointing to the glove in his own
   hat*⌝   Sir, know you this glove?
FLUELLEN   Know the glove? I know the glove is a glove.
WILLIAMS   I know this, and thus I challenge it.
                              Strikes him.
FLUELLEN   'Sblood, an arrant traitor as any 's in the
   universal world, or in France, or in England!   10
GOWER, ⌜*to Williams*⌝   How now, sir? You villain!
WILLIAMS   Do you think I'll be forsworn?
FLUELLEN   Stand away, Captain Gower. I will give trea-
   son his payment into plows, I warrant you.
WILLIAMS   I am no traitor.   15
FLUELLEN   That's a lie in thy throat.—I charge you in
   his Majesty's name, apprehend him. He's a friend
   of the Duke Alençon's.

Enter Warwick and Gloucester.

29. **this:** i.e., the **glove** in Fluellen's cap
30. **gave . . . change:** i.e., exchanged gloves with
34. **saving:** i.e., with all due respect to

"Every rub is smoothèd on our way." (2.2.197)
From *Le centre de l'amour . . .* [1650?].

WARWICK   How now, how now, what's the matter?

FLUELLEN   My Lord of Warwick, here is, praised be   20
God for it, a most contagious treason come to
light, look you, as you shall desire in a summer's
day.

Enter King ⌐of England⌐ and Exeter.

Here is his Majesty.

KING HENRY   How now, what's the matter?   25

FLUELLEN   My liege, here is a villain and a traitor, that,
look your Grace, has struck the glove which your
Majesty is take out of the helmet of Alençon.

WILLIAMS   My liege, this was my glove; here is the fellow
of it. And he that I gave it to in change promised to   30
wear it in his cap. I promised to strike him if he did.
I met this man with my glove in his cap, and I have
been as good as my word.

FLUELLEN   Your Majesty, hear now, saving your Majesty's manhood, what an arrant, rascally, beggarly,   35
lousy knave it is. I hope your Majesty is pear me
testimony and witness and will avouchment that
this is the glove of Alençon that your Majesty is give
me, in your conscience now.

KING HENRY, ⌐to Williams⌐   Give me thy glove, soldier.   40
Look, here is the fellow of it.
'Twas I indeed thou promised'st to strike,
And thou hast given me most bitter terms.

FLUELLEN   An please your Majesty, let his neck answer
for it, if there is any martial law in the world.   45

KING HENRY, ⌐to Williams⌐   How canst thou make me
satisfaction?

WILLIAMS   All offenses, my lord, come from the heart.
Never came any from mine that might offend your
Majesty.   50

KING HENRY   It was ourself thou didst abuse.

WILLIAMS   Your Majesty came not like yourself. You

54. **lowliness:** low state or condition
55. **suffered under:** endured in
70. **will:** i.e., will take
72. **wherefore:** i.e., why
74. **silling:** shilling (twelve pence)
78. **good sort:** i.e., high rank
82. **Full:** i.e., fully

A "christom child." (2.3.12)
From [Richard Day,] *A booke of christian prayers . . .* (1578).

appeared to me but as a common man; witness the
night, your garments, your lowliness. And what
your Highness suffered under that shape, I beseech   55
you take it for your own fault and not mine, for, had
you been as I took you for, I made no offense.
Therefore, I beseech your Highness pardon me.

KING HENRY
Here, uncle Exeter, fill this glove with crowns
And give it to this fellow.—Keep it, fellow,   60
And wear it for an honor in thy cap
Till I do challenge it.—Give him the crowns.—
And, captain, you must needs be friends with him.

FLUELLEN   By this day and this light, the fellow has
mettle enough in his belly.—Hold, there is twelve-   65
pence for you, and I pray you to serve God and keep
you out of prawls and prabbles and quarrels and
dissensions, and I warrant you it is the better for
you.

WILLIAMS   I will none of your money.   70

FLUELLEN   It is with a good will. I can tell you it will
serve you to mend your shoes. Come, wherefore
should you be so pashful? Your shoes is not so
good. 'Tis a good silling, I warrant you, or I will
change it.   75

Enter ⌐an English⌐ Herald.

KING HENRY   Now, herald, are the dead numbered?
HERALD, ⌐giving the King a paper⌐
Here is the number of the slaughtered French.
KING HENRY, ⌐to Exeter⌐
What prisoners of good sort are taken, uncle?
EXETER
Charles, Duke of Orléans, nephew to the King;
John, Duke of Bourbon, and Lord Bouciqualt.   80
Of other lords and barons, knights and squires,
Full fifteen hundred, besides common men.

85. **bearing banners:** i.e., entitled to lead into battle vassals under their own banner

87. **esquires:** squires, those aspiring to be knights

93. **blood and quality:** i.e., high descent and rank

102. **lusty:** handsome (especially in dress)

105. **a royal . . . death:** i.e., many nobles dying together

109. **name:** i.e., high social rank; **other men:** i.e., commoners

112. **stratagem:** (1) cunning trick; (2) act of generalship that deceives the enemy (Whether or not Henry used tricks, he certainly, according to contemporary report, used brilliant acts of generalship in the way he deployed his archers.)

113. **plain shock:** direct charge; **even:** equal

Grafting (3.5.5–9).
From Marco Bussato, *Giardino di agricoltura . . .* (1599).

KING HENRY
  This note doth tell me of ten thousand French
  That in the field lie slain. Of princes in this number
  And nobles bearing banners, there lie dead   85
  One hundred twenty-six. Added to these,
  Of knights, esquires, and gallant gentlemen,
  Eight thousand and four hundred, of the which
  Five hundred were but yesterday dubbed knights.
  So that in these ten thousand they have lost,   90
  There are but sixteen hundred mercenaries.
  The rest are princes, barons, lords, knights, squires,
  And gentlemen of blood and quality.
  The names of those their nobles that lie dead:
  Charles Delabreth, High Constable of France;   95
  Jacques of Chatillon, Admiral of France;
  The Master of the Crossbows, Lord Rambures;
  Great Master of France, the brave Sir Guichard
    Dauphin;
  John, Duke of Alençon; Anthony, Duke of Brabant, 100
  The brother to the Duke of Burgundy;
  And Edward, Duke of Bar. Of lusty earls:
  Grandpré and Roussi, Faulconbridge and Foix,
  Beaumont and Marle, ⌜Vaudemont⌝ and Lestrale.
  Here was a royal fellowship of death.   105
  Where is the number of our English dead?
              ⌜*Herald gives him another paper.*⌝
  Edward the Duke of York, the Earl of Suffolk,
  Sir Richard Ketly, Davy Gam, esquire;
  None else of name, and of all other men
  But five and twenty. O God, thy arm was here,   110
  And not to us, but to thy arm alone
  Ascribe we all! When, without stratagem,
  But in plain shock and even play of battle,
  Was ever known so great and little loss
  On one part and on th' other? Take it, God,   115
  For it is none but thine.

118. **village:** Maisoncelles
122. **an:** i.e., if it
128. **Non nobis:** a hymn that begins "Not unto us, O Lord, not unto us, but unto Thy name give the praise" (Psalm 115, Book of Common Prayer); **Te Deum:** a hymn that begins "We praise thee, O God"
131. **happy:** fortunate

"The game's afoot" (3.1.35).
From [George Turberville,] *The noble art of . . . hunting . . .* (1611).

EXETER 'Tis wonderful.

KING HENRY
Come, go ⌜we⌝ in procession to the village,
And be it death proclaimèd through our host
To boast of this or take that praise from God   120
Which is His only.

FLUELLEN   Is it not lawful, an please your Majesty, to
tell how many is killed?

KING HENRY
Yes, captain, but with this acknowledgment:
That God fought for us.   125

FLUELLEN   Yes, my conscience, He did us great good.

KING HENRY   Do we all holy rites.
Let there be sung *Non nobis*, and *Te Deum*,
The dead with charity enclosed in clay,
And then to Calais, and to England then,   130
Where ne'er from France arrived more happy men.
                                        They exit.

The Life of

HENRY V

ACT 5

5.Chorus The Chorus describes the great welcome accorded the English army when it returns home, the visit by the Holy Roman Emperor to establish peace between England and France, and the return of Henry to France.

---

1. **Vouchsafe:** grant as an act of condescension
2. **prompt them:** tell them what comes next; **of such as:** i.e., as for those who
3. **admit:** allow (i.e., as my **excuse** for what I'm doing in condensing things)
4. **time:** This chorus swallows up the many events of the five years between the Battle of Agincourt (1415), represented in Act 4, and the Treaty of Troyes (1420), represented in Act 5.
5. **proper life:** i.e., the **life** that actually belonged to them
10. **Pales in the flood:** encloses, or fences in, the ocean; **wives:** i.e., women
11. **claps:** applause; **outvoice:** i.e., drown out; **deep-mouthed:** sonorous
13. **whiffler:** official charged with clearing the way for a royal or civic procession
17. **Blackheath:** open space southeast of London
18. **Where that:** i.e., from where; **to have borne:** i.e., order to be carried
19. **bruisèd, bended:** i.e., battle-damaged
22–23. **Giving . . . God:** i.e., attributing the triumph (referred to here in terms of the symbols of it—**trophy, signal, and ostent**) entirely **to God signal:** sign, token **ostent:** show, display

ACT 5

Enter Chorus.

⌜CHORUS⌝
Vouchsafe to those that have not read the story
That I may prompt them; and of such as have,
I humbly pray them to admit th' excuse
Of time, of numbers, and due course of things,
Which cannot in their huge and proper life   5
Be here presented. Now we bear the King
Toward Calais. Grant him there. There seen,
Heave him away upon your wingèd thoughts
Athwart the sea. Behold, the English beach
Pales in the flood with men, wives, and boys,   10
Whose shouts and claps outvoice the deep-mouthed
    sea,
Which, like a mighty whiffler 'fore the King
Seems to prepare his way. So let him land,
And solemnly see him set on to London.   15
So swift a pace hath thought that even now
You may imagine him upon Blackheath,
Where that his lords desire him to have borne
His bruisèd helmet and his bended sword
Before him through the city. He forbids it,   20
Being free from vainness and self-glorious pride,
Giving full trophy, signal, and ostent
Quite from himself, to God. But now behold,

205

24. **workinghouse:** workshop
26. **brethren:** i.e., aldermen; **in best sort:** i.e., dressed in their best
27. **th' antique:** ancient
28. **plebeians:** ordinary people
30. **a lower . . . likelihood:** i.e., a similarity of persons lower in rank, but a similarity much to be desired
31. **general:** perhaps Essex; perhaps Mountjoy (See longer note, page 245.) **empress:** Queen Elizabeth I
33. **rebellion:** i.e., the Irish **rebellion** against England; **broachèd:** spitted
35. **much:** i.e., for **much**
37. **they:** i.e., **they** welcome
40. **Emperor:** Sigismund, the Holy Roman **emperor,** visited London to treat for peace in May 1416.
41. **order:** arrange
44–45. **myself . . . past:** i.e., I have performed what has happened since he was last in France **by** reminding **you** that it is now **past**
46. **brook abridgment:** perhaps, tolerate the omission from our performance of the events just narrated; or, perhaps, tolerate what I have done in thus digesting history

5.1 Fluellen avenges Pistol's insults by making Pistol eat a leek. Pistol, humiliated, plans to return to England in the guise of a wounded soldier.

---

4. **ass:** i.e., as
5. **scald:** scabby; mean

In the quick forge and workinghouse of thought,
How London doth pour out her citizens. 25
The Mayor and all his brethren in best sort,
Like to the senators of th' antique Rome,
With the plebeians swarming at their heels,
Go forth and fetch their conqu'ring Caesar in—
As, by a lower but by loving likelihood 30
Were now the general of our gracious empress,
As in good time he may, from Ireland coming,
Bringing rebellion broachèd on his sword,
How many would the peaceful city quit
To welcome him! Much more, and much more 35
    cause,
Did they this Harry. Now in London place him
(As yet the lamentation of the French
Invites the King of England's stay at home;
The Emperor's coming in behalf of France 40
To order peace between them) and omit
All the occurrences, whatever chanced,
Till Harry's back return again to France.
There must we bring him, and myself have played
The interim, by remembering you 'tis past. 45
Then brook abridgment, and your eyes advance
After your thoughts, straight back again to France.

                                        He exits.

⌜Scene 1⌝
Enter Fluellen and Gower.

GOWER Nay, that's right. But why wear you your leek
    today? Saint Davy's day is past.
FLUELLEN There is occasions and causes why and
    wherefore in all things. I will tell you ass my
    friend, Captain Gower. The rascally, scald, beggar- 5
    ly, lousy, pragging knave Pistol, which you and

15. **swelling:** i.e., puffing himself up

20. **bedlam:** mad (**Bedlam** refers to London's Bethlehem Hospital for the insane.)

20–21. **base Trojan:** a bombastic insult

21. **fold up Parca's fatal web:** i.e., kill you (a mistaken reference to the Parcae, or Fates, of classical mythology, who did not **fold up** the **web** of life but cut its thread)

22. **qualmish:** nauseated

29. **Cadwallader:** seventh-century Welsh hero, characterized by Pistol as a goatherd

37. **mountain squire:** i.e., owner of worthless mountain land

38. **squire . . . degree:** (1) in contrast to **mountain squire;** (2) the name of a popular medieval romance   **degree:** rank

The three Fates. (3.6.45; 5.1.21)
From Vincenzo Cartari, *Imagines deorum . . .* (1581).

yourself and all the world know to be no petter than
a fellow, look you now, of no merits, he is come to
me and prings me pread and salt yesterday, look
you, and bid me eat my leek. It was in a place where   10
I could not breed no contention with him, but I will
be so bold as to wear it in my cap till I see him once
again, and then I will tell him a little piece of my
desires.

Enter Pistol.

GOWER   Why here he comes, swelling like a turkey-   15
cock.

FLUELLEN   'Tis no matter for his swellings, nor his
turkey-cocks.—God pless you, Aunchient Pistol,
you scurvy, lousy knave, God pless you.

PISTOL   Ha, art thou bedlam? Dost thou thirst, base   20
Trojan, to have me fold up Parca's fatal web? Hence.
I am qualmish at the smell of leek.

FLUELLEN   I peseech you heartily, scurvy, lousy knave,
at my desires and my requests and my petitions, to
eat, look you, this leek. Because, look you, you do   25
not love it, nor your affections and your appetites
and your disgestions does not agree with it, I would
desire you to eat it.

PISTOL   Not for Cadwallader and all his goats.

FLUELLEN   There is one goat for you. (*Strikes him*   30
⌜*with a cudgel.*⌝) Will you be so good, scald knave,
as eat it?

PISTOL   Base Trojan, thou shalt die.

FLUELLEN   You say very true, scald knave, when God's
will is. I will desire you to live in the meantime and   35
eat your victuals. Come, there is sauce for it. ⌜*Strikes
him.*⌝ You called me yesterday "mountain squire,"
but I will make you today a squire of low degree. I
pray you, fall to. If you can mock a leek, you can eat
a leek.   40

41. **astonished:** stunned

43. **pate:** head

44. **green:** fresh

45. **coxcomb:** head (literally, a fool's cap) (See picture, below.)

47. **out of:** without

55. **do:** i.e., may it **do**

61. **Hold you:** i.e., wait; **groat:** coin worth only four pence

64. **verily:** truly

67. **in earnest of revenge:** i.e., as a promise of the revenge to come

69. **woodmonger:** seller of wood

75. **respect:** consideration

76. **predeceased valor:** i.e., brave men who have died; **avouch:** affirm

A fool wearing a coxcomb. (5.1.45)
From George Wither, *A collection of emblemes . . .* (1635).

GOWER   Enough, captain. You have astonished him.

FLUELLEN   I say I will make him eat some part of my
leek, or I will peat his pate four days.—Bite, I pray
you. It is good for your green wound and your
ploody coxcomb.   45

PISTOL   Must I bite?

FLUELLEN   Yes, certainly, and out of doubt and out of
question, too, and ambiguities.

PISTOL   By this leek, I will most horribly revenge.
⌜*Fluellen threatens him.*⌝ I eat and eat, I swear—   50

FLUELLEN   Eat, I pray you. Will you have some more
sauce to your leek? There is not enough leek to
swear by.

PISTOL   Quiet thy cudgel. Thou dost see I eat.

FUELLEN   Much good do you, scald knave, heartily.   55
Nay, pray you throw none away. The skin is good for
your broken coxcomb. When you take occasions to
see leeks hereafter, I pray you mock at 'em, that is
all.

PISTOL   Good.   60

FLUELLEN   Ay, leeks is good. Hold you, there is a groat
to heal your pate.

PISTOL   Me, a groat?

FLUELLEN   Yes, verily, and in truth you shall take it, or I
have another leek in my pocket, which you shall   65
eat.

PISTOL   I take thy groat in earnest of revenge.

FLUELLEN   If I owe you anything, I will pay you in
cudgels. You shall be a woodmonger and buy
nothing of me but cudgels. God be wi' you and   70
keep you and heal your pate.   *He exits.*

PISTOL   All hell shall stir for this.

GOWER   Go, go. You are a counterfeit cowardly knave.
Will you mock at an ancient tradition begun upon
an honorable respect and worn as a memorable   75
trophy of predeceased valor, and dare not avouch in

78. **gleeking and galling:** jesting and scoffing
82. **correction:** punishment
83. **condition:** moral nature
84. **play...with:** i.e., betray
85. **Doll:** In 2.1 and 2.3, Pistol is represented as married to the Hostess, Nell Quickly, not to Doll Tearsheet, a prostitute associated with Falstaff in *Henry IV, Part 2.* This incongruity in the Folio text has not been satisfactorily explained.
85–86. **i' th' spital...France:** in the hospital with venereal disease
86. **rendezvous:** retreat to safe haven
88–89. **something...cutpurse:** somewhat incline to (being a) pickpocket
91. **patches:** medicated paste; **unto:** i.e., for
92. **Gallia:** a mistake for "Gallic" or French

5.2 The Duke of Burgundy has brought about a meeting between French and English to sign a peace treaty. Henry delegates negotiation of the treaty to his nobles while he woos Katherine, Princess of France, who agrees to marry him. The French are brought to accept all English terms, including Henry's right to succeed to the French throne.

---

1. **wherefor:** i.e., for which reason (i.e., of making peace) (The language of these opening courtly speeches is marked by highly formal diction and contorted word order.)
2. **our...sister:** the king and queen of **France**
5. **royalty:** royal family
6. **contrived:** managed, brought about

your deeds any of your words? I have seen you
gleeking and galling at this gentleman twice or
thrice. You thought because he could not speak
English in the native garb, he could not therefore   80
handle an English cudgel. You find it otherwise, and
henceforth let a Welsh correction teach you a good
English condition. Fare you well.   *He exits.*
PISTOL   Doth Fortune play the huswife with me now?
News have I that my Doll is dead i' th' spital of a   85
malady of France, and there my rendezvous is quite
cut off. Old I do wax, and from my weary limbs
honor is cudgeled. Well, bawd I'll turn, and something lean to cutpurse of quick hand. To England
will I steal, and there I'll steal.   90
And patches will I get unto these cudgeled scars,
And ⌜swear⌝ I got them in the Gallia wars.
                             He exits.

⌜Scene 2⌝
Enter at one door, King Henry, Exeter, Bedford,
Warwick, ⌜Westmoreland,⌝ and other Lords. At another,
Queen Isabel ⌜of France,⌝ the King ⌜of France, the
Princess Katherine and Alice,⌝ the Duke of Burgundy,
and other French.

KING HENRY
Peace to this meeting wherefor we are met.
Unto our brother France and to our sister,
Health and fair time of day.—Joy and good wishes
To our most fair and princely cousin Katherine.—
And, as a branch and member of this royalty,   5
By whom this great assembly is contrived,
We do salute you, Duke of Burgundy.—
And princes French, and peers, health to you all.

10. **Fairly met:** i.e., welcome

12. **issue:** outcome; **Ireland:** This word was changed to "England" in the Second Folio of 1632, and has appeared thus in all subsequent editions. The name **Ireland** could, however, have been understood as a name for Henry V in plays onstage in the early seventeenth century. See longer note, page 245.

13. **gracious:** fortunate, prosperous

15–16. **have borne . . . in their bent:** i.e., have carried in them . . . when you directed your eyes **(against the French)**

17. **balls:** (1) cannonballs; (2) eyeballs; **basilisks:** (1) large cannon; (2) fabulous creatures whose glance was fatal (See picture, page 220.)

18. **fairly:** with respect

19. **quality:** i.e., venomous **quality**

23. **on:** i.e., based on

28. **bar:** tribunal

29. **Your . . . parts:** i.e., your Majesties both English and French

30. **office:** service or duty toward you

32. **congreeted:** greeted each other

34. **rub:** obstacle (See 2.2.197 and picture, page 194.)

36. **nurse:** nourisher

38. **put up:** raise

KING OF FRANCE
  Right joyous are we to behold your face,
  Most worthy brother England. Fairly met.—   10
  So are you, princes English, every one.
QUEEN OF FRANCE
  So happy be the issue, brother Ireland,
  Of this good day and of this gracious meeting,
  As we are now glad to behold your eyes—
  Your eyes which hitherto have borne in them   15
  Against the French that met them in their bent
  The fatal balls of murdering basilisks.
  The venom of such looks, we fairly hope,
  Have lost their quality, and that this day
  Shall change all griefs and quarrels into love.   20
KING HENRY
  To cry "Amen" to that, thus we appear.
QUEEN OF FRANCE
  You English princes all, I do salute you.
BURGUNDY
  My duty to you both, on equal love,
  Great kings of France and England. That I have
    labored   25
  With all my wits, my pains, and strong endeavors
  To bring your most imperial Majesties
  Unto this bar and royal interview,
  Your Mightiness on both parts best can witness.
  Since, then, my office hath so far prevailed   30
  That face to face and royal eye to eye
  You have congreeted, let it not disgrace me
  If I demand before this royal view
  What rub or what impediment there is
  Why that the naked, poor, and mangled peace,   35
  Dear nurse of arts, plenties, and joyful births,
  Should not in this best garden of the world,
  Our fertile France, put up her lovely visage?
  Alas, she hath from France too long been chased,

40. **husbandry:** agriculture; **on:** i.e., in
42. **merry cheerer:** i.e., when the grape from the vine becomes wine
43. **even-pleached:** uniformly interlaced
45. **fallow leas:** unplanted fields
46. **darnel . . . fumitory:** weeds **rank:** overgrown, rotten
47. **coulter:** vertical blade on the front of a plow
48. **deracinate:** tear up by the roots
49. **even mead:** level meadow; **erst:** formerly
50. **freckled:** spotted
51. **Wanting:** lacking; **withal uncorrected:** i.e., therewith uncontrolled
52. **Conceives:** reproduces
53. **docks:** weeds; **kecksies:** dry, hollow plant stems
55. **fallows:** unplanted lands; **meads:** meadows
57. **houses:** households
58. **want:** lack
59. **sciences:** learning; knowledge acquired through study; **become:** grace, adorn
61. **blood:** bloodshed
62. **diffused:** disordered
64. **reduce . . . favor:** i.e., bring into the favorable condition that formerly prevailed
66. **let:** hindrance
67. **inconveniences:** harms, troubles
69. **would:** i.e., wish to have
72. **accord:** agreement
73. **tenors . . . effects:** general substance and details
74. **enscheduled:** listed

And all her husbandry doth lie on heaps,   40
Corrupting in its own fertility.
Her vine, the merry cheerer of the heart,
Unprunèd, dies. Her hedges, even-pleached,
Like prisoners wildly overgrown with hair,
Put forth disordered twigs. Her fallow leas   45
The darnel, hemlock, and rank fumitory
Doth root upon, while that the coulter rusts
That should deracinate such savagery.
The even mead, that erst brought sweetly forth
The freckled cowslip, burnet, and green clover,   50
Wanting the scythe, withal uncorrected, rank,
Conceives by idleness, and nothing teems
But hateful docks, rough thistles, kecksies, burrs,
Losing both beauty and utility.
And all our vineyards, fallows, meads, and hedges,   55
Defective in their natures, grow to wildness.
Even so our houses and ourselves and children
Have lost, or do not learn for want of time,
The sciences that should become our country,
But grow like savages, as soldiers will   60
That nothing do but meditate on blood,
To swearing and stern looks, diffused attire,
And everything that seems unnatural.
Which to reduce into our former favor
You are assembled, and my speech entreats   65
That I may know the let why gentle peace
Should not expel these inconveniences
And bless us with her former qualities.
KING HENRY
    If, Duke of Burgundy, you would the peace,
Whose want gives growth to th' imperfections   70
Which you have cited, you must buy that peace
With full accord to all our just demands,
Whose tenors and particular effects
You have, enscheduled briefly, in your hands.

79. **cursitory:** cursory
80. **articles:** terms of peace; **Pleaseth:** if it pleases
81. **presently:** immediately
82. **better heed:** greater attention
83. **suddenly:** shortly
84. **Pass:** give; **accept:** i.e., accepted; **peremptory:** decisive, final
90. **advantageable for:** advantageous to
92. **consign:** subscribe
95. **Haply:** perhaps
96. **nicely:** precisely; **stood on:** insisted upon
98. **capital:** chief; **comprised:** included
99. **forerank:** first row (i.e., the first article of the treaty; see line 345)
100. **good leave:** permission

Paíx.

Peace. (5.2.66)
From Gilles Corrozet, *Hecatongraphie* . . . (1543).

BURGUNDY
The King hath heard them, to the which as yet   75
There is no answer made.
KING HENRY
Well then, the peace which you before so urged
Lies in his answer.
KING OF FRANCE
I have but with a ⌜cursitory⌝ eye
O'erglanced the articles. Pleaseth your Grace   80
To appoint some of your council presently
To sit with us once more with better heed
To resurvey them, we will suddenly
Pass our accept and peremptory answer.
KING HENRY
Brother, we shall.—Go, uncle Exeter,   85
And brother Clarence, and you, brother Gloucester,
Warwick, and Huntington, go with the King,
And take with you free power to ratify,
Augment, or alter, as your wisdoms best
Shall see advantageable for our dignity,   90
Anything in or out of our demands,
And we'll consign thereto.—Will you, fair sister,
Go with the princes or stay here with us?
QUEEN OF FRANCE
Our gracious brother, I will go with them.
Haply a woman's voice may do some good   95
When articles too nicely urged be stood on.
KING HENRY
Yet leave our cousin Katherine here with us.
She is our capital demand, comprised
Within the forerank of our articles.
QUEEN OF FRANCE
She hath good leave.   100
All but Katherine, and the King ⌜of England,
and Alice⌝ exit.
KING HENRY   Fair Katherine, and most fair,

111. **Pardonnez-moi:** pardon me

115–16. **Que . . . anges:** What is he saying? That I am like the angels? (Here even the supposedly French-speaking princess speaks broken French.)

117. **Oui . . . il:** Yes, truly, saving your Grace, thus he says.

120. **Ô bon Dieu:** O good God (The rest of this speech is correctly translated in lines 122–23.)

126–27. **Englishwoman:** i.e., a woman allegedly suspicious of flattery

132. **mince it in love:** i.e., speak elegant love-talk

134. **wear . . . suit:** exhaust my expressions of love

135. **clap:** i.e., clasp

137. **Sauf . . . honneur:** saving your honor (i.e., with all due respect to you)

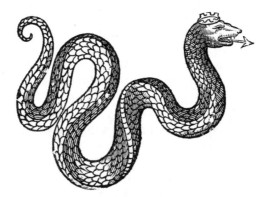

A basilisk. (5.2.17)
From Edward Topsell, *The history of . . . beasts
and serpents . . .* (1658).

Will you vouchsafe to teach a soldier terms
Such as will enter at a lady's ear
And plead his love-suit to her gentle heart?

KATHERINE Your Majesty shall mock at me. I cannot 105
speak your England.

KING HENRY O fair Katherine, if you will love me
soundly with your French heart, I will be glad to
hear you confess it brokenly with your English
tongue. Do you like me, Kate? 110

KATHERINE *Pardonnez-moi,* I cannot tell wat is "like
me."

KING HENRY An angel is like you, Kate, and you are
like an angel.

KATHERINE, ⌜*to Alice*⌝ *Que dit-il? Que je suis semblable à* 115
les anges?

ALICE *Oui, vraiment, sauf votre Grâce, ainsi dit-il.*

KING HENRY I said so, dear Katherine, and I must not
blush to affirm it.

KATHERINE *Ô bon Dieu, les langues des hommes sont* 120
pleines de tromperies.

KING HENRY, ⌜*to Alice*⌝ What says she, fair one? That the
tongues of men are full of deceits?

ALICE *Oui,* dat de tongues of de mans is be full of
deceits; dat is de Princess. 125

KING HENRY The Princess is the better Englishwoman.—I' faith, Kate, my wooing is fit for thy
understanding. I am glad thou canst speak no
better English, for if thou couldst, thou wouldst
find me such a plain king that thou wouldst think I 130
had sold my farm to buy my crown. I know no ways
to mince it in love, but directly to say "I love you."
Then if you urge me farther than to say "Do you, in
faith?" I wear out my suit. Give me your answer, i'
faith, do; and so clap hands and a bargain. How say 135
you, lady?

KATHERINE *Sauf votre honneur,* me understand well.

139. **you undid me:** i.e., you would ruin me

140. **measure:** meter, poetic rhythm

141. **measure:** rhythmical motion, dancing

143. **leapfrog:** i.e., leaping or vaulting (as in the game of leapfrog)

144. **under . . . of:** i.e., at the risk of

146. **buffet:** fight with my fists; **for my love:** to win my lady

146–47. **bound my horse:** make **my horse** leap

147. **favors:** i.e., favor; **lay on:** fight with my fists; **like a butcher:** i.e., slaughtering an animal

148. **jackanapes:** monkey; **never off:** i.e., never falling off my horse

149. **greenly:** as if I had greensickness (a form of anemia)

152. **for urging:** no matter how I am urged

153. **temper:** i.e., temperament

154. **glass:** looking **glass,** mirror

155. **let . . . cook:** Proverbial: "**Let** his **eye be** the best **cook.**"

160. **uncoined:** Henry compares his **constancy** to metal in its natural state before it is turned into coin. **perforce:** necessarily

161. **do thee right:** i.e., be faithful to you

165. **prater:** chatterer

166. **fall:** shrink

171. **his course:** its **course**

KING HENRY Marry, if you would put me to verses or
to dance for your sake, Kate, why you undid me.
For the one, I have neither words nor measure; and   140
for the other, I have no strength in measure, yet a
reasonable measure in strength. If I could win a
lady at leapfrog or by vaulting into my saddle with
my armor on my back, under the correction of
bragging be it spoken, I should quickly leap into a   145
wife. Or if I might buffet for my love, or bound my
horse for her favors, I could lay on like a butcher
and sit like a jackanapes, never off. But, before God,
Kate, I cannot look greenly nor gasp out my elo-
quence, nor I have no cunning in protestation, only   150
downright oaths, which I never use till urged, nor
never break for urging. If thou canst love a fellow of
this temper, Kate, whose face is not worth sunburning, that never looks in his glass for love of
anything he sees there, let thine eye be thy cook. I   155
speak to thee plain soldier. If thou canst love me for
this, take me. If not, to say to thee that I shall die is
true, but for thy love, by the Lord, no. Yet I love thee
too. And while thou liv'st, dear Kate, take a fellow of
plain and uncoined constancy, for he perforce must   160
do thee right because he hath not the gift to woo in
other places. For these fellows of infinite tongue,
that can rhyme themselves into ladies' favors, they
do always reason themselves out again. What? A
speaker is but a prater, a rhyme is but a ballad, a   165
good leg will fall, a straight back will stoop, a black
beard will turn white, a curled pate will grow bald,
a fair face will wither, a full eye will wax hollow, but
a good heart, Kate, is the sun and the moon, or
rather the sun and not the moon, for it shines bright   170
and never changes but keeps his course truly. If
thou would have such a one, take me. And take me,
take a soldier. Take a soldier, take a king. And what

175. **fairly:** with kindness
180. **should love:** i.e., would be loving
189–90. **Je ... moi: I,** when on the possession of France, and when you have possession of me (One of Henry's errors is making **possession** a masculine rather than a feminine noun.)
191. **Saint Denis:** patron saint of France; **be my speed:** help me
191–92. **donc ... mienne:** then France is yours, and you are mine
194. **move thee:** (1) persuade you; (2) stir your emotions
196–97. **Sauf ... parle:** Saving your honor, the French that you speak is better than the English that I speak.
199. **truly-falsely:** sincerely but ungrammatically
200. **at one:** the same
206. **closet:** private room
208. **parts:** qualities

Henry V: "a fellow . . . whose face
is not worth sunburning." (5.2.152–54)
From John Taylor, *All the workes of . . .* (1630).

say'st thou then to my love? Speak, my fair, and
fairly, I pray thee.   175

KATHERINE   Is it possible dat I sould love de enemy of
France?

KING HENRY   No, it is not possible you should love the
enemy of France, Kate. But, in loving me, you
should love the friend of France, for I love France   180
so well that I will not part with a village of it. I will
have it all mine. And, Kate, when France is mine
and I am yours, then yours is France and you are
mine.

KATHERINE   I cannot tell wat is dat.   185

KING HENRY   No, Kate? I will tell thee in French,
which I am sure will hang upon my tongue like a
new-married wife about her husband's neck, hardly to be shook off. *Je quand sur le possession de
France, et quand vous avez le possession de moi*—let   190
me see, what then? Saint Denis be my speed!—*donc
vôtre est France, et vous êtes mienne.* It is as easy for
me, Kate, to conquer the kingdom as to speak so
much more French. I shall never move thee in
French, unless it be to laugh at me.   195

KATHERINE   *Sauf votre honneur, le français que vous
parlez, il est meilleur que l'anglais lequel je parle.*

KING HENRY   No, faith, is 't not, Kate, but thy speaking
of my tongue, and I thine, most truly-falsely must
needs be granted to be much at one. But, Kate, dost   200
thou understand thus much English? Canst thou
love me?

KATHERINE   I cannot tell.

KING HENRY   Can any of your neighbors tell, Kate? I'll
ask them. Come, I know thou lovest me; and at   205
night, when you come into your closet, you'll question this gentlewoman about me, and, I know, Kate,
you will, to her, dispraise those parts in me that you
love with your heart. But, good Kate, mock me

211. **cruelly:** excessively

212. **a saving faith: a faith** that protects me from anything undesirable

213. **scambling:** scrambling, scuffling (an understatement for warfare)

215–16. **compound:** i.e., create (literally, put together)

217. **take ... beard:** i.e., humiliate **the Turk** (Constantinople did not fall to the Turks until 1453, some thirty-three years after the setting of this scene.)

218–19. **flower de luce:** i.e., fleur-de-lis, emblematic of France

224. **moiety:** half

225–26. **la plus ... déesse:** the most beautiful Katherine in the world, my very dear and divine goddess (Again Henry gets the gender of a noun, **déesse,** wrong.)

227. **Majesté:** Majesty; **fausse:** false

228. **demoiselle:** young woman; **en:** in

231. **blood:** passion

233. **untempering:** unappeasing

234. **beshrew:** curse

235. **got:** begot

236. **stubborn:** stiff, rigid; **aspect:** appearance; expression

239. **ill layer-up:** poor preserver

242. **wear me:** possess and enjoy me as your own

244. **avouch:** affirm

mercifully, the rather, gentle princess, because I 210
love thee cruelly. If ever thou beest mine, Kate, as I
have a saving faith within me tells me thou shalt, I
get thee with scambling, and thou must therefore
needs prove a good soldier-breeder. Shall not thou
and I, between Saint Denis and Saint George, com- 215
pound a boy, half French, half English, that shall go
to Constantinople and take the Turk by the beard?
Shall we not? What say'st thou, my fair flower de
luce?

KATHERINE I do not know dat. 220

KING HENRY No, 'tis hereafter to know, but now to
promise. Do but now promise, Kate, you will
endeavor for your French part of such a boy; and
for my English moiety, take the word of a king and
a bachelor. How answer you, *la plus belle Katherine* 225
du monde, mon très cher et divin déesse?

KATHERINE Your *Majesté* 'ave *fausse* French enough to
deceive de most sage *demoiselle* dat is *en* France.

KING HENRY Now fie upon my false French. By mine
honor, in true English, I love thee, Kate. By which 230
honor I dare not swear thou lovest me, yet my blood
begins to flatter me that thou dost, notwithstanding
the poor and untempering effect of my visage. Now
beshrew my father's ambition! He was thinking of
civil wars when he got me; therefore was I created 235
with a stubborn outside, with an aspect of iron, that
when I come to woo ladies, I fright them. But, in
faith, Kate, the elder I wax, the better I shall appear.
My comfort is that old age, that ill layer-up of
beauty, can do no more spoil upon my face. Thou 240
hast me, if thou hast me, at the worst, and thou shalt
wear me, if thou wear me, better and better. And
therefore tell me, most fair Katherine, will you have
me? Put off your maiden blushes, avouch the
thoughts of your heart with the looks of an empress, 245

248. **withal:** with

250. **Plantagenet:** the name of the English royal family from the twelfth to the fifteenth centuries

251. **fellow with:** equal to

252. **good fellows:** drinkers, partygoers (an allusion to Henry's youthful wildness, as presented in Shakespeare's *Henry IV, Parts 1* and *2*)

253. **broken music: music** in parts

255. **break:** open

257. **roi mon père:** king my father

258. **shall:** must

263–67. **Laissez . . . seigneur:** Let go, my lord, let go, let go! My faith, I do not wish in the least that you abase your greatness in kissing the hand of one—Our Lord!—unworthy servant. Pardon me, I beg you, my very powerful lord.

269–70. **Les . . . France:** For ladies and young women to be kissed before their weddings, it is not the French custom.

272. **pour les:** for the

275. **entendre:** i.e., understands; **que moi:** than I

278. **Oui, vraiment:** yes, indeed

279. **nice:** strict

281. **list:** barrier

take me by the hand, and say "Harry of England, I
am thine," which word thou shalt no sooner bless
mine ear withal, but I will tell thee aloud "England
is thine, Ireland is thine, France is thine, and Henry
Plantagenet is thine," who, though I speak it before　250
his face, if he be not fellow with the best king, thou
shalt find the best king of good fellows. Come, your
answer in broken music, for thy voice is music, and
thy English broken. Therefore, queen of all, Katherine, break thy mind to me in broken English. Wilt　255
thou have me?

KATHERINE　Dat is as it shall please de *roi mon père.*

KING HENRY　Nay, it will please him well, Kate; it shall
please him, Kate.

KATHERINE　Den it sall also content me.　260

KING HENRY　Upon that I kiss your hand, and I call you
my queen.

KATHERINE　*Laissez, mon seigneur, laissez, laissez! Ma
foi, je ne veux point que vous abaissiez votre gran-
deur, en baisant la main d' une—Notre Seigneur!—*　265
*indigne serviteur. Excusez-moi, je vous supplie, mon
très puissant seigneur.*

KING HENRY　Then I will kiss your lips, Kate.

KATHERINE　*Les dames et demoiselles, pour être baisées
devant leurs noces, il n'est pas la coutume de France.*　270

KING HENRY　Madam my interpreter, what says she?

ALICE　Dat it is not be de fashion *pour les* ladies of
France—I cannot tell wat is *baiser en* Anglish.

KING HENRY　To kiss.

ALICE　Your *Majesté entendre* bettre *que moi.*　275

KING HENRY　It is not a fashion for the maids in France
to kiss before they are married, would she say?

ALICE　*Oui, vraiment.*

KING HENRY　O Kate, nice customs curtsy to great
kings. Dear Kate, you and I cannot be confined　280
within the weak list of a country's fashion. We are

283. **follows our places:** waits upon our positions

284. **I will do yours:** Henry plays here with the phrase "stop the mouth," which also means "kiss."

297. **apt:** ready to learn

298–99. **condition:** disposition, temper

301–2. **he, his:** i.e., it, its (referring to **the spirit of love**)

305. **circle:** i.e., a magic **circle** (The obscene implication of these lines to 335—Burgundy's **frankness**—is carried on in the words "naked," "hard," "handling," "latter end," "entered.") **Love:** Cupid, the Roman god of love, is often depicted as naked and blindfolded.

307–8. **yet rosed over:** still blushing

311. **consign:** subscribe

312. **they:** maids, virgins; **wink:** close their eyes

313. **blind:** heedless, inconsiderate

Cupid, that "naked blind boy." (5.2.309)
Anonymous engraving inserted in Jacques Callot,
[*La petite passion* (n.d.)].

the makers of manners, Kate, and the liberty that
follows our places stops the mouth of all find-faults,
as I will do yours for upholding the nice fashion of
your country in denying me a kiss. Therefore, 285
patiently and yielding. ⌜*He kisses her.*⌝ You have
witchcraft in your lips, Kate. There is more elo-
quence in a sugar touch of them than in the tongues
of the French council, and they should sooner
persuade Harry of England than a general petition 290
of monarchs.

Enter the French power, ⌜*the French King and Queen
and Burgundy,*⌝ *and the English Lords* ⌜*Westmoreland
and Exeter.*⌝

Here comes your father.
BURGUNDY God save your Majesty. My royal cousin,
teach you our princess English?
KING HENRY I would have her learn, my fair cousin, 295
how perfectly I love her, and that is good English.
BURGUNDY Is she not apt?
KING HENRY Our tongue is rough, coz, and my condition is not smooth, so that, having neither the voice
nor the heart of flattery about me, I cannot so 300
conjure up the spirit of love in her that he will
appear in his true likeness.
BURGUNDY Pardon the frankness of my mirth if I
answer you for that. If you would conjure in her,
you must make a circle; if conjure up Love in her in 305
his true likeness, he must appear naked and blind.
Can you blame her, then, being a maid yet rosed
over with the virgin crimson of modesty, if she deny
the appearance of a naked blind boy in her naked
seeing self? It were, my lord, a hard condition for a 310
maid to consign to.
KING HENRY Yet they do wink and yield, as love is
blind and enforces.

318. **wink on her:** i.e., **wink** at **her**

320. **summered:** pastured

321. **Bartholomew-tide:** the time around St. Bartholomew's day, August 24, when flies are allegedly sluggish

324. **moral:** instructive example; **ties:** binds

326. **latter end:** (1) conclusion; (2) posterior, buttocks

332–33. **perspectively:** in such a way that, from the single viewpoint from which you look, the cities are resolved into the image of a single maiden

337. **So:** i.e., if it

339. **wait on:** attend, accompany

341. **will:** desire

342. **terms of reason:** reasonable terms

346. **their firm proposèd natures:** i.e., the terms in which they were firmly proposed

A city "girdled with maiden walls." (5.2.334)
From Henry Peacham, *Minerua Britanna* . . . [1612].

BURGUNDY   They are then excused, my lord, when they
   see not what they do.   315
KING HENRY   Then, good my lord, teach your cousin to
   consent winking.
BURGUNDY   I will wink on her to consent, my lord, if
   you will teach her to know my meaning, for maids
   well summered and warm kept are like flies at   320
   Bartholomew-tide: blind, though they have their
   eyes; and then they will endure handling, which
   before would not abide looking on.
KING HENRY   This moral ties me over to time and a hot
   summer. And so I shall catch the fly, your cousin,   325
   in the latter end, and she must be blind too.
BURGUNDY   As love is, my lord, before it loves.
KING HENRY   It is so. And you may, some of you, thank
   love for my blindness, who cannot see many a fair
   French city for one fair French maid that stands in   330
   my way.
KING OF FRANCE   Yes, my lord, you see them perspectively, the cities turned into a maid, for they are all
   girdled with maiden walls that war hath ⌜never⌝
   entered.   335
KING HENRY   Shall Kate be my wife?
KING OF FRANCE   So please you.
KING HENRY   I am content, so the maiden cities you
   talk of may wait on her. So the maid that stood in
   the way for my wish shall show me the way to my   340
   will.
KING OF FRANCE
   We have consented to all terms of reason.
KING HENRY   Is 't so, my lords of England?
WESTMORELAND
   The King hath granted every article,
   His daughter first, and, in sequel, all,   345
   According to their firm proposèd natures.

347. **subscribèd:** assented to
349–50. **matter of grant:** consent, permission
351. **addition:** title
351–52. **Notre . . . France:** our very dear son Henry, king of England, heir to France
353–54. **Praeclarissimus . . . Franciae:** our most excellent son Henry, king of England and heir to France
360. **from her blood:** i.e., **from her** (as a member of the royal blood of France)
361. **Issue:** i.e., descendants; **that:** i.e., so that
362. **pale:** a reference to the chalk cliffs on both sides of the English Channel
365. **neighborhood:** neighborliness
367. **His:** i.e., its
374. **spousal:** marriage
375. **ill office:** i.e., evil acts; **fell:** fierce

A tennis match. (1.2.272–78)
From *Le centre de l'amour . . .* [1650?].

EXETER
Only he hath not yet subscribèd this:
Where your Majesty demands that the King of
France, having any occasion to write for matter of
grant, shall name your Highness in this form and 350
with this addition, in French: *Notre très cher fils*
Henri, roi d' Angleterre, héritier de France; and thus
in Latin: *Praeclarissimus filius noster Henricus, rex*
Angliae et hæres Franciae.

KING OF FRANCE
Nor this I have not, brother, so denied 355
But your request shall make me let it pass.

KING HENRY
I pray you, then, in love and dear alliance,
Let that one article rank with the rest,
And thereupon give me your daughter.

KING OF FRANCE
Take her, fair son, and from her blood raise up 360
Issue to me, that the contending kingdoms
Of France and England, whose very shores look pale
With envy of each other's happiness,
May cease their hatred, and this dear conjunction
Plant neighborhood and Christian-like accord 365
In their sweet bosoms, that never war advance
His bleeding sword 'twixt England and fair France.

LORDS Amen.

KING HENRY
Now welcome, Kate, and bear me witness all
That here I kiss her as my sovereign queen. 370
⌜*He kisses her.*⌝ *Flourish.*

QUEEN OF FRANCE
God, the best maker of all marriages,
Combine your hearts in one, your realms in one.
As man and wife, being two, are one in love,
So be there 'twixt your kingdoms such a spousal
That never may ill office or fell jealousy, 375

377. **paction:** compact, agreement

378. **make . . . league:** i.e., cause their embodied alliance to come apart (The **league** is **incorporate** or embodied in the metaphorically single flesh of the married couple, Henry and Katherine.)

380. **speak this Amen:** say "Amen" to **this**

384. **surety of our leagues:** security of our compacts

386. SD. **Sennet:** trumpet signal for a ceremonial exit

Epilogue The Chorus reminds the audience that Henry died very young, leaving the kingdom to his infant son, during whose reign France was lost and England did "bleed."

---

1. **all-unable:** utterly inadequate

2. **bending:** (1) bowing, as if to receive applause; (2) straining

3. **room:** space

4. **by starts:** i.e., **by** fits and **starts** (perhaps, i.e., broken up into scenes)

5. **Small:** i.e., short (Henry lived to be only 35, dying in 1422.)

9. **infant bands:** swaddling clothes

13. **Which . . . shown:** a reference to such plays as *Henry VI, Parts 1, 2,* and *3*; **their sake:** the sake of those plays

14. **let . . . take: let this** play be accepted

Which troubles oft the bed of blessèd marriage,
Thrust in between the paction of these kingdoms
To make divorce of their incorporate league,
That English may as French, French Englishmen,
Receive each other. God speak this Amen!   380
ALL   Amen.
KING HENRY
Prepare we for our marriage; on which day,
My Lord of Burgundy, we'll take your oath,
And all the peers', for surety of our leagues.
Then shall I swear to Kate, and you to me,   385
And may our oaths well kept and prosp'rous be.
                              Sennet. They exit.

              Enter Chorus ⌜*as Epilogue.*⌝

⌜CHORUS⌝
Thus far with rough and all-unable pen
Our bending author hath pursued the story,
In little room confining mighty men,
Mangling by starts the full course of their glory.
Small time, but in that small most greatly lived   5
This star of England. Fortune made his sword,
By which the world's best garden he achieved
And of it left his son imperial lord.
Henry the Sixth, in infant bands crowned King
Of France and England, did this king succeed,   10
Whose state so many had the managing
That they lost France and made his England bleed,
Which oft our stage hath shown. And for their sake,
In your fair minds let this acceptance take.
                              ⌜*He exits.*⌝

HENRY THE FIFTH
KING OF ENGLAND
And FRANCE,
LORD OF IRELAND.

FRom my Lancaſtrian Sire ſucceſſiuely,
I Englands glorious golden Garland got:
I temper'd Iuſtice with mild clemency,
Much blood I ſhed,yet blood-ſhed loued not,
Time my Sepulchre and my bones may rot,
But Time can neuer end my endleſſe fame.
Obliuion cannot my braue acts out blot,
Or make Forgetfulneſſe forget my name.
I plaid all *France* at Tenniſe ſuch a game,
With roaring Rackets,bandied Balls and Foyles :
And what I plaid for,ſtill I won the ſame,
Triumphantly tranſporting home the ſpoyles.
  But in the end grim death my life aſſail'd,
  And as I liu'd,I dy'd,belou'd,bewail'd.

From John Taylor, *All the workes of* . . . (1630).

Longer Notes

1.2.70–82. Pepin ... Tenth: Canterbury's long speech sweeps across three dynasties of French kings who ruled from the eighth century to the thirteenth century. The three dynasties are the Merovingian (the name deriving from Merovich, of whom nothing is known), including **Clothair** and **Childeric;** the Carolingian (**Pepin, Charlemagne, Lewis the Emperor, Charles II**); and the Capetian (**Hugh Capet, King Lewis the Tenth**). For Canterbury's account of these kings, Shakespeare closely follows the chronicler Holinshed and reproduces many of the mistakes in his source, such as misnaming Louis IX **Lewis the Tenth.** (Since Shakespeare's play is already fiction and not history, we do not correct these mistakes.) **Clothair** is **Clothair** I, who reigned from 511 to 561; **Childeric,** the last of the Merovingian kings, reigned from 743 to 751, when he was deposed by the first of the Carolingian kings, **Pepin** III. Otherwise known as Pepin the Short, he ruled from 751 to 768, when he was succeeded by his son **Charlemagne** or **Charles the Great.** The rule of **Charlemagne,** by far the most famous of all these kings, lasted until 814. His son, **Lewis the Emperor** or Louis I, succeeded him and ruled until 840. The last of the Carolingian kings mentioned by Canterbury is **Charles** II or Charles the Bald, whose rule extended from 843 to 877. The Carolingian dynasty continued beyond **Charles** II until 987, and it would have gone on beyond this date had not the Carolingian heir to the throne, **Charles the Duke of Lorraine,** been rejected in favor of **Hugh Capet,** founder of the Capetian dynasty. Among **Capet's** successors was Louis IX or St. Louis (misnamed by Holinshed and Shakespeare

King Lewis the Tenth), whose reign lasted from 1226 to 1270. Queen **Blithild** belongs to the first of these dynasties, the Merovingian; she was the consort of Clovis II (reigning 639–57) and the mother of Clothair III (reigning 657–73).

2.Chorus.41–42.
But, till the King come forth, and not till then, Unto Southampton do we shift our scene.
The awkwardness of these lines has suggested to some editors that Act 2, scene 1, was a late addition, and that these lines were added to explain the delay in the scene shift promised in lines 34–35.

2.1.28–29. **How . . . Pistol:** Many editors follow the quarto and assign this line to Nym, whom they see as deliberately insulting Pistol by calling him **mine host** (i.e., innkeeper), rather than addressing him by his military title. Pistol is, in fact, insulted by the term **mine host,** but there is no need to suppose the insult intended and, therefore, no need to depart from the Folio.

2.1.60. **that's the humor of it:** In early usage, **humor** referred to the bodily fluids of blood, phlegm, black bile, and yellow bile; later, the term referred to the dispositions, character traits, or moods thought to be caused by these fluids, and then to moods or whims in general. In Nym's language, the term becomes so vague as to have no real meaning.

2.1.75. **lazar:** The story of Troilus and Cressida was told by Chaucer and dramatized by Shakespeare; both represent Cressida as unfaithful to her lover Troilus. In Robert Henryson's fifteenth-century Scottish poem *Testament of Cresseid,* she is a begging leper. Her name came to mean "prostitute."

2.3.9–10. Arthur's bosom: In the story of the rich man and the beggar—Luke 16.22–31—the beggar at death is carried by angels "into Abraham's bosom." The marginal note in the Geneva Bible of 1560 reads: "whereby is signified that most blessed life which they that die in the faith that Abraham did shall enjoy after this world."

2.3.17. talked: We believe that the manuscript reading that lies behind the Folio's "Table" is now beyond recovery and prefer the more straightforward substitution **talked,** which was first suggested to Theobald by an anonymous correspondent.

In discussing possible emendations for the Folio's "Table," some critics have argued that Q1 would support the emendation **talked.** Our choice of **talked,** however, is based not on Q1 but on the fact that this is the most straightforward substitution of a needed past-tense verb for the noun *table.* Q1 reads not **talked** but "talk," and Q1, here and elsewhere, is so different from the Folio that it seems irrelevant to the discussion. Q1 reads: "I saw him fumble with the sheetes, / And talk of floures, and smile vpo[n] his fingers ends."

3.2.55 SD. He exits: The Folio text provides ambiguous signals about the possible staging of the sequence from line 28 to line 55 SD. As editors have long since recognized, the Boy's speech (lines 29–55) is a soliloquy. The stage should then be empty when the boy exits at line 55, and a new scene should begin then. However, the Folio's entrance direction after line 55, immediately preceding the conversation between Fluellen and Gower, reads simply *Enter Gower,* thus indicating that Fluellen has remained onstage throughout the Boy's speech, and that the scene therefore continues. There is no simple way to reduce the Folio's indeterminacy about staging, and so this edition, like many before it, reproduces the Folio's mixed signals by making the

Boy's speech a soliloquy while, at the same time, continuing the scene (after the Boy exits) with the entrance of Fluellen and Gower and their conversation.

3.3.35. **Desire:** Since Rowe's 1714 edition, editors have emended **Desire** to "Defile." It has been argued that this emendation was inspired by Alexander Pope's poem *The Rape of the Lock* (1712). Perhaps Rowe's change has also persisted through the continuing influence of Pope's poem (Catherine Bates, "Pope's Influence on Shakespeare?" *Shakespeare Quarterly* 42 [1991]: 57–59).

3.3.43. **guilty in defense:** In international law of the time, the governor of a town could be charged as **guilty in defense** if he continued to defend the town even when his king failed to provide him the resources necessary for its defense (E. A. Rauchut, "'Guilty in Defence': A Note on *Henry V*," *Shakespeare Quarterly* 42 [1991]: 55–57).

3.4.50. *Le foot, et le count:* These words apparently sound to her like the French words *foutre* and *con*. Cotgrave's 1611 *Dictionarie of the French and English Tongues* defines *foutre* as "to leacher" (i.e., to play the lecher) and defines *con* as "a woman's etc."

3.5.63. **ransom:** According to the rules of warfare of the period, prisoners of war could be ransomed for sums often negotiated between the warring parties prior to their battle. The higher the rank of the prisoner, the higher the ransom. "Prisoner ransom comprised war's greatest gain" (E. A. Rauchut, "Hotspur's Prisoners and the Laws of War in *1 Henry IV*," *Shakespeare Quarterly* 45 [1994]: 96–97).

3.7.14. **Pegasus:** The Dauphin's high praise for his horse (lines 11–25) draws both from classical mythology and from the Bible. In classical mythology, when Perseus killed the Gorgon Medusa, the winged horse Pegasus sprang to life from her blood. Then, when the hoof of Pegasus struck Mount Helicon, there was created Hippocrene, the fountain of the Muses (the nine sister-goddesses who inspire the arts, including music). Hence the reference to the musicality of **Pegasus's horn** or hoof. In all accounts before Ovid's *Metamorphoses*, Bellerophon alone was the rider of Pegasus, but Ovid had Perseus ride the winged horse in his rescue of Andromeda from the dragon. It is also in Ovid that Hermes lulls the monster Argus asleep by playing a pipe (line 18).

In Job 39.24–28, the horse in battle is described as follows: "He goeth forth to meet the harnessed man. He mocketh at fear and is not afraid and turneth not back from the sword, though the quiver rattle against him, the glittering spear and the shield. He swalloweth the ground for fierceness and rage. . . . He saith among the trumpets, Ha, ha; he smelleth the battle afar off, and the noise of the captains and the shouting."

4.1.309–13. **Five . . . soul:** Henry's words are informed by the Roman Catholic doctrine of purgatory, which would still have been in place during his reign more than a hundred years before the English Reformation. According to this doctrine, the souls of those who avoided damnation upon their deaths nonetheless were obliged to atone for the sins that had been forgiven them in confession by enduring punishment for them in the fires of purgatory, which cleansed these souls of sin and guilt and readied them for heaven. Also according to this doctrine, the living could assist individual souls of the dead in their passage through purgatory by saying prayers and by having masses offered up on their behalf. Hence Henry's reference to the **five hundred poor** whom he employs to pray for the dead King Richard and to the **priests** who **sing** masses for him.

According to *Britannica Academia,*

The idea of purification or temporary punishment after death has ancient roots and is well attested in early Christian literature. The conception of purgatory as a geographically situated place is largely the achievement of medieval Christian piety and imagination. Beliefs and practices relating to purgatory profoundly affected Western society in the Middle Ages and beyond. As the focus of a complex system of suffrages (intercessory prayers, masses, alms, and fasting on behalf of the dead), penitential practices, and indulgences, purgatory strengthened the bond between the living and the dead, provided motivation for works of social philanthropy as well as for pilgrimages and Crusades, and furnished abundant matter for visionary and imaginative literature.

In general, the origins of purgatory may be sought in the worldwide practice of praying for the dead and caring for their needs. Such ministrations presuppose that the dead are in a temporal state between earthly life and their final abode and that they can benefit from the generosity or transferred merit of the living. Purgatory answers the human need to believe in a just and merciful cosmos, one in which ordinary people, neither hardened sinners nor perfect saints, may undergo correction, balance life's accounts, satisfy old debts, cleanse accumulated defilements, and heal troubled memories. Since these are universal concerns, there are parallels to the Christian conception of purgatory in many religious and cultural traditions.

4.3.56. **Warwick and Talbot:** Both are English heroes in the wars against the French represented by Shakespeare in *Henry VI, Part 1*. Neither fought in the Battle of Agincourt about to be presented here in *Henry V*.

5.Chor.31. **general:** Most editors and critics have long assumed that this **general** must be Robert Devereux, Earl of Essex, whom Elizabeth sent to secure her Irish colony against native rebellion in 1599, and who looms so large in our perspective of Elizabethan history because of his subsequent unauthorized return in failure and his equally unsuccessful rebellion, for which he was executed in 1601. A consequence of linking these lines to Essex's Ireland expedition is to date the writing of these lines with great precision, since they would have been written while Essex was in Ireland and before his return and his rebellion. However, Essex was not the only general that Elizabeth sent to Ireland; Essex's successor, Lord Mountjoy, was, in his time, just as famous as Essex, not least because, unlike Essex, Mountjoy actually managed to put down rebellion. See, for example, Warren D. Smith, "The *Henry V* Choruses in the First Folio," *Journal of English and Germanic Philology* 53 (1954): 38–57.

5.2.12. **Ireland:** Henry was described as "Lord of Ireland" in, for example, the collection of pictures of English monarchs included in the 1630 *All the workes of John Taylor* (see above, page 238), and as *Henricus V, Angliae et Franciae Rex, Dominus Hiberniae* (i.e., Henry V, King of England and France, Lord of Ireland) in an engraving published in William Martin, *The Histories and Lives of the Kings of England* (1628), which probably dates from the 1618 work *Baziliwlogia* compiled by Henry Holland. See also lines 248–49 below, where Henry offers Katherine all that is "his" in the following order, "England is thine, Ireland is thine, France is thine. . . ."

For an analysis of the complex and contradictory Elizabethan English attitudes toward Ireland that might permit the representation of Ireland in the same play both in insulting terms in the character Macmorris and in honorable terms in King Henry's title "Brother Ireland," see Michael Neill, "Broken English and Broken Irish: Nation, Language, and the Optic of Power in Shakespeare's Histories," *Shakespeare Quarterly* 45 (1994): 1–32.

Textual Notes

The reading of the present text appears to the left of the square bracket. Unless otherwise noted, the reading to the left of the bracket is from **F,** the First Folio text (upon which this edition is based). The earliest sources of readings not in **F** are indicated as follows: **Q** is the quarto of 1600; **F2** is the Second Folio of 1632; **F3** is the Third Folio of 1663–64; **F4** is the Fourth Folio of 1685; **Ed.** is an earlier editor of Shakespeare, beginning with Rowe in 1709. No sources are given for emendations of punctuation or for corrections of obvious typographical errors, like turned letters that produce no known word. **SD** means stage direction; **SP** means speech prefix; **uncorr.** means the first or uncorrected state of the First Folio; **corr.** means the second or corrected state of the First Folio; ~ stands in place of a word already quoted before the square bracket; ʌ indicates the omission of a punctuation mark.

1.1. 18. besides] F (beside)
1.2. 1 *and hereafter to 5.2.1.* SP KING HENRY] Ed.; *King.* F   42. *succedant*] *succedaul* F   49, 57. Elbe] F (Elue)   91. So that] ~, ~ F   95–96. day, | Howbeitʌ] ~. ~, F   120. SP BISHOP OF ELY] Ed.; *Bish.* F   137. blood] F3; Bloods F   170. her] Ed.; their F   175. begin] *begia* F   180. 'tame] Ed.; tame F   181. then] theu F   205. majesty] Q; Maiesties F   220. End] Q; And F   248. meaning] meauing F   254. then] F2; than F   282. therefore,] ~ʌ F   298. husbands] hnsbands F   323. SD *Flourish. They exit.*] Ed.; *Exeunt.* | *Flourish.* F
2.Chorus. 25. knight,] ~ʌ F   28. die,] ~. F
2.1. 25. mare] Q; name F   42–43. Iceland . . . Iceland] F (Island . . . Island)   78. too! Go] ~ʌ ~ F   102.

Corporal] Corporall F   113. that's] F2; that F   115.
Ah] F (A)

2.2.   31. SP GREY] F4; *Kni.* F   46. much] mueh
F   94. him] Q; *omit* F   102. inhuman] F (inhumane)
114. a] F2; an F   115. whoop] F (hoope)   121. All]
Ed.; And F   128. demon] F (Dæmon)   146. mark the]
Ed.; make thee F   155. Henry] Q; *Thomas* F   155.
Masham] *Marsham* F   157. knight,] ~ʌ F   166. I] F2;
omit F   184. must] uust / F   185. have] Q; *omit* F
190. SD *They . . . guard.*] Ed.; *Exit.* F

2.3.   17. talked] Ed.; Table F   18. o'] F (a)   25.
upward] Q; vp-peer'd F   31. devils] F (Deules)   33.
SP HOSTESS] Ed.; *Woman* F   35. devil] F (Deule)   49.
word] Q; world F   51. dog,] ~: F

2.4.   1 *and hereafter to 3.5.69.* SP KING OF FRANCE]
Ed.; *King.* F   15 *and hereafter.* SP DAUPHIN] Ed.; *Dolphin* F   114. privèd] Ed.; priuy F   141. Louvre] Ed.;
Louer F   143. difference] diff'rence F   155. SD *Flourish. They exit.* Act 3 *Enter Chorus.*] Ed.; *Exeunt.* | *Actus
Secundus.* | *Flourish. Enter Chorus.* F

3.Chorus.   7. fanning] Ed.; fayning F   27. ordnance] F (Ordenance)

3.1.   8. summon] Ed.; commune F   16. nostril] F
(Nosthrill)   18. noblest] F2; Noblish F   25. men] F4;
me F   35. Straining] Ed.; Straying F   37. Saint] S. F

3.2.   18. hie] F (high)   32. antics] F (Antiques)
70–140. SP FLUELLEN] Ed.; *Welch.* F   85–138. SP JAMY]
Ed.; *Scot.* F   90–135. SP MACMORRIS] Ed.; *Irish.* F   138.
Ah] F (A)

3.3.   23. career] F (Carriere)   32. heady] F2; headly F

3.4.   *See Appendix.*

3.5.   7. scions] F (Syens)   11. *de*] F2; *du* F   27.
may] F2; *omit* F   40. hie] F (high)   44. Vaudemont]
F2; *Vandemont* F   46. Foix] Ed.; *Loys* F   46. Bouciqualt] *Bouciquall* F   48. knights] Ed.; Kings F

3.6.   8. life] F (liue)   30. her] Q; his F   85. SD *2*

lines later in F.   87. God] Ed.; *Flu.* God F   105. o'] F
(a)   114. lenity] Q; Leuitie F   127. cue] F (Q.)
   3.7.   12–13. pasterns] F2; postures F   13. *Çà*] Ed.;
ch' F   14. *volant*] F2; *volante* F   14–15. *qui a*] Ed.; *ches*
F   61. lief] F (liue)   66–67. *vomissement*] F2; *vemisse-
ment* F   67. *et*] Ed.; *est* F   67. *truie*] Ed.; *leuye* F
Act 4] Ed.; *Actus Tertius.* F
   4.Chorus.   28. Presenteth] Ed.; Presented F   47.
define,] ~. F
   4.1.   3. Good] F (God)   19. example.] ~, F   37.
Qui] Ed.; *Che* F   57. Saint] F (S.)   65. SD *He steps
aside.*] Ed.; *Manet King.* F   97. Thomas] Ed.; *Iohn* F
108. human] F (humane)   129–30. alone, . . . minds.]
~: . . . ~, F   231. enough] F (enow)   237. SD *5 lines
earlier in* F   253. What∧] ~? F   253. adoration] Odora-
tion F   261. Think'st] F (Thinks)   284. Hyperion] *Hip-
erio* F   302. or] Ed.; of F   302. numbers∧] ~: F   320.
friends] Q; friend F
   4.2.   1. armor. Up] ~∧ ~ F   2. *Montez à cheval*]
Monte Cheual F   2. varlet] F (*Verlot*)   2. Lackey] F (*Lac-
quay*)   4. *eaux*] *ewes* F   5. *puis?*] ~∧ F   6. *Cieux*] *Cein*
F   11. dout] F (doubt)   29. enough] F (enow)   36.
sonance] Sonuance F   44. bankrupt] F (banqu'rout)
48. drooping] F2; dropping F   50. gemeled] F (Iymold)
56. lifeless] liuelesse F
   4.3.   6. be wi'] F (buy')   22. Westmoreland?] ~.
F   23. enough] F (enow)   45. o'] F (a)   51. forgot,] ~:
F   61. rememberèd] remembred F   135. SD *Montjoy
exits.*] This ed.; *Exit* F *after line 133.*   140. pleasest,]
~∧ F
   4.4.   2–3, 11–12, 20, 24, 39–42, 50–57. *See Appendix.*   13. or] Ed.; for F   16. *la*] *le* F   26, 27. Master] F
(M.)   34. *disposé . . . à cette heure*] *disposee . . . asture* F
66. *See Appendix.*
   4.5.   2, 3. *See Appendix.*   13. die. . . . more! . . .
again!] ~∧ . . . ~∧ . . . ~, F   17. by a slave] Q; a base

slaue F   18. contaminate] Ed.; contaminated F   21. enough] F (enow)

4.6.   3. Duke] F (D.)   22. grip] F (gripe)   35. my full] This ed.; mixtfull F

4.7.   *Actus Quartus.* F   17. great] grear F   69. this,] ~ʌ F   73, 91, 94. SP MONTJOY] Ed.; *Her.* F   81. the] This ed.; with F   109. Saint] F (S.)   116. countryman] Q; Countrymen F   122. God] F3; Good F   124. SD *Enter Williams*] *3 lines earlier in* F   135. o'] F (a)   181. o'] F (a)

4.8.   9. any 's] F (anyes)   23. SD *1 line later in* F.   45. martial] F (Marshall)   103. Foix] F (*Foyes*)   104. Vaudemont] F2; *Vandemont* F   114–15. lossʌ ... other?] ~? ... ~, F   118. we] F2; me F

5.Chorus.   10. floodʌ] ~; F   18. Whereʌ ... himʌ] ~, ... ~, F   37. himʌ] ~. F

5.1.   2. Saint] F (S.)   49. revenge.] ~ʌ F   70. be wi'] F (bu'y)   74. begun] F (began)   92. swear] Q; swore F

5.2.   1. wherefor] F (wherefore) 9 *and hereafter to* 79. SP KING OF FRANCE] Ed.; *Fra.* (or *France.*) F   12 *and hereafter.* SP QUEEN OF FRANCE] Ed.; *Quee.* F   21 *and hereafter to* 97. SP KING HENRY] Ed.; *Eng.* (or *England.*) F   23. love,] ~. F   41. its] F (it)   46. fumitory] F (Femetary)   62. diffused] F (defus'd)   79. cursitory] Ed.; curselarie F   95. Haply] F (Happily)   100. SD *All ... exit.*] This ed.; *Exeunt omnes. Manet King and Katherine.* F   101 *and hereafter to 328.* SP KING HENRY] Ed.; *King.* F   111. Pardonnez] F (*Pardonne*)   117 *and hereafter.* SP ALICE] Ed.; *Lady.* F   117. *vraiment*] *verayment* F   121. *pleines*] Ed.; *plein* F   124. tongues] tongeus F   145. spoken,] ~. F   158. Lord] F (L.)   190. *avez*] F (*aues*)   196–97. See Appendix.   227, 275. *Majesté*] F (Maiestee)   227. *fausse*] F (fause)   228. *demoiselle*] F (Damoiseil)   263–67. See Appendix.   269–70. See Appendix.   272. fashion] fashon F   272. *les*] F (le)   273. *baiser*] Ed.; buisse F   278. *vraiment*] F

(*verayment*) 291. SD *1 line later in* F 332. SP KING OF
FRANCE] *French King.* F 334. never] Ed.; *omit* F 336
and hereafter to 357. SP KING HENRY] Ed.; *England.* F
337 *and hereafter.* SP KING OF FRANCE] Ed.; *France.* F
352. *héritier*] Ed.; *Heretere* F 369, 382. SP KING HENRY]
Ed.; *King.* F 377. paction] Pation F

Appendix

3.4

Enter Katherine and an old Gentlewoman.
Kathe. Alice, tu as este en Angleterre, & tu bien par-
las le Language.
Alice. En peu Madame.
Kath. Ie te prie m' ensigniez, il faut que ie apprend a
parlen: Comient appelle vous le main en Anglois? 5
Alice. Le main il & appelle de Hand.
Kath. De Hand.
Alice. E le doyts.
Kat. Le doyts, ma foy Ie oublie, e doyt mays, ie me
souemeray le doyts ie pense qu'ils ont appelle de 10
fingres, ou de fingres.
Alice. Le main de Hand, le doyts le Fingres, ie pense
que ie suis le bon escholier.
Kath. I'ay gaynie diux mots d' Anglois vistement,
coment appelle vous le ongles? 15
Alice. Le ongles, les appellons de Nayles.
Kath. De Nayles escoute: dites moy, si ie parle bien:
de Hand, de Fingres, e de Nayles.
Alice. C'est bien dict Madame, il & fort bon Anglois.
Kath. Dites moy l' Anglois pour le bras. 20
Alice. De Arme, Madame.
Kath. E de coudee.
Alice. D' Elbow.
Kath. D' Elbow: Ie men fay le repiticio de touts les mots
que vous maves, apprins des a present. 25

Alice. Il & trop difficile Madame, comme Ie pense.

Kath. Excuse moy Alice escoute, d' Hand, de Fingre, de
    Nayles, d' Arma, de Bilbow.

Alice. D' Elbow, Madame.

Kath. O Seigneur Dieu, ie men oublie d' Elbow, coment 30
    appelle vous le col.

Alice. De Nick, Madame.

Kath. De Nick, e le menton.

Alice. De Chin.

Kath. De Sin: le col de Nick, le menton de Sin.   35

Alice. Ouy. Sauf vostre honneur en verite vous pronoun-
    cies les mots ausi droict, que le Natifs d' Angleterre.

Kath. Ie ne doute point d' apprendre par de grace de
    Dieu, & en peu de temps.

Alice. N' aue vos y desia oublie ce que ie vous a   40
    ensignie.

Kath. Nome ie recitera a vous promptement, d' Hand, de
    Fingre, de Maylees.

Alice. De Nayles, Madame.

Kath. De Nayles, de Arme, de Ilbow.   45

Alice. Sans vostre honeus d' Elbow.

Kath. Ainsi de ie d' Elbow, de Nick, & de Sin: coment
    appelle vous les pied & de roba.

Alice. Le Foot Madame, & le Count.

Kath. Le Foot, & le Count: O Seignieur Dieu, il sont le 50
    mots de son mauvais corruptible grosse & impudi-
    que, & non pour le Dames de Honeur d' vser: Ie ne
    voudray pronouncer ce mots deuant le Seigneurs de
    France, pour toute le monde, fo le Foot & le Count,
    neant moys, Ie recitera vn autrefoys ma lecon en-   55
    sembe, d' Hand, de Fingre, de Nayles, d' Arme, d'
    Elbow, de Nick, de Sin, de Foot, le Count.

Alice. Excellent, Madame.

Kath. C'est asses pour vne foyes, alons nous a
    diner.   60

                                              Exit.

4.4 Speeches by the French Soldier and the Boy.

*French. Ie pense que vous estes le Gentilhome de bon
    qualitee.*   (2–3)

French. O prennes miserecordie aye pitez de moy.
                                    (11–12)

French. O perdonne moy.   (20)

Boy. Escoute comment estes vous appelle?   (24)

*French. O Ie vous supplie pour l' amour de Dieu: ma
    pardonner, Ie suis le Gentilhome de bon maison,
    garde ma vie, & Ie vous donneray deux cent escus.*
                                      (39–42)

*Boy. Encore qu'il et contra son Iurement, de pardonner
    aucune prisonner: neant-mons pour les escues que
    vous layt a promets, il est content a vous donnes le
    liberte le franchisement.*   (50–53)

*French. Sur mes genoux se vous donnes milles remer-
    cious, et Ie me estime heurex que Ie intombe, entre
    les main. d' vn Cheualier Ie peuse le plus braue val-
    iant et tres distime signieur d' Angleterre.*   (54–57)

Boy. Saaue vous le grand Capitaine?   (66)

Speeches from 4.5

Orl. O sigueur le iour et perdia, toute et perdie.

Dol. Mor Dieu ma vie   (2–3)

Speeches from 5.2

*Kath. Sauf vostre honeur, le Francois ques vous parleis,
    il & melieus que l' Anglois le quel Ie parle.* (196–97)

*Kath. Laisse mon Seigneur, laisse, laisse, may foy: Ie ne
    veus point que vous abbaisse vostre grandeus, en
    baisant le main d' une nostre Seigneur indignie seru-
    iteur excuse moy. Ie vous supplie mon tres-puissant
    Seigneur.*   (263–67)

*Kath. Les Dames & Damoisels pour estre baisee deuant
    leur nopcese il net pas le costume de Fraunce.*
                                      (269–70)

Henry V:
A Modern Perspective

Michael Neill

"It is not the literal past, the 'facts' of history, that shape us, but images of the past embodied in language."
—Brian Friel, *Translations*

The Life of Henry V is a "history play" in more senses than one: it is a play about how history is made, and also how it is remade; it is a representation of past events while being at the same time an examination of the uses of the past; and it is a play whose own reconstruction of history consciously intervened in the historical process.

As the text itself reminds us, *Henry V* was the latest of a series of English history plays in which Shakespeare had dramatized the fifteenth-century conflict between the royal families of York and Lancaster. This century-long period of turmoil had already received considerable attention from such chroniclers as Edward Halle and Raphael Holinshed, the creators of what is sometimes called the "Tudor myth" of English history. They described a long-drawn-out dynastic crisis that followed the deposition and murder of Richard II—a crisis that, after the brief heroic respite achieved by the Lancastrian Henry V, erupted in civil war (the Wars of the Roses) under his son, Henry VI. Reaching its bloody climax in the reign of the Yorkist Richard III, the national ordeal was at last brought to an end by Richard's overthrow at the hands of the first Tudor king, Henry VII, grandfather of Elizabeth I.

(See "The Line of Edward III," page 2.) In the narrative constructed by these chroniclers, the murderous confusions of fifteenth-century history served only to demonstrate the providential scheme by which God revenged the murder of a rightful king (Richard II) and purged the nation of its crimes before placing the Tudors on the throne and restoring the English people to their status as God's elect.

Shakespeare's English history plays absorb this reading of past events from Holinshed, their principal source, but they also subject its assumption to skeptical questioning. The Tudor myth and its lessons about God's special providence to the English are particularly prominent in *Richard II* and *Richard III*, the dramas that mark the historical beginning and end of the cycle; but one finds traces of the myth even in *Henry V*, whose hero, facing overwhelming odds at Agincourt, broods "upon the fault / My father made in compassing the crown" and promises to redouble his penance for Richard II's death (4.1.303–16). Nevertheless, the plays differ so markedly in their approach to history that it is difficult to subject the entire cycle to the unifying interpretive scheme once promoted by such scholars as E. M. W. Tillyard and Lily Bess Campbell.[1] Indeed, like the "Shakespeare" who was said to have produced it, the "cycle" is something of an artificial construct, since the plays were not even composed in chronological sequence. Shakespeare turned his attention to the supposed "original sin" of Richard's murder only *after* his so-called "first tetralogy"—the group of plays dealing with the reigns of Henry VI and Richard III—was written. As a result the "second tetralogy," composed of *Richard II, Henry IV, Parts 1* and *2*, and *Henry V*, seems in many ways less like the first half of a cycle than the second part of a deliberately parallel sequence, whose ending conspicuously undercuts the explicit providentialism of *Richard III* (the culminating play of the first tetralogy) by presenting Henry V's victories as a triumph of de facto power.

In all of Shakespeare's histories, moreover, we are repeatedly made aware of competing schemes of explanation that undercut the public certainties of official history. Nowhere are such conflicting explanations more apparent than in *Henry V.* This play is, admittedly, often staged as a piece of patriotic pageantry; but such a staging is possible only if (as in Laurence Olivier's 1944 film) the text undergoes extensive and highly selective cutting. In the uncut script, the heroic values and high rhetoric that glamorize King Henry's conquests are exposed to repeated interrogation by the down-to-earth skepticism of Henry's common soldiers and by scenes of parodic satire featuring his former Eastcheap companions, Pistol, Bardolph, and Nym. Yet there is no denying the persuasive power of the famous set speeches for which the play is most often remembered: neither the unheroic realism favored by Kenneth Branagh's post-Falklands film (1989), nor even the mud-stained antiheroics of the Royal Shakespeare Company's Vietnam-era version (1964), were sufficient to silence the work's emotional nationalism.[2] Any production that is true to the text must take account of its conflicting voices; and the inevitable effect is to confront the audience with the fact that "history," after all, consists not of objective events but of the stories that are told about them.

This makes *Henry V* seem suspiciously close to the work of such contemporary dramatists as Brian Friel, whose *Making History* presents the sacred narratives of Irish nationalism as simply another form of ideologically motivated storytelling. Yet that resemblance may be less anachronistic than it appears. National history has always been an instrument of nation-building, and this was something the Renaissance well understood.

For in contrast to post-Enlightenment historians, with their pretense to scientific "objectivity," Renaissance writers were perfectly frank about the ideological purposes of history. (This was true whether they saw the past as a demonstration of Christian providence, a storehouse of morally instructive examples, or a testing ground of political theory.)

For those who wrote defending Elizabethan theater, indeed, the capacity of historical drama to arouse patriotic fervor was one of its principal justifications. "What can be a sharper reproof to these degenerate effeminate days of ours," demands Thomas Nashe in his *Pierce Pennilesse* (1592), than to witness "our forefathers' valiant acts, that have long lain in rusty brass and worm-eaten books, . . . raised from the grave of oblivion"; and Nashe singles out the presentation of Henry V and of Talbot (the hero of Shakespeare's *Henry VI, Part 1*) as outstanding examples of such theatrical consciousness-raising.[3] The play in which Nashe saw Henry V "leading the French King prisoner, and forcing both him and the Dolphin [i.e., Dauphin] to swear fealty" must have been one of the earlier dramatizations of Henry's reign; but it was surely Shakespeare's *Henry V* that Thomas Heywood remembered when he returned to the same theme in his *Apology for Actors* (1612):

> . . . what English blood seeing the person of any bold Englishman presented . . . doth not hug his fame, and honey at [i.e., delight in] his valor, pursuing him in his enterprise with his best wishes, and as being rapt in contemplation, offers to him in his heart all prosperous performance, as if the personator were the man personated, so bewitching a thing is lively and well-spirited action, that it hath power to new mold the hearts of the spectators and fashion them to the shape of any noble and notable attempt. What

coward, to see his countryman valiant, would not be ashamed of his own cowardice? What English prince, should he behold the true portraiture of that famous King *Edward* the Third, foraging France, taking so great a king captive in his own country, quartering English lions with the French flower-de-luce, and would not be suddenly inflamed with so royal a spectacle, being made apt and fit for the like achievement? So of *Henry* the fifth.[4]

Heywood has in mind precisely the kind of patriotic pageant that the Chorus is so anxious to have the audience discover in Shakespeare's *Henry V*; and just as Heywood's spectators find themselves "pursuing" their ancestral heroes on their triumphant path of French conquest, so the members of Shakespeare's audience are urged to "follow" Henry's fleet to Harfleur, imaginatively enlisting themselves in the ranks of England's "culled and choice-drawn cavaliers" (3.Chor.18–25). In all of this, *Henry V* deliberately appealed to the patriotic emotions of a country whose national identity had been shaped by a long war with Catholic Spain. Nothing is more characteristic of the English self-image in this period than the simultaneous sense of aggressive triumphalism and besieged vulnerability that characterizes the play's treatment of the French war. At one moment the Chorus's imagination catches fire at the "majestical" spectacle of Henry's vast invasion fleet ("A city on th' inconstant billows dancing," 3.Chor.17, 16); at another the Chorus stresses the pathos of an island nation imagined as a "little body with a mighty heart" (2.Chor.17), its predicament epitomized in the plight of the "poor condemnèd English" at Agincourt (4.Chor.23), a tiny "band of brothers" (4.3.62) surrounded by a sea of hostile foreigners. For the Elizabethan audience, Henry's insistence that the victory has been God's work (4.8.110–25) must have echoed similar explanations for the miraculous defeat of the overwhelmingly powerful Spanish Armada a decade before the play was written; and the appeal was not merely a nostalgic one, but seems designed to muster support for what was seen as the latest phase in the struggle against the Catholic enemy—Elizabeth's attempt to complete the conquest of Ireland. The Act 5 Chorus invited them to recognize in Henry's successes a pattern for the crucial Ulster campaigns of the Earl of Essex and his successor, Lord Mountjoy. Just as Henry's return from France is presented as a Roman triumph in which the citizens of London "Go forth and fetch their conqu'ring Caesar in," so, the Chorus suggests, they may soon pour out to welcome a successful Elizabethan general "Bringing rebellion broachèd on his sword" (5.Chor.29, 33). Plainly the Queen's Irish wars provided an essential context for the play's original reception, just as Churchill's struggle against Hitler in the 1940s did for Olivier's film.

The Chorus's attempts to recruit the "imaginary puissance" of an audience whose "thoughts . . . must deck our kings" (Pro.26–30) are couched as an apology for the technical limitations of Shakespeare's playhouse, but they are actually an assertion of its power, insisting on drama's active participation in the shaping of history. We may see this power emblematized in the third-act Chorus. There, in a trick of remarkable theatrical bravura, the Chorus (in collaboration with the stage technician) makes it appear as if the power of the audience's patriotic imagination has succeeded in bringing to life onstage the noisy assault of Henry's siege artillery:

> Work, work your thoughts, and therein see a
> siege[.]

....

Suppose th' ambassador from the French comes
   back[.]
....
The offer likes not, and the nimble gunner
With linstock now the devilish cannon touches,
              Alarum, and chambers go off.
And down goes all before them.
                                          (3.Chor.26–36)

   That said, there remains something oddly tentative about the Chorus's encomium for its "general,"
with its careful parenthetical reservations ("by a *lower*
but by loving likelihood," "As in good time he *may,*"
5.Chor.30–32), which suggests a less than wholehearted
commitment to this "application" of history. Whether
we suppose these lines were written as a salute to
Essex recently departed for Ireland or as a gesture to
Mountjoy in the wake of Essex's disastrous return, the
entanglement of the Irish wars with the overreaching
designs of Elizabeth's former favorite, Essex, meant
that there were good reasons for circumspection. Perhaps the dramatist, sensing the risk of comparing an
ambitious contemporary "general" with a man who
made himself dictator of ancient Rome, was hedging
his bets.[5] Such hesitations might help to account for
a more general ambivalence in the play's treatment of
military expansionism. As we shall see, that ambivalence is reflected in sometimes glaring discrepancies
between the Chorus's heroic vision of history and the
actualities of Shakespeare's dramatization; but it is
also apparent in a pervasive skepticism about the way
in which the characters fashion history to their own
political purposes—one that inevitably reflects on the
play's own manipulation of the past.
   Thus, just as the Chorus uses Henry's victories to
rally enthusiasm for Elizabeth's Irish wars, so Henry

and his supporters use the stories of his heroic fore-bears, Edward III and Edward the Black Prince, to boost English morale and justify Henry's cause. A considerable portion of Act 1 is given over to the lengthy genealogical history by which the Bishops of Canterbury and Ely demonstrate the justice of Henry's claim to the French throne, firing up his ambition with strategic recollections of his "mighty ancestors[,] . . . these valiant [English] dead" whose histories of triumph on French soil will provide a pattern for his conquests (1.2.37–100, 107–26). The French, naturally, have a different narrative of that past—one that stresses French suffering and the "black name" of their enemy (2.4.53–66); but their version of history remains subordinate to that mobilized by Henry, who challenges his troops to model themselves upon their "fathers of war-proof, / Fathers that, like so many Alexanders, / Have in these parts from morn till even [i.e., evening] fought" (3.1.19–21). Such emulation, he insists—looking forward to a time when "our history shall with full mouth / Speak freely of our acts" (1.2.238–39)—will ensure that his knights in turn will become makers of history and figure in the heroic narratives of their own descendants.

The audience will of course be conscious that the "full mouth" of history has indeed found a voice in Shakespeare's own text—most notably in the vaunting speech of its Chorus. Yet the Chorus itself remains uneasily aware of other voices, as if remembering that "the life of Henry V" has already been the subject of numerous tellings and retellings in a whole variety of genres. Indeed, even to those in the original audience who had not "read the story" in the chronicles (5.Chor.1), it would have been familiar through numerous popular anecdotes, ballads, and (not least) earlier dramatic versions—no fewer than three of which had been staged in the previous twelve years, reflecting the

militant national mood created by the war with Spain.
Through its peculiar narrative self-consciousness, the
Chorus reminds the audience that what they are witnessing is not a transparent representation of "the very
casques / That did affright the air at Agincourt" (Pro.
14–15), but a piece of more or less inadequate historical reconstruction that can never fully satisfy the
expectations it exploits. The power and coherence of
the players' representation must depend not only on
the enlisted imaginations of the audience but (as the
Epilogue implies) on the careful shaping of history by
which Shakespeare has separated his material from
the mere contingency of events: "*Thus far* with rough
and all-unable pen / Our bending author hath pursued
the story" (Ep.1–2; emphasis added). The tone of the
Epilogue marks a surprising collapse in the rhetorical confidence of the Chorus: in the Epilogue he wanly
confesses that the dramatist *can* take the story no further because, beyond the celebratory-marriage ending, which gives the play its satisfying sense of formal
completeness, lies the debacle of Henry VI's reign. Only
upon the stage can *The Life of Henry V* end with the
hero at the height of his achievement, his betrothal
to the French princess apparently sealing his claim
to the throne of France; and the Chorus's disconcert-
ing reminder of the disintegration of Henry's empire
after his death emphasizes the arbitrary nature of
such closure. Where the French Queen has invited us
to see Henry's "incorporate league" of kingdoms as a
harmonious resolution instituted by divine providence
(5.2.371–80), the Chorus finally recognizes only the
erratic violence of "Fortune" (Ep.6).

Other details in the text remind us that the play's
beginning is as arbitrarily imposed as its ending: just as
the Epilogue looks forward to a future that has already
become history in *Henry VI's* spectacles of catastrophe

("Which oft our stage hath shown," Ep.13), so the Pistol scenes, with the nostalgically evoked death of the King's former archcrony, Sir John Falstaff, serve as an uncomfortable reminder that *Henry V* forms a sequel to the earlier histories of *Henry IV*—though the narrative it presents is not quite "the story, with Sir John in it" promised by the epilogue to the second part of that play. The survivors of Henry's former life, Pistol, Bardolph, Nym, and the dying Falstaff, represent the freight of personal history that the King carries into the play and that cannot be quite so easily banished as the Bishop of Canterbury's glib metaphors proclaim:

> The breath no sooner left his father's body
> But that his wildness, mortified in him,
> Seemed to die too. Yea, at that very moment
> Consideration like an angel came
> And whipped th' offending Adam out of him,
> Leaving his body as a paradise . . .   (1.1.27–32)

The Bishop's Garden-of-Eden allegory suggests a perfect congruence between Henry's Edenic self-restoration and the regal prowess through which his kingdom is transformed to "the world's best garden" (Ep. 7). But the persistence of the Eastcheap crew compromises both transformations. Falstaff, it is true, dies even before he can make his promised reappearance, and the other denizens of Eastcheap are progressively marginalized, degraded, and purged from the action: Lieutenant Bardolph and Corporal Nym are condemned for petty theft and consigned to humiliating offstage deaths, while Ancient Pistol is cudgeled out of the play to join the vicious ranks of discharged soldiery who haunted the streets and highways of Shakespeare's England (5.1.88–90). But this marginalization does not occur before these characters have enacted a counternarrative that is profoundly threatening to the predominant voice of official history.

Henry V lurches to and fro between, at the one extreme, the Chorus's intoxicated visions of chivalric glory and the King's charismatic oratory of martial brotherhood and, at the other, the degraded, increasingly vicious buffoonery of Eastcheap. Thus in Act 2 the Chorus's heady proclamation that "all the youth of England are on fire" (2.Chor.1) serves merely to usher in the burlesque fury of Pistol, Nym, and Bardolph: "Pistol's cock is up, and flashing fire will follow" (2.1.53–54); while, instead of Henry's brotherhood of eager knights, "Following the mirror of all Christian kings / With wingèd heels, as English Mercurys" (2.Chor.6–7), we are shown only this trio of cutpurses preparing to travel "sworn brothers to France," where "profits will accrue" (2.1.12–13, 109–10)—reminding us that Mercury was, among other things, the god of thieves.

War, wrote the Renaissance humanist Erasmus, citing such classical heroes as Alexander the Great, was the work of "insane robbers," a kind of "brigandage, all the more immoral from being wider spread."[6] When Bardolph is hanged for stealing "a pax" (a tablet imprinted with a crucifix), Henry declines to "know the man," coldly wishing "all such offenders so cut off" (3.6.104, 109–10); yet the detail of this trivial theft reminds us that the King himself has stolen the *pax* (peace) of two entire kingdoms. The implication that Henry's war of conquest may, when stripped of its rhetorical gilt, amount to nothing more than theft on a grand scale repeatedly surfaces through such ironic parallels between the heroic main plot and the scenes from Pistol's world. Early in the play an unlucky coincidence of metaphors threatens to collapse English martial prowess into the opportunist banditry attributed by the Bishop of Ely to the Scots:

BISHOP OF ELY
    For once the eagle England being in prey,
    To her unguarded nest the weasel Scot
    Comes sneaking and so sucks her princely eggs . . .
                           (1.2.176–78)
PISTOL . . . let us to France, like horse-leeches, my
    boys, to suck, to suck, the very blood to suck.
                           (2.3.53–55)

Pistol's summons is itself a perverted echo of Henry's own "Now, lords, for France, the enterprise whereof / Shall be to you as us, like glorious" (2.2.191–92); and the sequencing of scenes makes the French king's alarmed "*Thus* comes the English with full power upon us" (2.4.1) seem like a direct response more to Pistol's corrupt bravado than to Henry's earlier command, "Cheerly to sea. The signs of war advance" (2.2.201). At Harfleur the King's famous rallying cry "Once more unto the breach, dear friends, once more" (3.1.1–2) is almost immediately travestied in Bardolph's "On, on, on, on, on! To the breach, to the breach!" (3.2.1–2); while at Agincourt the King's stirring oratory and pious appeals to the god of battles ("And how Thou pleasest, God, dispose the day," 4.3.140) serve only to announce Pistol's grotesque victory over Monsieur Le Fer—a scene, whose literalization of Henry's promise to "cut French crowns, and . . . be a clipper" (4.1.236–37) further confuses the King's regal ambition with Pistol's mercenary desire for gold ("give me crowns, brave crowns," 4.4.37). Most damaging of all, perhaps, remembering Erasmus's adage that "war [is] but murder shared by many,"[7] is the way in which the heroic rage that causes Henry to order the killing of his French prisoners is parodied in Pistol's sanguinary cry of *"cuppele gorge"* (4.4.36)—a cry that in the quarto version is repeated at the end of 4.6 in response to the King's command.

The skeptical light in which such episodes cast the main action seems to confuse even the loyal Fluellen. His misguided effort to justify the butchery of the prisoners leads him to an embarrassing comparison between Henry and the classical hero whose name he unluckily pronounces as "Alexander the Pig" (4.7.14): through Alexander's murder of Cleitus, the Welshman stumbles on a history of betrayed friendship that the high plot has struggled hard to forget:

> As Alexander killed his friend Cleitus, being in his ales and his cups, so also Harry Monmouth, being in his right wits and his good judgments, turned away [Falstaff] the fat knight with the great-belly doublet[.]   (4.7.46–50)

Henry may not have killed Falstaff, but the Hostess has insisted that he "killed his heart" (2.1.86), and for a protagonist who constantly appeals to the values of the "heart" ("a good heart, Kate, is the sun and the moon," 5.2.169), the charge is extremely compromising. "Brotherhood" will be a recurrent theme of the democratic rhetoric with which Henry rallies his beleaguered troops in France; but the thieving "brotherhood" (2.1.107) of Eastcheap both devalues the term in advance and serves as a constant uneasy reminder of older claims upon a prince who once proclaimed himself "sworn brother to a leash of drawers" (*Henry IV, Part 1*, 2.4.6–7)—a prince whom Shakespeare first introduced talking about a highway robbery with the man who, in the early acts of *Henry V*, lies dying in Pistol's tavern, Sir John Falstaff.

Such destabilization of official history is by no means confined to the satiric world of Eastcheap. Thus the drum-roll of the opening Prologue, with its promise to introduce "the warlike Harry . . . assum[ing] the port of Mars" (Pro.5–6), gives way, in a carefully calculated anticlimax, to the self-interested scheming of the Bishops of Canterbury and Ely. Their primary motive for encouraging the King's French designs is, it rapidly emerges, simply to preserve the wealth of the Church; and for most audiences, the arguments by which the venal Canterbury seeks to vindicate Henry's claim to a foreign throne serve only to arouse, by their pompous contortions, the very doubts they profess to quell (1.2.37–100). The true function of Henry's spiritual counselors is nicely indicated by the Machiavellian twist that Canterbury gives to a piece of familiar Protestant doctrine: "miracles are ceased, / And therefore we must needs admit the means [i.e., acknowledge the natural ways] / How things are perfected" (1.1.70–72). This maxim of pragmatic wisdom might serve as a motto for the action that ensues, in which the rhetoric of God's special providence to the English is always accompanied by a hardheaded realism about the practicalities of war and politics.

The play, indeed, is full of demonstrations of the ruthless "means" by which power maintains itself: thus, for example, the penitent conspirator Scroop expresses gratitude that God has "discovered" his plotting (2.2.158), but we already know that it was actually the King's intelligence network that exposed the conspirators ("The King hath note of all that they intend, / By interception which they dream not of," 2.2.6–7). Even the comradely warmth of that "little touch of Harry in the night" celebrated by the Chorus (4.Chor.29–48) can be seen as another form of espionage, in which a disguised Henry sets about testing morale in his camp. Fittingly, however, the effect of his surveillance is to raise once again the very uncertainties about the justice of the war that Canterbury sought to allay. Brooding on the consequences of death in battle, the stubborn Williams demands to know what consequences soldiers must face "if the [King's] cause

be not good" (4.1.138)—a challenge to which, signifi-
cantly enough, Henry's elaborate reply can offer no real
answer. By the same token, the egalitarian language of
"brothers, friends, and countrymen" (4.Chor.35), which
the King uses to persuade his followers of the essential
unity of their common cause, is undercut by Williams's
sullen reminders of class difference: the King, Henry
declares, has vowed not to be ransomed; "he said so,"
Williams shrewdly replies, "to make us fight cheerfully,
but when our throats are cut, *he* may be ransomed, and
we ne'er the wiser" (4.1.199–201; emphases added).
Williams's suspicion about the manipulative character of Henry's rhetoric is justified, we might think, by a
telling linguistic detail: in the oration before Agincourt
the King proclaims that "he today that sheds his blood
with me / Shall be my brother; be he ne'er so vile, / This
day shall gentle his condition" (4.3.63–65); but once the
crisis has passed the language of brotherhood is conspicuously reserved for his royal peers—for his blood
brother Gloucester (4.7.178) and for his defeated rival,
"brother France" (5.2.2). No wonder that Williams
bristles at attempts to buy him off, refusing Fluellen's
twelve-penny blandishments and, by implication, the
King's crowns too ("I will none of your money," 4.8.70).

Recalcitrant as Williams may be, however, he can
maintain his resistance only by a retreat into silence.
His voice is suppressed as the other inconvenient
voices—like those of the Pistol crew, the Act 2 conspirators, and the turbulent Irishman Macmorris—are
variously suppressed or discredited. Yet the very fact
of such suppression can serve to draw attention to
the official narrative's management of historical fact.
Take, for example, the hidden story of the Earl of Cambridge. While the motives for Cambridge's conspiracy
are carefully excluded from the play, the Earl's hint—
his dark insistence that something other than "the gold
of France" (2.2.162) inspired his plotting—would have

been enough to remind better-informed playgoers of the intrafamilial struggles that motivated Cambridge and of the dynastic dispute that would ultimately lead to Cambridge's Yorkist descendants deposing Henry's own son. Just as Henry remains conspicuously deaf to Fluellen's enquiry about the condemned Bardolph— seeming as unwilling to "know" his disgraced friend as he is eager to "know" the gallant enemy, Montjoy (3.6.104, 118, 142)—so the play itself appears anxious not to "know" the truth of Cambridge's cause or even to acknowledge that Cambridge was the brother of the loyal Duke of York whose "testament of noble-ending love" bathes the field of Agincourt in the glow of eroticized sacrifice (4.6.27).

In such ways the text draws attention to the suppressions and elisions involved in its own shaping of the past. Rallying his dispirited followers before Agincourt, Henry seeks to persuade them that they too are makers of history and that their names are destined to become "familiar . . . as household words" in a narrative that they themselves will fashion:

> This story shall the good man teach his son,
> And Crispin Crispian shall ne'er go by,
> From this day to the ending of the world,
> But we in it shall be rememberèd[.]   (4.3.54,58–61)

In Henry's persuasive fantasy, the telling of this story will be the prerogative of those whose actions it records—veterans of the fight. But the play itself has already shown us that making history is never such a straightforward business; and that far from being privileged to fix the meaning of the events they help to create, the "makers" of history will always remain at the mercy of the true fashioners of history—politicians, chroniclers, and (not least) playwrights. Like the other survivors of the battle, Pistol will return to England with his own version of events ("patches will I get unto these cudgeled scars, / And swear I got them in the Gallia wars," 5.1.91–92); but neither his story nor those of the play's other common soldiers will be allowed the "full mouth" that is granted to the King's "history." And not even the King will remain immune from the distortions of representation; for even as Henry projects into an admiring future his "official" version of Agincourt, authenticated (like Pistol's) by the survivors' battle scars, the audience will be aware that what they are actually witnessing is someone else's telling of the story—a narrative mediated by the urgent interventions of a Chorus who openly strives to dictate their reading of events in the teeth of ambivalences that persistently outrun his control.

These ambivalences do more than call in question the play's apparent adulation of the hero; they cut to the very heart of the national project in whose cause his martialist values are enrolled. The words *England, English,* and *Englishman* appear more often in *Henry V* than in any other of Shakespeare's plays: repeated with incantatory insistence, they remind us of the play's deep involvement in that process of national self-definition which saw the emergence of England as Europe's first true nation-state.[8] The historical Henry V belonged to a late feudal world in which the boundaries of a state were still determined from the top by the accidents of dynastic inheritance; Shakespeare's king belongs to an emergent world of nation-states whose boundaries would increasingly be legitimated by appeal to a shared history and heritage, a common language and culture. For such states, foreign wars became the anvil on which ideas of national difference were hammered out. It is through their confrontation with the French that Henry's followers experience what it means to be English.

The nationality they discover is one that claims their allegiance by right of nature; and it is only the failure of all England's children to be "kind and natural," the Chorus insists, that prevents this small nation from fulfilling its imperial destiny (2.Chor.19). In fact, however, the play puts too much pressure on the definitions of nationality to allow such ideas of "natural" allegiance to remain self-evident. Henry seeks to knit up the internal divisions of his kingdom by following his father's advice to "busy giddy minds / With foreign quarrels" (*Henry IV, Part 2*, 4.3.372–73). Yet his foreign war, ironically enough, also serves to expose contradictions in the very idea of "foreign" and "native."

The problematic nature of "English" identity has been foregrounded from the beginning by reminders that Henry's kingdom (like Elizabeth's) consists not of a single, united people but of two only partially unified islands, in which the interests of several ethnic groups exist in uneasy association or open conflict. Across the northern border lies that "giddy neighbor" Scotland, whose predatory history (as Henry tells it) dangerously mimics England's relations with France—

> For you shall read that my great-grandfather
> Never went with his forces into France
> But that the Scot on his unfurnished kingdom
> Came pouring like the tide into a breach . . .
> Girding with grievous siege castles and towns
> (1.2.151–58)

—prompting the aggressive domino theory articulated by the Bishop of Ely: "If that you will France win, / Then with Scotland first begin" (1.2.174–75). This is the logic of expansion that has already brought under English control two other Celtic territories whose rep-

resentatives figure prominently in the play—figures
through whom the very notion of "Englishness" is subject to significant interrogation.

The troops of "noblest English" whom Henry urges
into the breach at Harfleur (3.1.18) prove, when we
actually encounter them in 3.3, to be a volatile mixture of Scots, Irish, Welsh, and English—an ill-assorted
company who seem as likely to turn their swords on
one another as upon the French. Among them are two
men, Fluellen and Macmorris, in whom the dream
of ethnic incorporation is respectively represented as
dream and nightmare. It was no accident that Shakespeare should have chosen a Welshman and an Irishman to fill these roles. For if Wales, where the Tudors
were able to capitalize on their own Welsh origins,
had been absorbed with relative ease into the English
body politic, Ireland (as Elizabeth's campaigns demon-
strated) remained an intractable anomaly—in name a
separate kingdom attached to the English crown, but
in practice a colony subject to the full rigor of military conquest. While the compliant Welsh were merely
mocked as provincial mountain men, the "wild Irish"
were demonized as a savage and disorderly people
whom only the force of imposed English law could
redeem from feuding barbarity.[9] Thus while Fluellen
and Macmorris are both characterized by a dangerous
wildness of temper, Fluellen's irascibility is shown to
arise only from his passionate excess of loyalty, while
Macmorris's reveals him as a true denizen of what
Elizabethans dubbed "the Land of Ire." The Welsh captain is received into full membership of the English
nation—first by Henry's graceful acknowledgment that
his natal Welshness makes them fellow countrymen
(4.7.111), and then by Fluellen's demonstration that his
"native garb" is no more than a comic disguise for an
Englishness more real than Pistol's jingoistic counter-
feiting:

GOWER You thought because he could not speak
English in the native garb, he could not therefore
handle an English cudgel. You find it otherwise,
and henceforth let a Welsh correction teach you a
good English condition.   (5.1.79–83)

Macmorris, by contrast, is reduced to spitting incoher-
ence by the very mention of the word "nation": "What
ish my nation? Ish a villain and a basterd and a knave
and a rascal. What ish my nation? Who talks of my
nation?" (3.2.125–27).

His sensitivity is perhaps understandable, given the
hybrid surname (a Gaelicized version of Anglo-Norman
Fitzmaurice) that appears to identify him with a group
who inspired particular horror in English propaganda
about Ireland—members of English settler families
who, by adopting the manners, customs, and language
of the natives, had become "more lawless and licentious than the very wild Irish" themselves.[10] Like the
fantasy of "going native" in later times, the spectacle
of such "degeneration" opened the imperial imagination to the disturbing possibility that the project of
incorporating conquered peoples might lead only to a
fatal corruption of the national body politic that it was
designed to enlarge. So potentially disruptive to the
idea of national harmony fostered in the play is this
frustrated English-Irishman that he must be banished
from the action. The problems raised by Macmorris,
however, do not vanish with his disappearance at the
end of 3.3.

In the immediate wake of Agincourt, Fluellen demonstrates his impassioned loyalty by bringing to light
what he takes to be Williams's participation in "a most
contagious treason" (4.8.21). The reassuring effect of
this comic replay of the Cambridge conspiracy is com-
promised, however, by Williams's surly resistance to
the Welshman's blandishments. That this rebuff (echo-

ing the quarrel with Macmorris) should be delivered to Fluellen is especially significant, given the Welshman's pivotal position in the play's construction of national identity. Moreover, if the play has difficulty convincing itself that to be Welsh, or Scots, or perhaps even Irish, is only to belong to a subspecies of English, it has even greater problems accommodating the French, who are assigned a dangerously contradictory role in the play's treatment of nationality. On the one hand, Henry's policy is meant to draw together his subjects (English, Scots, Welsh, and Irish) by violently enacting their difference from the French—arrogant and caste-conscious foreigners; on the other, his conquest is aimed at abolishing that very difference through an "incorporate league" in which "English may as French, French Englishmen, / Receive each other" (5.2.379–80).

This contradiction (a significant one, given the play's immediate political context) is of precisely the same kind that appears in contemporary English accounts of the Irish question. In Edmund Spenser's *View of the Present State of Ireland,* for example, at one moment the Irish are represented as irremediably alien barbarians who can be dealt with only by conquest and extirpation; at the next they are merely errant subjects who need only be brought within the fold of English law, language, and culture "to bring them to be one people [with their conquerors], and to put away the dislikeful concept [i.e., hostility] both of the one and the other." [11] In *Henry V* the tensions between nationalist exclusivism and imperial expansionism are smoothed away by the convenient device of a marriage between Henry and the French princess, which symbolically reconciles the paradox of "French Englishmen" through the sacramental fiction of "one flesh."

But Shakespeare is too honest a dramatist to give himself entirely to the finessing involved in this sly appropriation of the conventional ending of romantic comedy. Indeed, the play makes it apparent that the ideal of a hybrid nation, ruled over by "a boy, half French, half English" (5.2.216), is only the mask for an incorporation as violent and peremptory as that which "the general of our gracious empress" (5.Chor.31) was trying to initiate across the Irish sea. Crucial here is the scene of translation (3.4) that immediately follows the siege of Harfleur—a scene that, like Pistol's encounter with Monsieur Le Fer, highlights the linguistic gulf between the rival kingdoms. In this brief but telling episode, the French princess, as if reading in the fate of Harfleur the sign of her own surrender, undertakes the Englishing of her own body, beginning with the hand (a metonymy for marriage) and ending (by accident of translation) in the middle region with "Le foot [i.e., the obscene *foutre*] *et* le count [i.e., gown, but also pudendum]" (3.4.54–55). The meaning of Katherine's carefully cataloged body will have been perfectly apparent to an audience accustomed to thinking of conquest in gendered metaphor in which the conquered is necessarily feminine. The effect here, in the wake of Henry's threats at Harfleur, is to emphasize the brutality of conquest by drawing attention to the work of nation-building and empire upon actual women's bodies:

> What is 't to me, when you yourselves are cause,
> If your pure maidens fall into the hand
> Of hot and forcing violation?
> ....
> . . . why, in a moment look to see
> The blind and bloody soldier with foul hand
> Desire the locks of your shrill-shrieking daughters.
> (3.3.19–35)

The point is disconcertingly reiterated in the final scene of national "spousal" (5.2.374). Though customarily played for its superficial charm, this scene is quite explicitly a scene of enforcement—a civil rape in which the conqueror's will is summarily imposed upon the conquered:

> KATHERINE   Dat is as it shall please de *roi mon père.*
> KING HENRY   Nay it *will* please him well, Kate; it *shall* please him, Kate.   (5.2.257–59; emphases added)

The language and bluff manners of this final scene troubled Dr. Johnson, who expressed his incomprehension that "Shakespeare now gives the King nearly such a character as he made him formerly ridicule in Hotspur" (the aggressive and blunt-spoken warrior of *Henry IV, Part 1*).[12] But (as Katherine's remark about the tongues of men being full of deceits [5.2.120–21] suggests) all Henry's "speak[ing] . . . plain soldier" (5.2.156) is by no means as plain as he pretends. As much "false French" as it is "true English" (5.2.229–30), more bluff than genuine bluffness, his transformation into blunt "King Harry" is another consciously contrived linguistic performance to add to Canterbury's admiring list (1.1.41–53)—a performance whose calculated naïveté allows him ("most truly-falsely," 5.2.199) to translate Katherine to his own purposes, converting her to "the better Englishwoman" in the process (5.2.126–27). "My royal cousin," asks Burgundy, "teach you our princess English?" And Henry's reply is perfectly nuanced: *"I would have her learn, my fair cousin, how perfectly I love her, and that is good English"* (5.2.293–96; emphases added). The bawdy transports of the conqueror's wooing make entirely plain what is at stake in the "possession" of this princess, what it means to "move [her] in French" (5.2.189, 194–95)—or, rather, to translate Katherine into English "Kate":

... I love France so well that I will not part with a village of it. I will have it all mine. And, Kate, when France is mine ... you are mine.... So the maid that stood in the way for my wish shall show me the way to my will. (5.2.180–84, 339–41)

Henry is determined to persuade us that even the French can be subsumed in an "English" empire— figuring Katherine's "broken English" not as the broken-hearted and confused speech of the country that he threatened to "break ... all to pieces" (1.2.233), but as the "broken music" of a French heart that may soon be Englished: "if you will love me soundly with your French heart, I will be glad to hear you confess it brokenly with your English tongue.... Therefore ... break thy mind to me in broken English" (5.2.107–10, 254–55). But after their one-sided linguistic duel, Katherine's mouth, like those of the play's other dissident voices, is effectually silenced—"stopped" by the kiss of possession that signals the end of her speaking part (5.2.286) and denies her any part in the political maneuvering that ties up the conditions of her marriage.

It would be misleading, of course, to pretend that *Henry V* is in any sense a pacifist play, much less that it is involved in some wholesale undoing of nationalist ideology. But it is remarkably open-eyed about the pragmatic necessities entailed by the cause it serves; it understands the cost of its ideals and it never shrinks from exposing who it is that will have to pay. Behind the merely rhetorical horrors of Harfleur lie the terrible, routine savageries of the European wars of religion and the indiscriminate massacres that defaced the progress of imperial expansion. Even as Shakespeare envisaged that scene of pillage in which old men are "taken by the silver beards / And their most reverend heads dashed to the walls" while "naked infants [are] spitted upon pikes" (3.3.36–38), the Irish cleric Peter Lombard was describing a similar massacre of the innocents visited on the Irish of Munster in the wake of the Desmond rebellion (1579–83). "Without distinction of age, sex, rank, or deserts," the English soldiery

> shot them with muskets, or ran them through with swords. Some they hung on trees by the wayside or on gallows, amongst whom was sometime seen the cruel spectacle of mothers hanging on crosses, the little one still lying or crying on their breasts strangled in their hair and hanging from this new fashioned halter; and other children wherever met or found it was an amusement and sport to toss in the air with spears or lances, or to pin them to the ground, or to dash them against rocks.[13]

The greatness of Shakespeare's play lies in its sober recognition that this, sooner or later, is how "culled and choice-drawn cavaliers" will behave—that "so many Alexanders" can also prove so many pigs.

———

1. See E. M. W. Tillyard, *Shakespeare's History Plays* (London: Chatto & Windus, 1943), and Lily B. Campbell, *Shakespeare's Histories: Mirrors of Elizabethan Policy* (San Marino, Calif.: Huntington Library, 1947).

2. For an account of Branagh's interpretation, usefully detailing his cuts to the text, see Robert Lane, "'When blood is their argument': Class, Character and Historymaking in Shakespeare's and Branagh's *Henry V*," *English Literary Renaissance* 61 (1994): 27–52; a more detailed political comparison between his film and Olivier's is offered by Graham Holderness, "Reproductions: *Henry V*," in his *Shakespeare Recycled:*

The Making of Historical Drama (Lanham, Md.: Barnes and Noble, 1992), 178–210.

3. Thomas Nashe, *Pierce Pennilesse, The Unfortunate Traveller and Other Works,* ed. J. B. Steane (Harmondsworth: Penguin, 1972), p. 113.

4. Thomas Heywood, *An Apology for Actors* (London, 1612), B4; spelling modernized.

5. For a discussion of the possible reference of these lines to the Earl of Essex or to Lord Mountjoy, see Warren D. Smith, "The *Henry V* Choruses in the First Folio," *Journal of English and Germanic Philology* 53 (1954): 38–57.

6. Erasmus, *"Dulce bellum inexpertis"* ("War is sweet to those who know nothing of it"), in *Adages,* ed. Margaret Mann Phillips (Cambridge: Cambridge University Press, 1964), pp. 333, 320.

7. Ibid., p. 320.

8. A fascinating account of how literature contributed to this process of national self-definition is to be found in Richard Helgerson, *Forms of Nationhood* (Chicago: University of Chicago Press, 1992).

9. See Michael Neill, "Broken English and Broken Irish: Nation, Language, and the Optic of Power in Shakespeare's Histories," *Shakespeare Quarterly* 45 (1994): 1–32.

10. Edmund Spenser, *A View of the Present State of Ireland* (c. 1596, pub. 1633), ed. W. L. Renwick (London: Eric Partridge, 1934), p. 82; spelling modernized.

11. Ibid., p. 197.

12. Cited from Arthur Sherbo, ed., *Johnson on Shakespeare,* The Yale Edition of the Works of Samuel Johnson, 16 vols. (New Haven: Yale University Press, 1958–90), 8:565.

13. Peter Lombard, *The Irish War of Defence 1598–1600,* tr. Matthew J. Byrne (Dublin: Cork University Press, 1930), pp. 15–17.

Further Reading

In addition to the following books and articles, see www.folger.edu/shakespeare and www.folger.edu/online-resources.

Henry V

Abbreviations: BBC = British Broadcasting Corporation; *FV* = *The Famous Victories of Henry the Fifth*; *1 and 2H4* = *Henry IV, Parts 1* and *2*; *H5* = *Henry V*; *1, 2, and 3H6* = *Henry VI, Parts 1, 2,* and *3*; *KJ* = *King John*; *Oth.* = *Othello*; *R2* = *Richard II*; *R3* = *Richard III*; RSC = Royal Shakespeare Company; *Wives* = *The Merry Wives of Windsor*

Altman, Joel B. "'Vile Participation': The Amplification of Violence in the Theater of *Henry V.*" *Shakespeare Quarterly* 42 (1991): 1–32.

For Altman, what distinguishes Hal's princely career in *1* and *2H4* is "vile participation" (*1H4* 3.2.89), the phrase used by Henry IV to rebuke his son for surfeiting the kingdom with his presence—a presence that partakes of the nature of low or vile persons, not only "sharing his presence with [them] but absorbing in return their private thoughts and words for his own use." It is therefore not surprising that a play about Harry as king "might offer itself to Shakespeare's imagination as . . . a problem of 'presencing,' with all the implications of psychic exchange and violation he had explored in the previous two plays." Altman argues that in *H5* Shakespeare taps the audience's emotions and directs their understanding so that they "admire the King and nurture hostile feelings toward him but

also transfer those feelings . . . to the foreign enemy";
this displacement is largely managed by means of
amplification, the rhetorical device used to "expand . . .
one's discourse by proliferating words and matter
and appreciating one's subject by representing it in
its fullest magnitude." Throughout the play, the King
is amplified by "serving him up in bits and pieces of
various shades and lusters . . . just as one may scatter
verbal images of throats cut or inventory parts of the
anatomy" (see, e.g., 2.1.70, 72; 3.2.114; 3.4; 4.1.139–40,
200). In 1599, when England's problems with Ireland
were proving particularly vexatious, Shakespeare
fashioned a play that presented to its actively participating audience—see the many choric urgings to
"suppose," "hear," "judge," "behold," "follow," "grant,"
and "place"—a dramatic mixture of heroism, patriotic
fervor, violence, and cunning policy. By "participating
[the king,] . . . digesting him, turning him to nourishment, Shakespeare's audience . . . is transformed into
a polity whose mind, filled with Harry, is historically
coextensive with Harry, sharing both the heroism and
the savagery of his French exploits while remaining
ineluctably Elizabethan."

Anonymous. *The Famous Victories of Henry the Fifth:
Containing the Honourable Battell of Agin-court.* . . . In
Narrative and Dramatic Sources of Shakespeare, edited
by Geoffrey Bullough, 4:299–343. New York: Columbia
University Press, 1975.

This short play, generally assigned to the late 1580s
and assumed to have been first performed in the same
time frame, is regarded as Shakespeare's primary theatrical source for the *H4* plays and *H5*, the chief historical sources being Raphael Holinshed's *Chronicles* (2nd
ed., 1587) and, by extension, Edward Hall's *Union of the
Two Noble and Illustre Families of Lancaster and York*

(1548), which Holinshed followed closely. The extant text of *FV*, registered for publication in 1594 and published as a quarto in 1598, is a corrupt version of what may have been a more substantial dramatic text, possibly even a two-part play; according to the title page, it was part of the repertory of the Queen's Men, a major acting company in London for almost a decade beginning in 1583. *FV* is a freewheeling popular treatment of the Henry V story that begins with Henry's youthful wildness as Prince Hal and continues into his reign as king (scenes ix to xx), compressing that reign into what is essentially the Agincourt campaign, followed quickly by the peace accord with France and Henry's pending marriage to Katherine (events that historically occurred five years after the success at Agincourt). Arguing for a greater connection between *H5* and *FV* than between the latter and the *H4* plays, Bullough notes verbal similarities and parallels between individual scenes: these include the Archbishop's justification of war with France, the tennis balls insult, the central battle at Agincourt, the courtship of Katherine, and the Treaty of Troyes. (See Bullough's introduction to *H5*, pp. 347–75, esp. 348–49.) *FV*'s low comic business involving Dericke and a French soldier may be behind Pistol's encounter with Monsieur Le Fer. Notable actions missing from *FV* include the conspiracy episode at Southampton, the disguised king's tour of the English camp on the eve of Agincourt, and Henry's order to kill the French prisoners. Although the Harfleur sequence is also omitted, a brief reference to it in *FV* (scene xii, lines 1–5) suggests that originally it may have been included. While not all of the parallels "are . . . close or sustained[,] . . . it can hardly be doubted that in writing *H5* Shakespeare was affected both positively (to accept) and negatively (to reject and replace) material found in . . . [*FV*]. But he transmuted almost everything that he touched" (see, for example, the barest suggestion of the St. Crispin's Day speech in scene xiv). Although his Henry V "retains some of the bluff, blunt masculinity of the earlier drama, [Shakespeare] gives him a high seriousness, a religious sense of responsibility, entirely lacking there, and also infuses the major scenes with a heroic quality unequalled even in his own earlier Histories" (Bullough, p. 349). (See Dutton and Ewert, below, for further discussion of the anonymous play.)

Baldo, Jonathan. "Wars of Memory in *Henry V*." Chapter 4 in *Memory in Shakespeare's Histories: Stages of Forgetting in Early Modern England*, pp. 102–30. New York: Routledge, 2012.

Drawing on the work of the anthropologist Ernest Gellner and the historian Ernest Renan, Baldo claims that Shakespeare's later histories (*KJ, R2, 1* and *2H4,* and *H5*) "reflect, help construct, and critically examine a growing sense of national identity in early modern England on [what has been identified] as the Western model," according to which "'the basis of national identity is not memory but amnesia'—or, at least, a complicated partnership of the two." Baldo focuses on the ways in which these plays "cast . . . remembering and forgetting in increasingly equivocal roles[,] . . . staging battles over memory and the uses of forgetting, and . . . exposing the degree to which national unity is produced by selective erasure of the past." The power to manipulate the memories of others as part of this erasure "becomes a critical aspect of state power, culminating in the charismatic Henry V, with reprises of the type in Prospero and Henry VIII." Baldo begins the chapter on *H5* with the observation that "most of the battles in the play are over memory": *H5*, "so singularly unimpressive as a representation of the epochal battle of Agincourt, is nonetheless a remarkable study of how a nation remembers." Baldo goes so far as to claim that "nowhere in the Shakespeare

canon is [the] struggle [of memory against forgetting]
more evident than in [*H5*]." The chapter explores both
Henry's manipulation of the national memory in pursuit
of his goal of a unified England and "the many points of
contention within Elizabethan memory" staged in the
play. To support his claim that *H5* "both mimics and to
some degree undoes Henry's role as choreographer of
the national memory," Baldo emphasizes the mnemonic
significance of both Calais (3.2.47, 3.57, 6.146; 4.8.130;
5.Cho.7) and the victory at Agincourt, each holding "an
ambiguous status as a memory common to Englishmen and promising to bind the nation together." The
former served as a "dubious memorial to England's
international affairs, capable of evoking memories of
some of England's greatest triumphs and failures";
and for an Elizabethan audience attending the play in
1599, the St. Crispin's Day speech would have reminded
them "not of Agincourt . . . but of the absence of any
national day of remembrance," annual celebrations of
Agincourt having long been omitted from the national
calendar. As "a minefield of counter-memories prepared
to detonate and to disrupt the appearance of a unified
public memory," *H5* challenges the English monarch's
seemingly unchallenged "master narrative" at the play's
conclusion: "The apparent triumph of unity—political,
artistic, and mnemonic—is qualified by manifold
reminders of elements of the past that the forces of
consolidation have tried to forget or suppress." To the
extent that Shakespeare "encourages us to hear those
reminders of history's remainders, those ghostly and
potentially rebellious mnemonic traces in *H5*, the early
modern nation remains a work-in-progress, an ongoing
fiction whose completion is always destined to lie in the
future."

Barton, Anne. "The King Disguised: The Two Bodies of
Henry V and the Comical History." In *The Triple Bond:*

Plays, Mainly Shakespearean, in Performance, edited by Joseph Price, pp. 92–117. University Park: Pennsylvania State University Press, 1975.

Barton examines *H5* in light of the motif of the disguised king who mingles with his subjects, a convention frequently used in English history plays from 1587 to 1600 and in popular ballads. While influenced by such plays as *George a Greene, Edward I, Fair Em,* and *The First Part of King Edward IV,* all of which depict kings whose disguises "demand . . . to be seen as a romantic gesture," Henry's meeting with Williams, Court, and Bates on the eve of Agincourt (4.1) lacks their "comical-historical tone." Instead of manifesting the "encouraging effect of 'a little touch of Harry in the night'" stressed by the Chorus (4.Cho.48), the opening scene of Act 4 exposes the "speciousness of Henry's pretense that he can really be the friend and brother of these soldiers, as well as their king" (4.1.204–9); for as Williams relentlessly asserts throughout the exchange, the gap between Henry's public and private natures— i.e., the public body of king and the private body of the man who wears the trappings of royal authority—is "unbridgeable." The nocturnal conversation thus ends not on a note of harmony but in a quarrel, "a failure to arrive at understanding which contradicts the romantic, ballad tradition." In summoning up "the memory of a wistful, naïve attitude toward history" in order to underscore its underlying "nostalgic but false romanticism," Shakespeare "question[s] rather than] celebrate[s] a folk convention," thereby achieving a tone that is "far more ironic and complicated" than that found in comical histories of the period. "The strain involved in maintaining . . . a constant ventriloquism" between the public and the private extends from the battlefield into Henry's wooing of Katherine in 5.2, where once again Henry finds himself in a situation demanding a personal response. Barton attributes his "blunders, his various solecisms," to his uncertainty "as to whether at a given instant he is speaking as Harry or as England, and whether the girl he addresses is the delectable Kate or the kingdom of France." Whatever this courtship scene was like in the lost original text of [*FV*; see above], "it has been made in Shakespeare's play to serve the [serious] theme of the king's two bodies: the dilemma of the man placed at a disadvantage in the sphere of personal relations by the fact of a corporate self." Barton concludes that Shakespeare's "atypical" handling of the motif of the disguised king calls attention to his interest in tragical, not comical, history, a dramatic form he exhausted both for himself and his contemporaries.

Berman, Ronald, ed. *Twentieth-Century Interpretations of "Henry V."* Englewood Cliffs, N.J.: Prentice-Hall, 1968.

Berman's collection provides an overview of early to mid-twentieth-century criticism. Part 1 consists of background material gathered from commentary by Lily Bess Campbell (from her chapter "The Victorious Acts of King Henry V," in *Shakespeare's Histories: Mirrors of Elizabethan Policy,* 1947) and Geoffrey Bullough (from his introduction to *H5* in *Narrative and Dramatic Sources of Shakespeare,* vol. 4, 1962). For Campbell, who reasserts the relevance of *H5* to "specific and contemporary situations in English life and politics," the theme of the play is "war, and the progress of the warrior-hero is the progress of the play. Thus [*H5*] becomes in form and content epic." The excerpt from Bullough discusses Shakespeare's debt to the anonymous *FV* (see item above) and to the work of Edward Hall, Raphael Holinshed, Samuel Daniel, and John Stowe. Part 2 presents excerpted interpretations by Charles Williams ("*Henry V,*" in *Shakespeare Criticism, 1919–35,* edited by Anne Ridler, 1936), E. M. W. Tillyard (*"Henry V,"* in *Shakespeare's History Plays,* 1944), Una Ellis-Fermor ("Shakespeare's Political Plays," in *The Frontiers of Drama,* 1945), Derek Traversi (*"Henry the Fifth,"* in *Shakespeare from Richard II to Henry V,* 1957), A. P. Rossiter ("Ambivalence: The Dialectic of the Histories," in *Angel with Horns,* 1961), and M. M. Reese (*"Henry V,"* in *The Cease of Majesty,* 1961). Part 3 excerpts individual perspectives from William Butler Yeats ("At Stratford-on-Avon" [1901], in *Essays and Introductions,* 1961), A. C. Bradley ("The Rejection of Falstaff," in *Oxford Lectures on Poetry,* 2nd ed., 1909), Elmer Edgar Stoll (*"Henry V,"* in *Poets and Playwrights,* 1930), Caroline F. E. Spurgeon ("Flight Images in *Henry V,"* in *Shakespeare's Imagery and What It Tells Us,* 1935), Mark Van Doren ("Henry V," in *Shakespeare,* 1939), J. Dover Wilson ("Introduction: Back to Johnson," in *The Fortunes of Falstaff,* 1943), and Paul Jorgensen ("Military Rank," in *Shakespeare's Military World,* 1956). In his introduction, Berman briefly addresses the play's plot ("deceptive" in that its "final cause . . . has occurred before the opening scene in the deposition of Richard II"), treatment of character (one of the play's consistent features is the "debate between character as a complex of individual motives and character as an emblem or epitome of historical experience"), images (the imagery of flight that "gives poetic sanction to the soaring spirit of the play's protagonist" and the contrasting kind of imagery that "dwells on the destruction of families, the slaughter of the innocent, the extinction of inheritance"), ideas (the rights and limits of monarchy and the tension between human will and divine prescription), and theme (identified variously as "la gloire," "machtpolitik," "burlesque," and "humanism"). Berman concludes that in *H5* Shakespeare "does not glorify war; he only comprehends it. It is equally clear that his very considerable accomplishment has been to unify the matter of epic and history; to make the former more credible and the latter more human than any of the sources available to him." A chronology of important dates and a selected bibliography round out the collection.

Clegg, Cyndia Susan. "Reading Italian Humanism: Elite Political Coteries and *Henry V.*" Chapter 3 in *Shakespeare's Reading Audiences: Early Modern Books and Audience Interpretation*, pp. 51–71. Cambridge: Cambridge University Press, 2017.

Concentrating on discrete reading communities, Clegg analyzes how Shakespeare's contemporary readers would have approached his works (whether printed or performed) through four lenses: Italian humanism, legal writing, religion, and politics. The focus of the chapter on *H5* is the importance of Machiavelli's political writings (available in manuscript and "cleverly marketed" by London stationers) to educated readers who "formed an important segment of Shakespeare's audience": the "elite reading clusters" associated with the court, the universities, and the Inns of Court. Members of an educated elite seeking advancement at court might well have found a humanist education coupled with knowledge of Machiavelli helpful in shaping how they approached a play "that participates in a distinctively Machiavellian rhetoric," noted for its lack of concern "with employing history in transparent exemplarity," favoring instead its use as "a humanist strategy of engaging its audience in an activity of prudent judgment." Such audience members would have "found themselves in the position of having to interrogate both Machiavelli's notion of virtù ['the amoral, flexible faculty of judgment . . . a faculty of deliberation'] and the humanist concept of virtue," which posits the inseparability of good rhetoric and ethical behavior (i.e., the Ciceronian conviction that the good man and the good orator are one and the same). "On one level Shakespeare's play may be seen as affirming the [latter] position: If he is nothing else, King Henry is a good rhetorician and a good man. Throughout the play, however, his goodness is in sufficient conversation with political reality to force the audience to resist accepting Henry as an example of either virtue or virtù": examples include the Archbishop of Canterbury's praise of Henry's virtue and rhetorical skills (1.1.24, 32–33, 50–55), followed by the ease with which the young king readily accepts the casuistic argument laid out in 1.2's Salic Law speech; the Southampton episode in which Henry models not humanist prudence but Machiavellian virtù (2.2); the matter of taking and ransoming prisoners, which captures the inherent conflict between "expediency and honor" (3.6.122–70; 4.1.88–237); the "Ceremony" soliloquy, in which Henry "completely ... embraces the political ironies of his circumstances" (4.1.238–93); and the Epilogue, which, in its ascription of Henry's victory to fortune, "render[s] both the king's virtue and virtù irrelevant," thereby "submit[ting] the play to the audience's judgment," and especially engaging those clusters "conversant in Machiavelli" in the kind of ethical and political discernment that "their humanist education intended." (*H5*, along with *Wives* and *Oth.*, is further discussed in chapter 4, where Clegg considers "how reading clusters knowledgeable about the status English women enjoyed under the law may have understood the sometimes problematic treatment of women across three genres of Shakespeare's plays: a comedy, a history, and a tragedy.") (For a view of Machiavelli in relation to *H5* that contrasts with Clegg's humanist reading, see Goddard and Greenblatt, below.)

Cottegnies, Line, and Karen Britland, eds. *King Henry V: A Critical Reader*. London: Bloomsbury Arden Shakespeare, 2018.

The Cottegnies and Britland reader surveys the play's critical and performance history, with a particular emphasis on its reputation in France as well as Britain and the United States. The table of contents reads as follows: Introduction (Karen Britland and Line Cottegnies); "The Critical Backstory" (James D. Mardock); "Performance History" (Gisele Venet and Anne-Marie Miller-Blaise); "The State of the Art" (Emma Smith); "*Henry V* on Screen" (Sarah Hatchuel); "New Directions: Shakespeare's *Henry V* and Religion" (John Drakakis); "New Directions: Making and Remaking the British Kingdoms—*Henry V*, Then and Now" (Christopher Ivic); "New Directions: 'His Bruised Helmet and His Bended Sword'—The Politics of Criminality and Heroism in *Henry V*" (Christine Sukic); New Directions: Agincourt and After: The Adversary's Perspective" (Elizabeth Pentland); and "Learning and Teaching Resources" (Gillian Woods and Laura Seymour). In their introduction, the editors discuss textual matters relating to the quarto and Folio versions of *H5*, address thematic and performance issues, note different readings that emerge when the play is read/seen by itself or as the culmination of a tetralogy, and provide an overview of the essays collected. Mardock's "Critical Backstory" reviews the "curiously polar" reception of *H5*—i.e., its "binary" view of both the play and its title character—from the seventeenth century to the end of the twentieth, with significant changes in perspective developing in the last two decades of the twentieth century as a result of new historicist, cultural materialist, and feminist studies, along with growing attention to the role of the play "in fostering a sense of nationhood" (see, respectively, Greenblatt, Dollimore and Sinfield, Howard and Rackin, and Neill, below). Picking up where Mardock's overview leaves off, Smith's chapter addresses scholarly approaches in the new millennium, noting that the impression of the play in the twenty-first century is "one of particular and pressing topicality, where the historicism that structured so much of the critical history prior to 2000 has ceded to more anxious forms of presentism." In addition to discussing insights gleaned from work in the areas of metatheater, memory, religion, gender, and a nationalism that expands beyond the play's concern with English and Irish identities to explore its "traces of Islam," Smith observes a trend away from an "either/or" stress on "irreconcilable polarities" (see the Rabkin entry, below) toward a "both/and" emphasis. The Venet and Miller-Blaise chapter guides the reader through the play's stage history from the Restoration to the present; under the final subheading "[*H5*] takes the world," the authors go beyond Anglophone productions in Australia and Canada to consider recent revivals in Japan and China. Hatchuel's chapter on cinematic treatments of the play provides "a contextual, aesthetic and ideological overview" of the productions by Laurence Olivier (1944), Michael Hayes (*An Age of Kings*, 1960), David Giles (BBC, 1979), Kenneth Branagh (1989), Michael Bogdanov (The Wars of the Roses cycle, 1989), Peter Babakitis (2007), Thea Sharrock (*Hollow Crown*, 2012), and Gregory Doran (RSC Live, 2016). A coda to the chapter considers how the play has been "cited and appropriated" in other films and popular television shows (e.g., *Star Trek*). The remaining four chapters under the heading "New Directions" begin with Drakakis's examination of "the various ways in which issues of a 'religious' nature are negotiated in relation to the new king Henry V's attempts to reinstate, and reinvigorate, and thereby reauthorize, the discourse of the Divine Right of Kings"; Drakakis contends that the play "balances the king's successes against his inner turmoil, with the result that we are never quite sure of the full extent of his reformation, or indeed, of the incontrovertible efficacy of providential power." Continuing the discussion of early modern kingship but now in the context of nation-building, Ivic situates *H5* "within a two-island (Britain and Ireland), three-kingdom (England, Ireland, and Scotland) and four-nation (England, Ireland, Scotland, and Wales) framework" to argue that the play was written at a moment in the nation's history when "matters English were giving way to matters British." Sukic's chapter uses the comic Fluellen subplot that "throws into relief both Henry's riotous past and his current legal infractions" to consider how the play "juxtaposes notions of heroism and criminality, underlying the fragility of Henry's status as a hero." As the final "new direction," Pentland's chapter examines contemporary responses to Agincourt as found in French medieval poetry and chronicle accounts; when viewed from the French side, "a startlingly different perspective from that familiar to Anglophone audiences of the play emerges, . . . open[ing] up many avenues for future work on this under-researched aspect of [*H5*]." Rounding out the volume is Woods and Seymour's guide to learning and teaching resources, which includes suggestions as to how these might be integrated into effective pedagogic strategies in the classroom; an extensive bibliography accompanies the guide.

Curry, Anne. *Agincourt: A New History*. Oxford: Oxford University Press, 2015.
    Curry re-creates the military campaign and battle from the perspectives of both the English and the French. Through an in-depth investigation of contemporary narrative sources as well as administrative records, and through a new look at the terrain where the battle was fought, she provides "firmer conclusions

on what exactly happened [at Agincourt] and why."
Acknowledging both key perceptions that continue to
prevail and myths that have developed, Curry warns
against taking a battle like Agincourt, with its great
imbalance in the mortality rates of the English and
the French, out of its context: "Agincourt took place
within a dramatic and complex period in English and
French history. Henry was the son of a usurper and still
insecure on his own throne in 1415. France had a king
who suffered from psychological illness, and in the
years leading up to Henry's invasion had been troubled by civil war." The aim of the book is to "examine Agincourt as the final stage of the whole campaign
and to attempt a balanced treatment of Henry's aims
and actions and of French responses to them." Curry
contends that the scale of the English victory and the
resulting eulogizing of Henry V "have disguised both
the potential insecurity of his position at home and the
failure of his campaign up to the point of the battle."
With respect to the French, the "disarray that defeat
caused . . . has likewise hidden the fact that, after years
of turmoil, the French were reasonably united in their
response": they had brought Henry to military action
at a battlefield of their choice and at a time when he
appeared desirous of avoiding a major confrontation.
And yet on October 25 they "found themselves in confusion and without the numbers they had hoped for.
Even then, Henry's response was symptomatic of panic
and uncertainty as much as military genius. Agincourt was and is shocking and amazing. It needs no
mythologising." The book's ten chapters are as follows:
(1) "Henry V's Inheritance: England and France 1399–
1413," (2) "Henry V and the Reopening of War, March
1413–August 1415," (3) "The Raising of Henry V's
Army, April–August 1415," (4) "The Siege of Harfleur,
13 August–22 September 1415," (5) "To Fight or Not
to Fight, 22 September–8 October 1415," (6) "From

Harfleur to the Crossing of the Somme, 8–19 October 1415," (7) "From the Crossing of the Somme to the Eve of Battle, 9–24 October 1415," (8) "The Armies Assemble, 24–25 October 1415," (9) "The Fight, 25 October 1415," and (10) "The Aftermath, 26 October–16 November 1415." In the epilogue titled "Battle or Murder?" Curry addresses Henry's decision to kill his French prisoners, an act that by boosting the mortality figures on the French side made the battle "truly distinctive": "No other medieval battle is known to have included the deliberate killing of a large number of men whom both sides believed would be ransomed." Coming down on the side of battle rather than murder, Curry contends that "the key to understanding Henry's bloody action is that he believed that he had already won," but fearing a French regrouping that could well lead to the prisoners forming a rearguard action, he "deliberately used an act of savagery to put pressure on the remaining French to withdraw, not wanting to risk the lives of his own men. . . . By the standards of the time Henry did not follow chivalric conventions, but his act was militarily necessary." The illustrated volume includes five appendices, maps and genealogical tables, and a bibliography. (On the issue of war crimes, see Warren's essay in the Hutson collection, below.)

Daniel, Drew. "Scambling Harry and Sampling Hal." In *Shakesqueer: A Queer Companion to the Complete Works of Shakespeare*, edited by Madhavi Menon, pp. 121–29. Durham: Duke University Press, 2011.

Daniel's essay appears in an anthology that attempts to integrate Shakespeare and queer theory, not to "provide 'queer readings'" of the texts but to bring the nonnormative stance of queerness into varied engagements with "the odd, eccentric, and unexpected" in the canonical Shakespeare. In the Chorus's "opening hymn to the signifying power of zero"—"O pardon, since a crookèd figure may / Attest in little place a million, / And let us, ciphers to this great account, / On your imaginary forces work" (Pro.16–19)—Daniel recognizes a "distinctly digital poetics." He posits that Henry is a cipher, "a desiring machine whose curious movement from sadistic fantasy to model pleading works on our 'imaginary forces' by producing in us as listeners a perverse fantasy of negation." Reviving and expanding on "queer theory" interpretations of *H5* (see the work of Jonathan Goldberg and Richard Corum), Daniel argues that the king's "practices of appropriation, mimicry, disguise, and simulation within this history play constitute an early modern practice of 'digital sampling,'" whereby Henry "extracts 'samples' of the behavior, habits, and sounds of others and willfully transforms them into his own use." There is "something rather queer about this promiscuity, this discursive restlessness, the itchy wanderlust that drives Harry to sidle up to others in disguise and attempt to 'blend in,' to slink alongside them, to ape their manners by sounding like them, to mirror and deceive his company with a series of passable approximations, imitations, and feints." When viewed in this context, "the exclusive thrust of the phrase 'we happy few' [4.3.62] seem[s] ever chillier and more distant." In Daniel's reading, the "digital sampler" is a type of internal electronic device for the storage and manipulation of audio signals that Henry uses for the purpose of charming and astonishing those around him. That he is successful in doing so is evidenced by the Archbishop of Canterbury, who says in wonderment, "Hear him but reason in divinity / And, all-admiring, with an inward wish / You would desire the King were made a prelate" (1.1.41–43). Daniel concludes that modern electronic digital sampling, operating through a pathway of sonic signals, serves to redesign the king's rhetorical skills as "the reproduction of a soldierly identity that is neither fully organic nor fully artificial." Invoking the artificial and fleetingly human voice of the computer Hal in Stanley Kubrick's 1968 film *2001: A Space Odyssey* and Roland Barthes' musing in "La musique, la voix, la langue" (1977) that a truly "neutral voice" would be a terror that would petrify the world, Daniel speculates that the voice of Henry, after he had seduced all comers and all the sampling was done, would be dead to its own desires and consume itself: the Hal of *1* and *2 Henry IV*, in other words, would become the Hal of Kubrick's film. In the course of the essay, Daniel cites Francis Bacon's "eerily prophetic" imagining of modern studio practices of sound manipulation in his 1626 utopian work *New Atlantis*: "We have also soundhouses, where we practice and demonstrate all sounds and their generation . . . and represent and imitate all articulate sounds and letters."

Dollimore, Jonathan, and Alan Sinfield. "History and Ideology: The Instance of *Henry V.*" In *Alternative Shakespeares*, edited by John Drakakis, pp. 206–27. London: Methuen, 1985.

In their frequently cited cultural materialist study of *H5*, Dollimore and Sinfield tease out the contradictions and conflicts that disrupt a play "assumed to be the [one text] where Shakespeare is closest to state propaganda." For critics who hold to a fixed and single "Elizabethan world picture" (see Campbell and Tillyard in Berman, above), "[*H5*] was a powerful Elizabethan fantasy simply because it represented a single source of power in the state. Nothing is allowed to compete with the king." Dollimore and Sinfield, however, focusing on *H5*'s "obsessive preoccupation" with instances of insurrection, demonstrate that the play's "construction of ideology is complex—even as it consolidates, it betrays inherent instability." Set against the arguments of self-serving clergymen, the suppression of the rebellious noblemen, the exclusion of Bardolph, Pistol, and Nym, and the quarrel with the skeptical Williams that puts the king on the defensive, Henry's consolidation of power and his victory over the French become for the authors a "re-presentation of the attempt to conquer Ireland and the hoped-for unity of Britain." The human cost of such imperial ambition, however, ultimately becomes visible and undermines the state's ideological justifications of national unity, a claim the authors further buttress by observing the play's pervasive imagery of slaughter. "[*H5*] can be read to reveal not only the strategies of power but also the anxieties informing both them and their ideological representation." As the play relentlessly "circles . . . around the inseparable issues of unity and division," *H5* exposes its own telos of national unity as a myth.

Dutton, Richard. "The Famous Victories of Shakespeare's *Henry V.*" In *Shakespeare, Court Dramatist*, pp. 173–200. Oxford: Oxford University Press, 2016.

The argument of Dutton's book is that Shakespeare's plays were frequently and specifically revised for presentation at the courts of Elizabeth I and James I and the texts that have come down to us often bear the marks of those revisions. "One of these marks . . . is the sheer length of many of Shakespeare's plays, which far exceed the norms of the public stage but would have found a ready audience in the royal palaces." According to Dutton, *H5*—which he considers a "succession play" within the chronicle rather than "political history" genre—is the most revealing Shakespeare play in relation to his argument because of the following extant texts: the anonymous *FV* (see item above), the comparatively short 1600 quarto version of *H5* (1,623 lines), and the much longer 1623 Folio text (3,166 lines), the third longest in the canon. For the quarto text, Shakespeare worked within the narrative structure of *FV* (reworking the verse and prose) while following Holinshed as to the history. Only later, for the text published in the Folio (none of which is based on the anonymous play except material deriving from the First Quarto), did he develop "a much more nuanced portrait of Henry, one that more forcefully locates it (rewriting history if needs be) in the longer pattern of English medieval history; a portrait in which the adulation of the Chorus is repeatedly in tension with what we see of [Henry's] actions and their consequences." The Folio text suggests that it was expanded for a court performance because it is "an epic that would unfold much more comfortably for a seated audience indoors through the dark hours of a winter's night, with breaks to trim the candles and to enjoy a light [banquet]." There are also indications that at least some of the Chorus's speeches may have been added for specific performances. Dutton thinks that the older Shakespeare was not afraid when creating the Folio text to sacrifice some of the historical accuracy he had achieved in the quarto; see, for instance, his shuffling of the aristocrats who accompany Henry to France so as to make the play the centerpiece in that span of histories that runs from the deposition of Richard II to the death of Richard III. It is less credible that Shakespeare erased the complexity he created in the Folio to produce the quarto "than that it was an achievement forged progressively and with increasing rhetorical and poetic skills, in two major creative phases": "[T]he most compelling reason to develop such sophistication would be to meet the tastes of an audience trained to appreciate it, in a venue where time was no object." As comparative analysis of the quarto and Folio texts demonstrates, the court "loomed much larger in Shakespeare's creative life than is usually appreciated." For Dutton, the quarto and Folio *H5*s, each with its own "register" of the succession theme, are different works and should not be conflated. [The chapter incorporates two of Dutton's earlier essays: (1) "'Methinks the truth should live from age to age': The Dating and Contexts of *Henry V*," *Huntington Library Quarterly* 68 (2005): 173–204, and (2) "*The Famous Victories* and the 1600 Quarto of *Henry V*," in *Locating the Queen's Men, 1583–1603: Material Practices and Conditions of Playing*, edited by Helen Ostovich, Holger Schott Syme, and Andrew Griffin (Farnham, Eng.: Ashgate, 2009), pp. 135–44.]

Ewert, Kevin. *Henry V.* Shakespeare Handbooks. New York: Palgrave Macmillan, 2006.

The core of Ewert's handbook, a performance-oriented introduction to *H5*, is a scene-by-scene commentary (chapter 3) that encourages readers to "envisage the words . . . unfurling in performance," thereby opening up the "environment for which [the play was] written and [offering] an experience as close as possible to an audience's progressive experience of a production." Other chapters address the authority of the dramatic text and early performances, sources and cultural context, key stage and cinematic revivals, and major trends in modern critical approaches. After briefly noting differences between the 1600 quarto text and the much longer 1623 Folio version and concluding that "neither . . . gives us Shakespeare's definitive intentions," Ewert turns to the matter of compositional date and first performance: "Most likely . . . the play was written early in 1599 and first performed in late spring or early summer." The chapter on sources and cultural context focuses on Shakespeare's borrowings from and transformations of the anonymous *FV* (see item above) and Holinshed's *Chronicles*, both of which "make clear . . . the strategies and tactics" that made possible the victory at Agincourt but that Shakespeare omits in favor of having Henry ascribe his victory to God alone; Ewert singles out Shakespeare's "most distinctive addition" to the historical and theatrically based story he inherited: the disguised king's encounters in the English camp on the eve of battle (4.1), a scene that reflects early modern ideas about a "good death," "dismemberment and dispersal of the body," and the fate of the soul. This second chapter concludes with a discussion of *H5*'s relationship to its "precursor plays," *1* and *2H4*. Key productions receiving special attention in chapter 4 are those directed by Adrian Noble (RSC, 1984), Michael Bogdanov (English Shakespeare Company, 1986–89), Matthew Warchus (RSC, 1994), Richard Olivier (The Globe Theatre, 1997), and Nicholas Hytner (National Theatre, 2003); playing the title role in each of these revivals were, respectively, Kenneth Branagh, Michael Pennington, Iain Glen, Mark Rylance, and Adrian Lester. The four cinematic and television versions of *H5* discussed in chapter 5 are Laurence Olivier's "fanciful" treatment (1944), the BBC/Time-Life's "dutiful" rendering (1979), the video-taped record of the English Shakespeare Company's 1986 "sceptical" staging (1989), and Kenneth Branagh's feature film, which offers "an often close-up account of what it feels like to be Henry" (1989). The final section of the chapter provides direct comparisons of the killing of Bardolph and the wooing of Catherine in each of the four versions reviewed. Ewert organizes his critical assessment of *H5* (chapter 6) under the following headings: "Early Assessments of the Genre," "Tillyard, Old / New World Order, Serial Thinking," "Ambivalence and Ambiguity," "Politics, Ideology, Power, Dissent," and "Performance Criticism." For Ewert, "the best critical assessments of the play are ones that implicate the audience, implicate us, in the play's ideals, cynicism, violence, bad faith, brotherhood, compelling ideologies and tentative dissent. Perhaps more than any other play by Shakespeare, *H5* is about its audience." An annotated bibliography keyed to chapter headings rounds out the volume.

Goddard, Harold C. *"Henry V."* In *The Meaning of Shakespeare*, 1:215–68. Chicago: University of Chicago Press, 1951.

Goddard questions the likelihood that Shakespeare would have written *R3* as a "pitiless exposure of the hollowness and rottenness of power, only to turn a few years later to a glorification of it on an imperialist scale" in *H5*. Consequently, he devotes the chapter on the latter play to demonstrating that any reading of it presenting Henry as the model of an ideal Christian king ignores its many ironies and contradictions. Central to Goddard's argument is the disconnection between the Chorus's commentary on the king and the actual words and deeds of Henry himself. In its role as "abstract of average public opinion," the Chorus presents the popular and exhilarating idea of Henry V as a glorious hero; the play minus the Chorus "tells the truth about him." Therein lies *H5*'s distinctive trait: "an irony that imparts intense dramatic value to practically every one of its main scenes." Act 1, for example, is suffused with irony in Henry's mixture of questionable personal motives and his professed devotion to God's will, and in the Archbishop's long legalistic justification of war with France (1.2.37–100): a "colossal piece of ecclesiastical casuistry with a highly ironical application to the situation in which Henry [the son of a usurper] finds himself." Goddard goes on to discuss the underplot of *H5* involving the tavern characters from the *H4* plays, especially Pistol's boasting, as ironic commentary on the upper plot and its warrior-hero, who is never shown in actual combat (a far cry from his Shrewsbury scenes in *1H4*). A close look at the Agincourt sequence (4.4 through 4.8)—particularly the king's order to kill the prisoners and the exchange between Henry and Williams in 4.8 (which proves the common man greater than a king)—leads Goddard to conclude that "if Shakespeare had deliberately set out to deglorify the Battle of Agincourt in general and King Henry in particular it would seem as if he could hardly have done more." Recalling that Machiavelli advised rulers in *The Prince* always to demonstrate mercy, faith, integrity, humanity, and religion but to be ready to change to the opposite when needed, Goddard writes, "Not maliciously and in cold blood but against the grain of his own nature and by insensible degrees, the man who began as Hal and ended as Henry V made himself into something that comes too close for comfort to Machiavelli's ideal prince." (Norman Rabkin [see below] regards Goddard's analysis as an "intemperate but necessary reading.")

Greenblatt, Stephen. "Invisible Bullets." In *Shakespearean Negotiations: The Circulation of Social Energy in Renaissance England*, pp. 21–65. Berkeley: University of California Press, 1988.
In this influential example of new historicism, Greenblatt pursues a poetics of Elizabethan power, one inseparable from a poetics of the theater. Finding parallels between the English incursions into the New World and Shakespeare's second Henriad (*1* and *2H4* and *H5*), he juxtaposes Thomas Harriot's *A Brief and True Report of the New Found Land of Virginia* (1588) with Shakespeare's plays to argue that the playwright's transformation of Hal from "rakehell" to monarch mirrors the tactics outlined by Harriot in his account of English colonization. (The title of Greenblatt's article derives from the success of the English in persuading

the natives of Virginia to accept the superiority of the European God, who, they believed, had struck down their tribe by means of "invisible bullets," when in reality the cause was the spread of measles, smallpox, and other diseases brought by the English.) Contemporaries accused Harriot of aping the Machiavellian hypothesis that princely power relies on subversion and containment. In the *H4* plays, Hal's subversive behavior represents the tactics of a counterfeit and a mimic who studies people in order to dominate them. Both the English colonizers, in their attempts to subdue the native inhabitants of the Americas, and Hal, in his efforts to control the domestic underworld associated with the taverns of Eastcheap, paradoxically encourage opposition in order to reaffirm their authority over those confined to the margins of society (the Indians in the former; the vagabonds, thieves, and prostitutes in the latter). According to Greenblatt, in *1H4* the audience does what Harriot did in Virginia: survey and test the waters. In *2H4*, the audience is like the tribe, paying homage to a fraudulent system. In *H5*, the audience finds "that we have all along been the colonizer and the colonized, king and subject. The play deftly registers every nuance of royal hypocrisy, ruthlessness, and bad [faith]." Greenblatt locates a pattern of "anticipatory subversion" of each of the play's central claims: Henry, who leads an invading army, repeatedly warns his victims that they are bringing pillage and rape upon themselves; Gower asserts that the king has ordered the killing of the prisoners in retaliation for the attack of the baggage train, although the audience has been shown that the king's order preceded the attack. "The charismatic authority of the king, like that of the stage, depends on falsification," thus confirming "the Machiavellian hypothesis that princely power originates in force and fraud even as [the Henriad] draw[s] the audience toward an acceptance of that power." *H5*, in particular, is dependent on the gap between the "real and ideal," as the spectators—both in the play and of the play—are induced to make up the difference, "to be dazzled by their own imaginary identification with the conqueror." Manifest in the Chorus's appeal "'tis your thoughts that now must deck our kings" (Pro.29–30) is the implication that all kings are "decked" out by imaginary forces and, therefore, that a sense of the limitations of king or theater "excites a more compelling exercise of these forces."

Howard, Jean E., and Phyllis Rackin. *Engendering a Nation: A Feminist Account of Shakespeare's English Histories*. New York: Routledge, 1997.

Employing a feminist analysis to examine the place of gender in "contesting representations of nationhood" in early modern England, Howard and Rackin argue that "the transition from dynastic kingdom to modern nation was integrally connected to shifts in cultural understandings of gender, and the social roles available to men and women. The cultural centrality of the Elizabethan theatre made it an important arena for staging the diverse and contradictory elements of this transition." The authors begin their study with commentary on Laurence Olivier's and Kenneth Branagh's cinematic versions of Shakespeare's *H5* (chapter 1, "Thoroughly Modern Henry," pp. 3–10). They contend that "Shakespeare's cultural authority is deeply implicated in the production of the very ideology that Branagh's film ['grittier' and more violent than Olivier's] expresses": "The history plays Shakespeare wrote in the 1590s helped produce what are now regarded as 'traditional' gender relations and the divisions between what we now call the public and private domains. The interconnections between Englishness, aggressive masculinity, and closeted womanhood that emerge so clearly in Branagh's film are present in Shakespeare's text marking it with a modernity that bears investigation." When the authors turn to the play itself (chapter 12, pages 186–215), they examine (1) the female gendering of France and Henry's view of his conquest as "the necessary validation of his manhood" (1.2.232–41); (2) the economic subjugation of a domesticated Mistress Quickly who is no longer in control of what was once her tavern, her new husband Pistol having taken ownership of both it and her as his property (2.3.48–53, 60–61); (3) the "pornographic redundancy" and violent rhetoric of the Harfleur speech (3.3.1–43); (4) Princess Katherine's anatomical language lesson (3.4); and (5) the courtship scene (5.2.101–291). Taken together, all of these passages further Howard and Rackin's argument that "in the struggle for power between men of two nations, the sexualized bodies of women become a crucial terrain where this battle is played out." In the language scene, no matter the vivacity of the actress, Katherine is a "woman preparing to be the bride of a conquering enemy, struggling to learn the language of that conqueror and to know her own body in the self-alienating terms provided by another's tongue. . . . Like the French territory she symbolizes, Katherine is preparing to be occupied, although her occupation will be called marriage." While the authors insist that the marriage itself is not a rape, they nonetheless argue that Henry's wooing is conducted in "the language of rape and warfare." *H5*, "more than any of Shakespeare's earlier English histories, . . . defines the roles of men and women in terms that clearly prefigure the performative masculinity and embodied female vulnerability of . . . our own historical situation." [For another feminist approach to the character of Katherine and the courtship scene, see Rubright, below.]

Hutson, Lorna, ed. *The Oxford Handbook of English Law and Literature, 1500–1700*. Oxford: Oxford University Press, 2017.

Included in this collection are two chapters on *H5*, both of which attempt to further our understanding of "the place of forensic modes of inquiry in the creation of imaginative fiction and drama": (1) Hutson's "Forensic History: *Henry V* and Scotland" (chapter 35, pp. 687–708), and (2) Christopher Warren's "*Henry V*, Anachronism, and the History of International Law" (chapter 36, pp. 709–27). Discussing the opening scene of *H5* in which the Archbishop of Canterbury outlines how he will persuade King Henry of the righteousness of his *casus belli* (cause of war), Hutson points out that the Latin word *causa* applied not only to the case being adjudged but also to the motive for the act being adjudicated. "The term *causa* thus straddles between the public and the private," between the question of why something was done and its purpose and cause as argued or justified in speech. According to Hutson, Shakespeare saw in the forensic materials of his chronicle sources "a chance to exploit the ambiguity of *causa*": dramatically speaking, this means "a chance to move us from asking the nation-imagining question 'is this cause just?' to asking the person-imagining question, 'what does he think?' thus deflecting legal questions about the justness of the national cause into characterological [psychological] questions" about Henry's motivation and "what it means to be human." When Henry debates with his soldiers and himself in 4.1 whether his war is just, it becomes "clear that the 'Englishness' of this play . . . has an inward, skeptical dimension that belies the idea of English nationalism, . . . actually, brilliantly, def[ying] it." As part of her discussion of Henry's "cause of war," Hutson recounts the disagreement described in the chronicles between England and Scotland over whether Scottish kings owed homage to the English monarch. She emphasizes how Shakespeare, through a process of selection and omission, presents the English viewpoint that Henry's taking of precautions against the Scots pouring over the border while he is in France (1.2.142–60) is a defense against rebels ("giddy neighbors") and not foreign invaders. The result reimagines a tripartite war of English, Scots, and French "as a vision of the plucky English against the might of foreign nations, thus covertly asserting English sovereignty over Scotland" and, in the process, assuring the audience that England's only historical enemies were overseas.

Warren begins his essay by asking (1) "Is Shakespeare's Henry V a war criminal?" and (2) Is it anachronistic to raise such a question? Taking the second question first, he cites the work of Anne Orford, who argues that modern contextualist historians think about concepts in their proper time and place while international lawyers think about how concepts move across time and space, making the international legal method "necessarily anachronistic" ("The Past as Law or History?," International Law and Justice Working Papers 2012/2 [Institute for International Law and Justice, New York University School of Law]). Law, which is understood as something binding in the present, is only possible precisely because historians have carved out a differentiated past. Noting that the first international war crime trial occurred in 1474 when the military lieutenant of Charles the Bold was tried for executing honorable men without benefit of law, Warren suggests that it is thus not anachronistic to ask whether Henry V was a war criminal, because the concept was understood at the time. (The same 1474 trial was introduced as an international law precedent at the Nazi Nuremberg trials after World War II.) As for literary studies, Warren writes that literature "can *mean* both synchronically and diachronically, in its own moment and potentially across vast temporal distances." Reading *H5* in the context of the writings of the early modern Oxford jurist Alberico Gentili—see his *De iure belli libri tres* (1598) and *De armis Romanis* (1599)—Warren states that both the playwright and the jurist "facilitate meaning-making" along the two temporal axes, thus allowing "for contemporary resonance" while also "transmitting legal meaning across time." Like Shakespeare in *H5*, Gentili in *De armis* was "engaged in a common project of transforming events of empire, whose role was to be narrated, into cases of empire, whose function was to be judged." In *De iure*, Gentili specifically denounced Henry V's execution of his French prisoners and compared his actions to those of barbarous Turks. Consequently, it may be argued that "Shakespeare's Henry . . . quite possibly was a war criminal for early modern elites, to say nothing of the moral intuitions of early audiences more generally." Shakespeare, however, creates ambiguity by twice ordering the French prisoners to be killed: the first time before he has heard that the English boys have been slaughtered (4.6.38–39), and the second afterward (4.7.1–11). As Warren reads these two passages, the first constitutes a war crime; the second, "lawful retaliation."

Kerrigan, John. "Oaths, Threats, and *Henry V.*" Chapter 9 in *Shakespeare's Binding Language*, pp. 237–55. Oxford: Oxford University Press, 2016.

Kerrigan understands "binding language" to mean "the whole array of utterances and acts by which people in early modern England committed themselves to the truth": i.e., oaths, vows, promises, asseverations, pledges, wagers, legal bonds, gages, and contracts. The chapter on *H5* focuses on the specific act of swearing and its varied dramatic potential: to attest to the truth of what is being said, as well as to cajole, persuade, intimidate, demand respect, deceive, evade, discredit, and, especially, threaten. Kerrigan begins with Macmorris's "tetchy" response to the crisis in the mines at Harfleur (3.2.90–95): "the heaviest concentration of swearing in all of Shakespeare—swearing both in the formal sense of oaths sworn by x or y and in the everyday sense of profanity." The "concentrated profanity" of the passage is significant not only because the "old-fashioned tenor" of the oaths reinforces the character's cultural otherness as an Irishman—the Irish were typically "represented as great swearers"—but because it underscores "in heightened form a broader presence of swearing in the play": "What [Macmorris] has in common with the other captains he also shares with Pistol, and, in a more exalted way, with Henry, whose rousing St. Crispin's Day speech, and response to Mountjoy's offer of ransom, are stiffened with such phrases as 'by the mass,' 'God's will,' 'By Jove,' 'faith,' and 'God's peace.' All of these characters demonstrate, in different ways and to different ends, the commonplace notion that soldiers were given to notorious swearing (see *AYLI* 2.7.156–57). They also show that, more often than not, swearing in *H5* becomes a threatening speech act: "Like blows struck by the word," aggressive oaths "assert a willingness to do physical damage." (Examples include the mix of swearing and drawing of swords among the tavern roisterers [2.1], Macmorris's threat to decapitate Fluellen [3.2.135–36], Henry's speech before the gates of Harfleur [3.3], and the leek episode between Fluellen and Pistol [5.1].) Kerrigan points to the young king's promise to "break [France] all to pieces" and "by God's grace, play a set / Shall strike [the French king's] crown into the hazard" (1.2.233, 273–74) as a reminder that "a formal asseveration can be designed less to bind the speaker than to rally good opinion among its auditors . . . and to function as a threat": "Whether in Eastcheap or before the walls of Harfleur, oaths that are threats can get things done in this play." As for Henry's quarrel with Williams (Act 4, scenes 1, 7, and 8), Kerrigan sums it up in this way: what was for the common soldier a matter of honor "has shrunk into a jest" for the English king, whose oath (sworn in disguise) was never intended to bind but always meant to mislead. In the final scene, peace is advanced through the courtship episode, but "the binding language of the sequence cannot, by now, reassure us. Oaths are not magic spells that secure truths and futures. Vows, articles, ransoms, and gages function in relation to larger forces, subject to displacement, performance, and error." Kerrigan returns to the Macmorris passage to argue that the captain's presence "shows an interest on Shakespeare's part [heightened by the Tudor wars in Ireland] in enemies sworn into friends, who might then turn back into enemies, and in oaths of fealty to the crown, as a seal of victory that comes unstuck once the power of binding words is unsupported by swords": as Pistol says in what may be the mantra of *H5*, "'Sword' is an oath, and oaths must have their course" (2.1.100–101). (The book chapter incorporates Kerrigan's earlier article of the same title in *Review of English Studies* 63 [2012]: 551–71.)

Loehlin, James N, *Shakespeare in Performance: Henry V.* Manchester: Manchester University Press, 1996.

Loehlin's modern performance history spanning the years 1944 to 1995 begins with an introductory chapter that contextualizes that history in terms of "innovations in theatrical theory and techniques, changing attitudes to war and politics, and new ideas about Shakespeare's histories" (especially those deriving from new historicist, cultural materialist, and feminist perspectives). Whereas the traditional approach to *H5* in performances from the eighteenth century through the first quarter of the twentieth viewed the play as a grand pageant and "a straightforward, nationalistic celebration of a great warrior-hero," later productions promoted what the playwright John Arden calls the "secret play within the official one" (see Ralph Berry, *Changing Styles in Shakespeare* [London: Allen and Unwin, 1981], pp. 77, 196), a play darker, more complicated, and more ironic. Loehlin's introduction briefly speculates on how Shakespeare's early audiences would have received the play and offers a concise commentary on late seventeenth- and early eighteenth-century adaptations before turning to elaborate productions "in the spectacular tradition" of William Charles Macready (1839); Charles Kean (1859), the "grandest" of the Victorian era; Charles Calvert (1872, 1879), "the first to acknowledge the play's anti-war aspects; and Lewis Waller, Frank Benson, and Richard Mansfield (1900)—all three "competing in their patriotic fervor." The seven-chapter chronological account that follows begins with Laurence Olivier's 1944 film, which both marked the culmination of the traditional approach and heralded "the move toward a complex twentieth-century Henry." The next five chapters discuss the productions of Terry Hands (RSC, 1975), David Giles (BBC Television, 1979), Adrian Noble (RSC, 1984), Michael Bogdanov (English Shakespeare Company, 1986), and Kenneth Branagh (Renaissance Films, 1989). A final chapter, "'Wish not a man from England,'" addresses productions outside the United Kingdom, particularly the "ground-breaking" revivals of Peter Zadek (*Henry the Hero*, Bremen, Germany, 1964—"an all-out assault on the whole idea of heroism") and Michael Kahn (the American Shakespeare Theater, 1969). The latter, with its vivid theatrical inventiveness . . . [and] strong statement of opposition to the Vietnam war," introduced the "secret" approach to *H5* on American stages. The same

chapter also briefly notes the revivals of Michael Lang-
ham (Stratford, Ont., 1956, 1966), Barry Kyle (Theatre
for a New Audience, New York, 1993), Maureen Shea
(an all-female production for Shakespeare & Company
[Lenox, Mass.], 1994), and Ron Daniels for American
Repertory Theater (Cambridge, Mass., 1995). Loehlin
ends his performance study with a question, now that
the "'secret' play has . . . become official": "What will
become of [*H5*] in the new millennium?" He envisions
as the next "paradigm shift" a decentering of Henry
as hero in favor of more attention being paid to the
Chorus, Pistol, the soldiers, and the female characters.
The volume includes two appendices: the first offers a
select list of significant twentieth-century productions
spanning the years 1900 to 1995; the second provides
cast and production staff information for the revivals
discussed in individual chapters.

Neill, Michael. "Broken English and Broken Irish:
Nation, Language, and the Optic of Power in Shakespeare's Histories." *Shakespeare Quarterly* 45 (1994):
1–32, esp. 18–32.

As part of a growing interest in *H5*'s role in promot-
ing a sense of nationhood, Neill surveys the discourse
about the English and Irish nations in the last years
of Elizabeth's reign, when debates about Irish identity and the Elizabethan colonization of Ireland were
intense and frequent. He finds in both the polemical
and literary discourse of the period a significant contradiction: namely, that Englishness was defined both
in opposition to Irishness—"stigmatized as a bar-
baric Other"—and through the desire to subdue and
incorporate the Irish "as a 'recalcitrant' part of the
nation . . . rather than [as] a foreign land to be subju-
gated. The effect of this peculiarly tense contradiction
was to produce a significant shift in English attitudes
toward Ireland over the course of the sixteenth cen-

tury." Neill then traces this discourse in several scenes in *H5*: the meeting of English, Irish, Welsh, and Scots, wherein the irascible Irishman Macmorris provokes a "crisis of nationality" (3.2.76–143), an encounter later recalled in the quarrel between Williams (the "recalcitrant English soldier") and the loyal Welsh Fuellen (4.8.1–75); Princess Katherine's language lesson (3.4), which makes clear the power of Henry's conquering tongue to dominate any linguistic threat to England's hegemonic goal; and the "ruthless" final scene in which Henry stages "a one-sided linguistic duel that claims to break the French princess to the discipline of 'broken English'" before silencing her "by the kiss of possession which signals the end of her speaking part" (5.2.268–91). When examined against the typical representation of colonial Ireland by imperial England as a woman requiring an (English)man, the wooing sequence figures the violent subduing of Ireland territorially, culturally, and linguistically. Finally, Neill contrasts the "extirpation" of Macmorris from the play with the "translation and incorporation" of Fluellen into "full membership of the English nation": "Indeed the arbitrary suppression of Macmorris only serves to draw attention to the uneasy marginal presence of Ireland as that which both defines and calls into question the idea of England." Given that the practicalities of English policy during the final years of Elizabeth's reign "more and more pressingly required that [the Irish] be absorbed within the boundaries of the nation-state," Neill's proposal of Ireland as an implicit point of reference in *H5* leads to understanding the play as a covert commentary on the "aggressive assimilation" at the core of England's colonial project in that neighboring but troublesome island to the west. (The article is incorporated in Neill's *Putting History to the Question: Power Politics and Society in English Renaissance Drama* [New York: Columbia University Press, 2002].)

Parker, Patricia. 'No Sinister Nor No Awkward Claim':
Theatrical Contexts and Preposterous Recalls in
Henry V." Chapter 4 in *Shakespearean Intersections:
Language, Contexts, Critical Keywords*, pp. 151–209.
Philadelphia: University of Pennsylvania Press, 2018.

Parker's interdisciplinary perspective on the Shakespeare canon examines historical intersections and
marginalized "critical keywords" to reveal how they
provide "a lens for interpreting the language, contexts,
and preoccupations of [the] plays." Zeroing in on the
word "preposterously" (2.2.118–20) in its etymologi-
cal yoking of "pre" and "post," "before" and "after," to
convey an "inversion of successor and ancestor"—the
sense of "coming from behind before"—Parker focuses
her reading of *H5* on the "recursive return or circling
back created by the fact that the death of Henry V,
projected as a future event in the play's epilogue, had
already occurred at the beginning of [*1H6*]," a play
"oft . . . shown" on the stage (Epi.13). She contends
that "[o]nce we take seriously [this theatrical] reversal
of chronological order in which the play of the father
(Henry V) comes after rather than before the plays of
the son (Henry VI), certain passages begin to appear
in a different light," with ironies and questions emerging that "undermin[e] the play's own apparently triumphant conclusion" and change our "apprehension of its
rhetoric of straightforward 'advance' and 'right.'" The
scene central to her argument is the Southampton episode involving the conspiracy of Cambridge, Grey, and
Scroop (2.2). Parker's detailed analysis illustrates how
its "pre" and "post" history are repressed by the "closure and enclosure of Henry's own forging, his exem-
plary humanist history moving in Aristotelian fashion
from fresh beginning to triumphant end." Lurking in
the margins of the scene, however, and "haunt[ing]
both the prologue and the sequel" to Henry V's reign,

is the "trace of a rival claim"—that of Edmund Mortimer, Earl of March and Richard II's designated heir. (Although Henry attributes the rebellion to a desire for "a few light crowns" [2.2.96], Mortimer's claim, championed by all three rebels but especially by Cambridge, was the real motive.) Reading the scene "preposterously," Parker argues that it looks to the past of Henry Bolingbroke's usurpation and the rebellions that plagued his reign in the *H4* plays and to the "theatrically past but historically future history" of Henry VI's reign, wherein the Earl of March's right is "repeatedly invoked" (most fully in *1H6* 2.5.61–100), the Lancastrian claim is acknowledged as weak by Henry VI himself (*3H6* 1.1.138, 199–200), and the grandson of the Cambridge executed at Southampton ultimately becomes "England's first Yorkist king" (*3H6* 5.7): the rebels in 2.2 "thus bring with them connections that exceed the boundaries of [*H5*]," connections that "throw . . . emphasis onto the motives and mechanisms of Henry's own suppression of the 'marches' or 'margins'" as he marches through France in pursuit of a questionable claim. Other examples of "preposterous recalls" or disruptions include (1) Exeter's declaration that Henry's right to the French throne is "no sinister nor no awkward claim" (2.4.92), two terms that for Shakespeare's audience would suggest the "inverse or underside of Henry's rhetoric of 'right'"—"sinister" meaning "crooked" and "illegitimate," and "awkward" signifying "the preposterously or 'awkly' reversed . . . awry"); (2) the "roll-call" of names singled out for remembrance in the St. Crispin's Day speech (4.3.55–56), "figures made famous in *1H6*"; and (3) the "most strikingly 'preposterous'" Burgundy, presented in Henry's closing lines (5.2.382–86) as a supporter of the diplomatic marriage between Henry and Katherine but who, as audiences familiar with *1H6* would have known, betrayed that union once he fell under the influence of Joan la Pucelle and came to side with the Dauphin, affirming him as "the rightful King of France" (*1H6* 3.3.37–84; 4.1.61). Reading the play "preposterously"—that is, with an eye to the subsequent undoing of Henry's triumph—reminds us that his seemingly "straightforward 'advance' and 'right,'" like the "O" or "crooked figure" of the Prologue, are not so straight and right after all: "Sometimes 'once more unto the breach' means moving 'awk,' or in reverse."

Rabkin, Norman. "Either/Or: Responding to *Henry V*." Chapter 2 in *Shakespeare and the Problem of Meaning*, pp. 33–62. Chicago: University of Chicago Press, 1981.

In what has become a seminal piece in *H5* scholarship, Rabkin argues that the ultimate power of the play "is precisely the fact that it points in two opposite directions, virtually daring us to choose one of the two opposed interpretations it requires of us," never allowing us to hold the two concurrently. Observing the irreconcilable "gestalts" of Henry as either ideal Christian king or Machiavellian prince, Rabkin maintains that neither conception—each persuasive in its own right—can be treated as the true interpretation: each is too reductive and, consequently, requires its respective proponents to exclude much of the play. Shakespeare deliberately prepares for this ambiguity by modifying Hal's character through *1* and *2H4*, making him less attractive in *Part 2*. Depending on which of the two histories one reads *H5* as a sequel to, two very different King Henrys emerge. Read as an "extension" of *Part 1*, we are "compelled to optimism"; read as a sequel to *Part 2*, we are made uneasy by the "dark shadows that cloud the comedy" of the earlier play. Among the dramatic moments that encourage us "to feel an eloquent discrepancy between the glamor of [*H5*'s] rhetoric and the reality of its action" are the "rapacious violence" of Henry's speech at Harfleur, his killing of the French prisoners, Pistol's pessimistic view of postwar life for the returning English veterans (5.1.84–92), the "unmistakable aggressiveness of [Henry's] sexual assault" on Katherine in Act 5, and the closing words of the Chorus. "The terrible fact about [*H5*] is that Shakespeare seems equally tempted by both its rival gestalts, the heroic versus the Machiavellian. And he forces us, as we experience and reexperience and reflect on the play, as we enter it in performances which inevitably lean in one direction or the other, to share his conflict." (The chapter is a revision of "Rabbits, Ducks, and *Henry V*," *Shakespeare Quarterly* 28 [1977]: 279–96.)

Rubright, Marjorie. "Incorporating Kate: The Myth of Monolingualism in Shakespeare's *Henry V.*" In *The Oxford Handbook of Shakespeare and Embodiment: Gender, Sexuality, and Race,* edited by Valerie Traub, pp. 468–90. Oxford: Oxford University Press, 2016.

Rubright's essay appears in a handbook that seeks "to situate feminist scholarship on the texts and legacies of Shakespeare within a broad conversation about the possibilities of and limits to politically engaged criticism." The editor characterizes the book's feminism as "broadband," borrowing the telecommunication term that suggests transmission of multiple signals and data simultaneously to indicate that "feminism functions most productively as a heuristic rather than a stand-alone method." The essay begins and ends with the Queen of France's use of the word "incorporate" (5.2.378) to describe the marriage of Henry and Katherine, a word that in the early modern period enjoyed a double and contradictory adjectival sense: on the one hand, it could mean a person or thing "united in one body," and, on the other, "one without a body or material substance: *in*corporeal, *un*embodied." Identifying Katherine "as both an embodied and unembodied subject," Rubright observes her three incorporations into marriage in 5.2 and how, in each instance, the marriage "materializes as a matter of language": first, at the level of dynastic politics; then, in the jarring of Katherine and Henry over whether it is possible for Katherine to love the "enemy of France" (5.2.176–77); and finally, with Katherine as a silent presence, in Queen Isabel's proclamation that the Anglo-French marriage will render both the king and princess, and their respective nations, an "incorporate league." While acknowledging a debt to the groundbreaking feminist scholarship of the 1990s that first addressed the relation of language and embodiment to the gender and sexual politics in *H5* (see, e.g., Howard and Rackin, above), Rubright focuses on the courtship sequence (5.2.101–291) to consider "what new feminist interpretations arise when we explore language itself as exceeding the agency of its speaker and take seriously the implications of the linguistic category confusions to which Kate's speech gives rise." Rubright's interrogation of "the ways in which bodies of language exceed the cultural stories and implicit genealogical principles that they are also invoked to define in [*H5*]" leads to an awareness of how Katherine's speech— both on stage and in the First Folio's "typographic embodiment" of it—challenges Henry's desire "to render England and France an 'incorporate league' on his terms." Henry's insistence that because he cannot speak French, Katherine must "break her mind to him in broken English" is the central "fiction" of their final dialogue. Broken as her English may seem, it offers her "a site of resistance[,] . . . a position from which she might enact a disruption to Henry's claims of monolingualism." To cast such resistance in the binary terms of English and French "misses an entire register of her resistance expressed through puns *in English*." The fact that "Kate's English is both broken and polyvalent . . . lends her speech the distinct advantage of breaking through the veneer of Henry's claims of 'plain soldier'-English-monolingualism to expose, instead, the doubleness always resident just on the tip of his tongue." When Henry adopts the half-English, half-French name "Harry le Roy" (4.1.50) on the eve of Agincourt, the linguistic disguise is revelatory of the "long history of cross-cultural Anglo-French linguistic 'incorporation'" that followed the Norman conquest and the Anglo-Norman genealogical intermixing that resulted. "What Henry attempts but fails to obscure in his dialogue with Katherine is the way in which Anglo-French linguistic relations are vexed through and through by sameness, by a fearful symmetry that risks undoing the premise of cultural and genealogical difference upon which his conquest is premised." Claiming that Katherine's English, broken English, and French "render her 'semblable' with England's King," Rubright concludes that her dialogue with Henry "peels back the national differences that their 'mother tongues' so imperfectly express, to reveal a 'Harry le Roy' and 'Princess English' who, when 'speaking of my tongue, and I thine, most truly-falsely must needs be granted to be much at one'" (5.2.198–200).

Watkins, John. "Shakespeare's Adumbrations of State-Based Diplomacy: *King John* and *Henry V.*" Chapter 5 in *After Lavinia: A Literary History of Premodern Marriage Diplomacy*, pp. 143–73, esp. 161–73. Ithaca: Cornell University Press, 2017.

In tracing the history of marriage treaties between royal families, Watkins explores "the unusually close relationship between diplomacy and literary production in Western Europe," from the time of the *Aeneid* (with its treatment of the marriage of Aeneas and Lavinia) through the late sixteenth-century works of

Spenser and Shakespeare to the plays of Corneille and Racine in seventeenth-century France, "when marriage began to lose its effectiveness and prestige as a tool of diplomacy." Chapter 5 examines Shakespeare's representations of marriage and politics and their wide dissemination through the public theater, focusing specifically on the relationship of marriage to the construction of national identity in *KJ* and *H5*. Watkins reads the latter as an "interrogation of just war theory in its conventional tripartite division: justice in waging, conducting, and ending war." While scholars have long noted how Henry and his English advisers "twist" tenets of international justice to defend a "legally dubious" war with France, they have neglected how the "weirdly comic turn" of the final sequence "presents the Treaty of Troyes as a violation of the third aspect of just war theory: justice in ending a war." Watkins contends that in *H5* Shakespeare uses the "conspicuous artifice" of the Elizabethan stage "to expose marriage diplomacy as a comic, even absurdist fiction . . . a practice [inadequate] to contain the mistrust, hatred, injustice, and inhumanity unleashed in war." That inadequacy is both poignantly and pointedly underscored in Katherine's simple question, "Is it possible dat I sould love de enemy of France?" (5.2.176–77). As a conclusion for the stage play, the pending marriage between a "dashing English king and a coy French princess . . . fails to resolve the tragic ambivalences raised in preceding scenes. As a conclusion for a war that in historical fact had already lasted over a century, it fails to resolve a series of insurmountable political conflicts that . . . threaten to disrupt [Act 5's] comic closure": see, for example, the lingering "messiness" of French factionalism hinted at in Burgundy's labors to secure peace (5.2.24–29); the "de facto exclusion" of the Dauphin from the succession (347–54); and the cryptic offer by Queen Isabel to use her "woman's voice" (94–96) to further negotiations:

does she want a seat at the table "as a natural champion of peace, or to maintain her own political interests?" The Epilogue's dire predictions support Watkin's claim that the romantic happy endings associated with comedy, especially Shakespeare's comedies, "have no place in [a] history play. Achieving them requires too many deletions and oversimplifications, too many distortions of the historical record." Watkins concludes that no other writer in English literary history did more "to dismantle a marriage ideology that dated back to the High Middle Ages" than Shakespeare. He gave that ideology eloquent voice in the speeches assigned to the King of France and Queen Isabel (5.2.360–67, 371–80). "But the action in which he embeds their hope for peace questions whether interdynastic marriages were ever a just or even reliable means to resolve hostilities between states. At best, his interdynastic brides were tragically ineffective. At their worst, they could subvert the integrity of proudly independent nations."

Films

For discussion of these films, see the Cottegnies and Britland, Ewert, and Loehlin entries above; Howard and Rackin's first chapter compares the Olivier and Branagh productions.

Branagh, Kenneth, director. *Henry V.* Renaissance Films, in association with BBC and Curzon Film Distributors, 1989. 137 min.
   Kenneth Branagh in the title role.

Giles, David, director. *Henry V.* BBC and Time-Life Television Productions, 1979. 166 min.
   David Gwillim in the title role.

Olivier, Laurence, director. *Henry V.* Two Cities Films, 1944. 137 min.

Olivier in the title role.

Shakespeare's Language

Abbott, E. A. *A Shakespearian Grammar.* New York: Haskell House, 1972.

This compact reference book, first published in 1870, helps with many difficulties in Shakespeare's language, especially with respect to syntax, grammar, and prosody. Abbott systematically accounts for a host of differences between Shakespeare's usage and sentence structure and our own. As he observes, Shakespearean English "presents the English language in a transitional . . . condition, rejecting and inventing much that the verdict of posterity has retained and discarded. It was an age of experiments, and the experiments were not always successful." For more than a century, Abbott's book was the chief resource for questions of grammar; see Jonathan Hope (below) for a twenty-first-century approach to the subject.

Adamson, Sylvia, Lynette Hunter, Lynne Magnusson, Ann Thompson, and Katie Wales, eds. *Reading Shakespeare's Dramatic Language: A Guide.* London: Arden Shakespeare, 2001.

This interdisciplinary collection draws on literary criticism, performance, and the history of language to explore both the similarities and differences between "the writing and language use" of Shakespeare's time and our own. The first part of the book, "The Language of Shakespeare's Plays," consists of twelve essays that bring together "an understanding of Renaissance rhetoric and modern conversation theory, with some issues of reading, writing, and staging": Ann Thompson, "Heightened Language"; Lynne Magnusson, "Style, Rhetoric and Decorum"; Sylvia Adamson, "The Grand Style"; George T. Wright, "Shakespeare's Metre Scanned"; Walter Nash, "Puns and Parody"; William C. Carroll, "Description"; David Scott Kastan, "Narrative"; Lynette Hunter, "Persuasion"; Lynne Magnusson, "Dialogue"; Pamela Mason, "Characters in Order of Appearance"; Peter Lichtenfels, "Shakespeare's Language in the Theatre"; and Keir Elam, "Language and the Body." The second part, "Reading Shakespeare's English," contains four essays that examine Shakespeare's sounds, grammar, and word-making strategies, in addition to his "rich repertoire of regional and social varieties": Katie Wales, "Varieties and Variation"; Sylvia Adamson, "Understanding Shakespeare's Grammar: Studies in Small Words"; Terttu Nevalainen, "Shakespeare's New Words"; and Roger Lass, "Shakespeare's Sounds." The volume also includes a list of rhetorical terms and an annotated bibliography.

Crystal, David. *"Think on my words": Exploring Shakespeare's Language.* Cambridge: Cambridge University Press, 2008.
   Crystal's introduction to the linguistic nuts and bolts of Shakespeare's language is governed by the principle that "one should never examine a linguistic nut or bolt without asking 'what does it do?' And 'what does it do?' means two things: how does it help us understand the meaning of what is said (a semantic explanation), and how does it help us appreciate the dramatic or poetic effect of what is said (a pragmatic explanation)?" The book's chapters cover Shakespearean graphology, punctuation, phonology, pronunciation, grammar, vocabulary, and conversational style. The epilogue, " 'Your daring tongue,' " locates the hall-

mark of Shakespearean linguistic creativity not in the words and expressions that Shakespeare coined but in an "economy of expression" that trades on the "relationship between lexicon and grammar" in "service of the poetic imagination." The appendix, "An A-to-Z of Shakespeare's False Friends," considers words that seem familiar but are not because their meanings have changed since Shakespeare's time (examples include "awful," "belch," "dainty," "ecstasy," "fancy," "honest," and "jog"). Two tables deal, respectively, with (1) shared lines in relation to the number of verse lines in the plays, and (2) the proportions of verse and prose in the plays. Notes, references, and suggested further reading conclude the study.

Crystal, David, and Ben Crystal. *Shakespeare's Words: A Glossary and Language Companion.* London: Penguin, 2002.

In this comprehensive compilation of Early Modern English vocabulary found in Shakespeare, the authors provide definitions of nearly 14,000 words along with treatments of selected language topics (e.g., frequently encountered words, archaisms, greetings, currency terms, and swearwords). To be included in the glossary, a word must "present . . . the reader with a difficulty arising out of the differences between Elizabethan and Modern English." Following the glossary is a series of "Shakespearean Circles" for each play, diagramming the family, social, and occupational relationships entered into by the characters; lines of connection between circles "identify important points of contact between different groups." Several appendices "collate . . . the way characters are named, the names of the people and places they talk about, and the foreign languages that some of them use." The editors also provide information on figures of classical mythology and nonclassical legend, religious beings and personalities, historical personages, and contemporary figures (factual and fictitious). The glossary is one part of the Crystals' larger digital project bringing computer-based Shakespeare resources into the Internet age. See their *Shakespeare's Words,* http://www.shakespearswords .com/, which provides a list of all the definitions associated with a word. When one clicks on a particular definition, the user is directed to other instances in the canon where the same meaning applies. A concordance accompanies the *Shakespeare's Words* website.

Hope, Jonathan. *Shakespeare's Grammar.* London: Arden Shakespeare, 2003.

Commissioned as a replacement for E. A. Abbott's *Shakespearian Grammar* (see above), Hope's book is organized in terms of the two basic parts of speech, the noun and the verb. After extensive analysis of the noun phrase and the verb phrase come briefer discussions of subjects and agents, objects, complements, and adverbials. The book targets three different audiences: Shakespeare specialists who will utilize it as a reference grammar, general readers/beginners who will benefit from the descriptive grammar provided, and literary critics who potentially will put the volume's stylistic overviews to good use in their analysis, explication, and interpretation of Shakespeare's plays and poems. Hope aims "to present Shakespeare's idiolect (that is, his particular version of Early Modern English) within a coherent linguistic structure" that will enable readers "to get a sense of the interrelatedness of many of the features of Early Modern English."

Houston, John. *Shakespearean Sentences: A Study in Style and Syntax.* Baton Rouge: Louisiana State University Press, 1988.

Houston studies Shakespeare's stylistic choices, considering matters such as sentence length, treatment of subordinate clauses, and the relative positions of subject, verb, and direct object. Examining plays throughout the canon in roughly chronological, developmental order, he analyzes how sentence structure is used in setting tone, in characterization, and for other dramatic purposes. Houston pays extensive attention to the effects of certain rhetorical devices— e.g., asyndeton, syndeton, polysyndeton, parataxis, and hypotaxis—on sentence construction.

Johnson, Keith. *Shakespeare's English: A Practical Linguistic Guide.* Harlow: Pearson, 2013.

With chapters on phonetics, grammar, vocabulary, word usage, pragmatics, rhetoric, the printed word, and prosody, this guide examines Shakespeare's early modern English within the history of the English language as a whole. In addition to discussing rhyme, meter, and pronunciation, Johnson specifically explores declensions, pronouns, compounds, speech acts (such as curses, insults, and commands), archaic word choices and forms, word clusters, word order, wordplay, spelling, punctuation, and Shakespeare's use of Anglo-Saxon, French, and Latinate vocabulary. Along with the pervasive influence of Cicero's *De inventione* and the pseudo-Ciceronian *Ad Herennium* on the writing practices of Shakespeare and his contemporaries, Johnson considers the importance of such humanist works as Thomas Wilson's *The Arte of Rhetorique* (1553) and George Puttenham's *The Arte of English Poesie* (1589). Although criticism is not the author's purpose, he does on occasion offer readings to illustrate how Shakespeare's linguistic and rhetorical choices chart changes in a character's trajectory.

Throughout the book Johnson reminds the reader of shifts in lexical meaning over the centuries.

Robinson, Randal. *Unlocking Shakespeare's Language: Help for the Teacher and Student.* Urbana, Ill.: National Council of Teachers of English and the ERIC Clearinghouse on Reading and Communication Skills, 1989.

Specifically designed for the high-school and undergraduate college teacher and student, Robinson's book addresses the problems that most often hinder present-day readers of Shakespeare. Through work with his own students, Robinson found that many readers today are particularly puzzled by such stylistic characteristics as subject-verb inversion, interrupted structures, and compression. He shows how our own colloquial language contains comparable structures, and thus helps students recognize such structures when they find them in Shakespeare's plays. This book supplies worksheets—with examples from major plays—to illuminate and remedy such problems as unusual sequences of words and the separation of related parts of sentences.

Williams, Gordon. *A Dictionary of Sexual Language and Imagery in Shakespearean and Stuart Literature.* 3 vols. London: Athlone Press, 1994.

Drawing on theatrical works, broadside ballads, newsbooks, jestbooks, and pamphlets, Williams provides a comprehensive list of words and expressions to which Shakespeare, his contemporaries, and later Stuart writers gave sexual meanings. He supports his identification of these meanings by extensive quotations, which, taken together, reveal how the language and imagery of sexuality reflect both linguistic development and sociocultural change across the early modern period.

Wright, George T. *Shakespeare's Metrical Art*. Berkeley: University of California Press, 1988. (Reissued as a paperback in 1991.)

Wright examines "the basic forms of Shakespeare's iambic pentameter line, its relation to other patterns (such as short lines, long lines, and prose), its changes over his career, and, most of all, the expressive gestures and powers this system provides for Shakespeare and his dramatis personae." To better understand Shakespeare's achievement (the primary focus of chapters 5 to 16), the author historicizes it in the "context of the decasyllabic line [Shakespeare] inherited and strongly influenced." For Wright, Shakespeare's metrical art is the culmination of a metrical chain that "runs back to Chaucer," through the verse of Thomas Wyatt, George Gascoigne, Henry Howard (Earl of Surrey), Philip Sidney, Edmund Spenser, and Christopher Marlowe. Chapter 17 considers the "extravagant turns" the pentameter line would take in John Donne and John Milton. Chapter 14, "The Play of Phrase and Line," explores the "creative equilibrium" Shakespeare maintains between "the continually recurring metrical pattern and the rhythmic phrase," a balance he achieves by varying the placement of the line break from the traditional fourth syllable slot of earlier poets to any position in the line, thereby yielding "phrases of three, five, or seven syllables as readily as phrases of four or six." The result of such freedom, especially in Shakespeare's later plays, is a more flexible and "sinuous" iambic pentameter line. For Wright, "the drama of Shakespeare is played out not only through a dialogue of characters but also through a dialogue of differently formed and framed verse lines, which speak to each other and to us of the variety, grace, and plenitude of human speech and trouble." Three appendices conclude the volume: (1) "Percentage Distribution of Prose in Shakespeare's

Plays," (2) "Main Types of Deviant Lines in Shakespeare's Plays," and (3) "Short and Shared Lines." (Chapter 14 first appeared in *Shakespeare Quarterly* 34 [1983]: 147–58.)

Shakespeare's Life

Baldwin, T. W. *William Shakspere's Petty School.* Urbana: University of Illinois Press, 1943.

Baldwin here investigates the theory and practice of the petty school, the first level of education in Elizabethan England, where boys from the ages of four or five until the age of seven would learn the rudiments of reading and writing, with the aid of a hornbook (a leaf of paper framed in wood and covered with a thin layer of translucent horn) that contained the letters of the alphabet (preceded by a cross), combinations of vowels, and the Lord's Prayer. Students also mastered ABC books (introductory books to a subject, usually in question and answer form), the Catechism from the Book of Common Prayer, and the Primer (a fuller version of the catechism with additional prayers and psalms). As Baldwin states, the goal of the petty school was "to teach to read and write always, and to cast accounts [numbers] frequently," but, more importantly, the "predominantly religious" curriculum aimed at providing children with the fundamentals (in both theory and practice) of their orthodox Protestant religion. Baldwin focuses on the petty school educational system primarily as it is reflected in Shakespeare's art; see, for example, references to the life of a typical schoolboy in *As You Like It* (2.7.152–54), to the hornbook in *Love's Labor's Lost* (5.1.46–49) and *Richard III* (1.1.58–63), and to the ABC book in *King John* (1.1.202).

Baldwin, T. W. *William Shakspere's Small Latine and Lesse Greeke.* 2 vols. Urbana: University of Illinois Press, 1944.

Baldwin refutes the view that Shakespeare was an uneducated genius—a view that had been dominant among Shakespeareans since the eighteenth century. Instead, Baldwin shows, the educational system of Shakespeare's time would have given the playwright a strong background in the classics, and there is much in the plays that shows how Shakespeare benefited from such an education. Volume 1 deals with the evolution of the grammar school curriculum in the sixteenth century from 1509 to 1600: Baldwin devotes chapters to the work of Erasmus; the education of royalty; specific models such as the Winchester, Eton, Westminster, and Paul's systems under Queen Elizabeth; the King's Free Grammar School at Stratford; and the Latin curriculum of the lower grammar school. Turning in volume 2 to the curriculum of the upper school (primarily Latin and, to a lesser degree, Greek), Baldwin considers the emphasis on rhetorical training (by way of the key texts of Cicero, Erasmus, Susenbrotus, and Quintilian), prose and verse composition, Latin poets (namely, Ovid, Virgil, Horace, Juvenal, Catullus, and Seneca), moral history, and moral philosophy. As Baldwin concludes, "If William Shakspere had the grammar school training of his day—or its equivalent—he had as good a formal literary training as had any of his contemporaries. At least, no miracles are required to account for such knowledge and techniques from the classics as he exhibits. Stratford grammar school will furnish all that is required. The miracle lies elsewhere; it is the world-old miracle of genius."

Beier, A. L., and Roger Finlay, eds. *London 1500–1700: The Making of the Metropolis.* New York: Longman, 1986.

Focusing on the economic and social history of early modern London, the nine essays in this collection probe aspects of metropolitan life under the headings "Population and Disease," "Commerce and Manufacture," and "Society and Change." The essays are as follows: Roger Finlay and Beatrice Shearer, "Population Growth and Suburban Expansion"; Paul Slack, "Metropolitan Government in Crisis: The Response to Plague"; Margaret Pelling, "Appearance and Reality: Barber-Surgeons, the Body and Disease"; A. L. Beier, "Engines of Manufacture: The Trades of London"; John Chartres, "Food Consumption and International Trade"; Brian Dietz, "Overseas Trade and Metropolitan Growth"; M. J. Kitch, "Capital and Kingdom: Migration to Later Stuart London"; M. J. Power, "The Social Topography of Restoration London"; and Stephen MacFarlane, "Social Policy and the Poor in the Later Seventeenth Century." The collection reveals a London caught up in the redistribution of socioeconomic and political power, the result of developments in capitalism and changes in class structure.

Callaghan, Dympna. *Who Was William Shakespeare? An Introduction to the Life and Works.* Oxford: Wiley-Blackwell, 2013.

Callaghan devotes the first part of her study to an examination of Shakespeare's life in the context of the social, cultural (particularly theatrical), political, intellectual, and religious climate of early modern England. She carries this focus on period and context into the second half of the volume in short essays on twenty-four plays, grouped under the following headings: "Comedies: Shakespeare's Social Life," "English and Roman Histories: Shakespeare's Politics," "Tragedies: Shakespeare in Love and Loss," and "Romances: Shakespeare and Theatrical Magic." The strictly biographical

portion of the book considers "three of the most significant issues that shaped Shakespeare's identity": education (chapter 2), religion (chapter 3), and social status
(chapter 4). Callaghan contends that Shakespeare's
grammar school education was "the most important
factor in allowing him as a gifted individual to become
a writer." Religion furnished more than the backdrop
for Shakespeare's canon, forming instead "the crucible
in which his secular drama was generated." Callaghan
is not concerned with Shakespeare's religious affilia-
tion ("staunch Protestant, devout crypto-Catholic, fur-
tive nonbeliever, or the holder of any one of a range of
positions in between"), but rather with the impact of
the Reformation and religious persecution on his theatrical practice and "identity as a professional writer."
Before turning to specific plays, Callaghan discusses
the nature of theater as a new urban institution with
a fixed location, the pressures of censorship on both
performance and print, "the social and professional
conditions that molded Shakespeare's theatrical career
in London," and the "competitive environment of early
modern theatre." Callaghan acknowledges that Shakespeare's life "cannot explain his works, but it can help
us to understand them."

Cressy, David. *Education in Tudor and Stuart England.*
London: Edward Arnold, 1975.

Cressy collects over 150 sixteenth-, seventeenth-, and
early eighteenth-century documents detailing aspects
of formal education that reflect "the efforts of govern-
ments, philanthropists, religious writers, social critics
and other leaders of opinion, as well as schoolmasters
themselves, to direct the educational enterprise" of
early modern England. Cressy groups the items under
eight categories: perspectives on education, control of

education, the organization of schools, schoolmasters, the curriculum, educational opportunity, education of women, and the universities. The selected documents "illustrate some of the social and political pressures bearing on education in the period."

Duncan-Jones, Katherine. *Shakespeare: An Ungentle Life.* London: Arden Shakespeare, 2010.

This biography, first published in a slightly different version in 2001 under the title *Ungentle Shakespeare: Scenes from His Life,* sets out to look into the documents from Shakespeare's personal life—especially legal and financial records—and it finds there a man very different from the one portrayed in more traditional biographies. He is "ungentle" in being born to a lower social class and in being a bit ruthless and more than a bit stingy. As the author notes, "three topics were formerly taboo both in polite society and in Shakespearean biography: social class, sex and money. I have been indelicate enough to give a good deal of attention to all three." She examines "Shakespeare's uphill struggle to achieve, or purchase, 'gentle' status." She finds that "Shakespeare was strongly interested in intense relationships with well-born young men." And she shows that he was "reluctant to divert much, if any, of his considerable wealth towards charitable, neighbourly, or altruistic ends." She insists that his plays and poems are "great, and enduring," and that it is in them "that the best of him is to be found."

Enterline, Lynn. *Shakespeare's Schoolroom: Rhetoric, Discipline, Emotion.* Philadelphia: University of Pennsylvania Press, 2012.

Two questions inform Enterline's study of Shakespeare's "career-long fascination" with the classical curriculum and humanist pedagogy of the early modern grammar school: "How did [such] training influence what counted as genteel masculinity in the period?" and "How did early modern pedagogy affect experiences of sexuality and desire?" Throughout the book, Enterline underscores "the significant difference between what humanists claimed their [pedagogical] methods would achieve [the formation of proper English gentlemen who would benefit the commonwealth] and what the texts of at least one former schoolboy reveal about the institution's unintended literary and social consequences"—namely, the undercutting of the patriarchal social order that the educational system was meant to reproduce. By assuming female roles in the classroom, the boys learned to "identify with women as they learned to voice the emotions needed for a persuasive oratorical performance." The introduction and first two chapters focus on Shakespeare's grammar school curriculum and Enterline's overall thesis concerning "gender instability" in the pedagogical tradition of the time. The remaining chapters illustrate the author's argument by way of particular poems or plays: Chapter 3 deals with *Venus and Adonis*; chapter 4, with *The Taming of the Shrew*; and chapter 5, with aspects of *Hamlet, Lucrece,* and *The Winter's Tale.*

Evans, Robert C. *Culture and Society in Shakespeare's Day.* New York: Chelsea House, 2012.

Part of a three-part series titled *Backgrounds to Shakespeare* (the other two volumes are *Shakespeare's Life* and *Literature and the Theater in Shakespeare's Day*), Evans's illustrated overview gives historical and social-political context to the period 1564 to 1616, describing daily life as it was lived in three major centers of English existence: the countryside, London, and the royal court. Citing contemporaneous reports and comments, Evans sheds light on a diversity of topics: education; the enclosure movement and its impact on agricultural life; industries such as fishing, mining, and bricklaying; the rural poor, the rural aristocracy, and the rural parson as lawyer and doctor; courtier life, royal progresses, and the royal palaces of White-hall, Hampton Court, and Greenwich; the road system to London, English inns, and livery companies; and meals, domestic furnishings, and "sumptuary laws" specifying the proper attire for people of different ranks and occupations. Evans also includes "special features" on the rituals and customs associated with birth, marriage, and death; religious conflict in Shake-speare's England, folklore, superstition, and witchcraft; disease and medicine; and major events of the period (such as explorations of the New World, the Spanish Armada, and the Gunpowder Plot). Frequent quota-tion from the plays underscores connections between topics discussed by Evans and their treatment in the Shakespeare canon.

Manley, Lawrence. *Literature and Culture in Early Mod-ern London.* Cambridge: Cambridge University Press, 1995.

Spanning the years 1475 to 1675, Manley's study of the image of London in and the city's influence on lit-erature in the early modern period examines a variety of writings: lyrics, ballads, epics, satires, praises, plays, chronicles, treatises, sermons, official documents, pag-eants, and mayoral shows. Within two hundred years London was transformed from "a late medieval com-mune" of 35,000 inhabitants into a "rapidly chang-ing metropolis of nearly half a million, the engine of an evolving early modern society, a capital . . . that would soon become the most populous in Europe," and a major European trading center. These changes brought "[n]ew possibilities . . . for cultural exchange and combination, social and political order, and literary expression." Among the many factors that led to making early modern London "the largest and most widely experienced human creation in Britain" were the rise of humanist learning and the impact of a print culture; "the emergence of . . . a national consciousness" that coincided with transformations of late medieval aristocracy; changes in the rural economy; the development of new class functions, "tied especially to commerce, bureaucracy, and law"; and "new types of religious . . . association." The volume's illustrations include representations of royal and civic ceremonies, emblematic images of personified early modern London, and contemporary maps of the city as a whole and of individual streets, processional routes, and areas such as Cheapside.

Manley, Lawrence, ed. *London in the Age of Shakespeare: An Anthology.* University Park: Penn State University Press, 1986.

A useful companion to Manley's later study (see above), this anthology seeks to "reflect the experience of London" during Shakespeare's time. The book's sixteen chapters excerpt writings published between 1485 and 1660; these include prose descriptions of the city, verse encomia, sermons, jestbooks, broadside ballads, satires and complaints, official records, civic myths, epigrams, poems of transit, erotica, and portrayals of London as found in stage comedy, character writing, and official pageantry. Challenges to social order—crime, disease, poor harvests, unemployment, and a growing and an increasingly diverse population—"animate the materials" gathered, underscoring how the literature of the period "amounts to a kind of city in itself, a polemical space in which competing visions and voices exert a productive influence on each other. . . . Emerging from the varied strands and forms of London life, and integrated with them, the London that was performed, imagined and sung was, in many ways, the London that was lived." As the items collected attest, Tudor-Stuart descriptions of London "reveal that a major corollary of the Renaissance discovery of man was the discovery of the city."

Potter, Lois. *The Life of William Shakespeare: A Critical Biography.* Malden, Mass.: Wiley-Blackwell, 2012.

This critical biography of Shakespeare takes the playwright from cradle to grave, paying primary attention to his literary and theatrical milieu. The chapters "follow a chronological sequence," each focusing on a handful of years in the playwright's life. In the chapters that cover his playwriting years (5–17), Potter considers events in Stratford-upon-Avon and in London (especially in the commercial theaters) while giving equal space to discussions of the plays and poems Shakespeare wrote during those years. Filled with information from Shakespeare's literary and theatrical worlds, the biography also shares frequent insights into how modern productions of a given play can shed light on the play, especially in scenes that Shakespeare's text presents ambiguously.

Schoenbaum, S. *William Shakespeare: A Compact Documentary Life.* New York: Oxford University Press, 1977.

Schoenbaum's evidence-based biography of Shakespeare is a compact version of his magisterial folio-size

Shakespeare: A Documentary Life (New York: Oxford University Press, 1975). Schoenbaum structures his readable "compact" narrative around the documents that still exist which chronicle Shakespeare's theatrical, legal, and financial existence. These documents, along with those discovered since the 1970s, form the basis of almost all Shakespeare biographies written since Schoenbaum's books appeared. For Schoenbaum, "The story of William Shakespeare's life is a tale of two towns. Stratford bred him; London gave him, literally and figuratively, a stage for his fortune."

Shapiro, James. *Contested Will: Who Wrote Shakespeare?* New York: Simon & Schuster, 2010.
This historical investigation of the authorship controversy and its history explains "what it means, why it matters, and how it has persisted despite abundant evidence that William Shakespeare of Stratford wrote the plays attributed to him." Shapiro is able to date the onset of the controversy to the middle of the nineteenth century; he exposes as forgery documents purporting to backdate it to the eighteenth century. What gave rise to the controversy were the combination of "the presumption that Shakespeare could only write about what he had felt or done rather than heard about, read about, borrowed from other writers, or imagined" and the coincident deification of Shakespeare. So great was Shakespeare's reputation and so rich his presumed experience as it was abstracted from his writings that it became impossible for some to persist in associating him with the Stratfordian Shakespeare whose documented life consisted only of narrow legal and commercial interests. Once skepticism about Shakespeare's claim to have written his plays arose, more and more candidates for authorship began to be proposed—an activity that continues right up to the present. Sha-

piro acknowledges such contenders as Christopher Marlowe, Mary Sidney, the Earl of Derby, the Earl of Rutland, Sir Walter Ralegh, and Queen Elizabeth; his emphasis, however, falls on only two candidates, each of whom is the subject of a full chapter: Francis Bacon and the Earl of Oxford. For Shapiro, their candidacies are "the best documented[,] . . . most consequential [and] representative." The epilogue explains why the author thinks William Shakespeare wrote the plays and poems attributed to him.

Wolfe, Heather, curator. *Shakespeare Documented.* Digital Project. 2016. The Folger Shakespeare Library. Washington, D.C. See http://www.shakespearedocumented.org.

Assembled by the Folger Shakespeare Library to commemorate the 400th anniversary of Shakespeare's death, this multi-institutional collaboration brings together the resources of the Folger, the Bodleian Library of Oxford University, the Shakespeare Birthplace Trust, the National Archives, and the British Library to provide the "largest and most authoritative" collection of primary source materials documenting the life of William Shakespeare. Materials include all known manuscripts and print references relating to the poet-playwright, his works, and family, including a letter addressed to him, manuscripts signed by him, and references to his coat of arms. Dating from his lifetime and shortly thereafter, the documents reveal a portrait of Shakespeare as a professional playwright, actor, poet, businessman, and family man who lived in both London and Stratford-upon-Avon. They trace his path "to becoming a household name," from the earliest reference to his father in Stratford (1552) through the publication of the First Folio in 1623 to the gossiping about him in the following decades. Images, descriptions, and transcriptions of 107 manuscripts that refer to Shakespeare by name, ninety-five printed books and manuscripts that mention or quote his plays or poems, and eighty-four printed editions of his plays and poems up to and including the First Folio point to "a remarkable legacy for someone of his socio-economic status and profession."

Shakespeare's Theater

Astington, John H. *Actors and Acting in Shakespeare's Time: The Art of Stage Playing.* Cambridge: Cambridge University Press, 2010.

Astington describes and analyzes the "cultural context of stage playing, the critical language used about it, and the kinds of training and professional practice employed" by actors on the early modern English stage from Richard Tarlton to Thomas Betterton. Drawing on recent discoveries "about actors and their social networks, about apprenticeship and company affiliations, and about playing [venues] outside" the theatrical center of London, this study compares "the educational tradition of playing in schools, universities, legal inns and choral communities . . . to the work of the professional players." In addition to portraying the early modern actor's versatility in playing many parts, Astington attends closely to the study of oratory in the grammar school curriculum and to the use of dramatic performance as a pedagogic tool, even at the university level, thereby underscoring the connection between "the performative arts of the stage and the select and remote realm of contemporary formal education." In the chapter "Players at Work," he uses Shackerley Marmion's *Holland's Leaguer* (1631) and Philip Massinger's *The Roman Actor* (1626) "to approach some of the pragmatics of a particular moment of theatrical production in the earlier seventeenth century." Astington concludes with commentary on changes in acting styles and the "social place" of actors: neither descendants from gentry nor university graduates, leading actors were, nevertheless, "of a social rank equal to the respectable citizens of London"; journeymen actors, however, lived "on the margins of poverty." An appendix provides a comprehensive biographical dictionary of all major professional actors in the years 1558 to 1660.

Berry, Herbert. *Shakespeare's Playhouses*. New York: AMS Press, 1987.

With illustrations by Walter Hodges, Berry's six essays collected here discuss varying aspects of the four playhouses in which Shakespeare had a financial stake: the Theatre of 1576 in Shoreditch (the subject of two essays), the Blackfriars of 1596, the Globe of 1599, and the Globe of 1614. The final essay, "A New Lawsuit about the Globe," addresses the legal action brought by the King's Men in their efforts to seek an extension of their lease on the Globe property, which was due to expire in 1635. The four theaters at the core of Berry's study "embrace and virtually define the whole of the most remarkable period in English theatrical history."

Berry, Herbert, William Ingram, and Glynne Wickham, eds. *English Professional Theatre, 1530–1660*. Cambridge: Cambridge University Press, 2000.

This study of the English professional theater in the years designated consists of three parts: "documents of control," "players and playing," and "playhouses," each part divided into chapters with their own subdivisions. Wickham presents the government documents designed to control professional players, their plays, and playing places. Ingram handles the professional actors, giving as representative a life of the actor Augustine Phillips, and discussing among other topics patrons, acting companies, costumes, props, playbooks, provincial playing, and child actors. Berry treats the twenty-three different London playhouses from 1560 to 1660 for which there are records, including four inns. As he reminds us, "Probably nothing of the kind had happened in any other city on earth." The documents supporting the third part are primarily legal.

Cook, Ann Jennalie. *The Privileged Playgoers of Shakespeare's London.* Princeton: Princeton University Press, 1981.

Cook sets out to answer the question, "Who were the people for whom Shakespeare, Marlowe, Jonson, Webster, and their fellow dramatists wrote plays?" Were they "ignorant or intelligent, riotous or refined, libertine or law abiding, plebeian or privileged?" In contrast to Alfred Harbage (see below), Cook argues, on the basis of sociological, economic, and documentary evidence, that Shakespeare's audience—and the audience for English Renaissance drama generally—consisted mainly of the "privileged," a group that ranged "from the threadbare scholar or the prospering landholder, newly risen from the yeomanry, all the way up to nobility and royalty itself." Such an audience was ready-made, given the fact that the "privileged had long fostered the drama as schoolboys, as patrons, and even as playwrights themselves." To claim that the "privileged" dominated the "plebeians" as playgoers is not to say that they did so exclusively: "Ordinary people who could afford the price of a ticket made their way to attend a play on any given day, especially on holidays, but not (as the economic and social pressures affecting them demonstrate) in the numbers or frequency previously thought."

Dutton, Richard, ed. *The Oxford Handbook of Early Modern Theatre.* Oxford: Oxford University Press, 2011.

Dutton divides his study of the theatrical industry of Shakespeare's time into the following sections: "Theatre Companies," "London Playhouses," "Other Playing Spaces," "Social Practices," and "Evidence of Theatrical Practices." Each of these sections is further subdivided, with subdivisions assigned to individual experts. W. R. Streitberger treats the "Adult Playing Companies to 1583"; Sally-Beth MacLean, those from 1583 to 1593; Roslyn L. Knutson, 1593–1603; Tom Rutter, 1603 to 1613; James J. Marino, 1613–1625; and Martin Butler, the "Adult and Boy Playing Companies 1625 to 1642." Michael Shapiro is responsible for the "Early (Pre-1590) Boy Companies and Their Acting Venues," while Mary Bly writes of "The Boy Companies 1599–1613." David Kathman handles "Inn-Yard Playhouses"; Gabriel Egan, "The Theatre in Shoreditch 1576–1599"; Andrew Gurr, "Why the Globe Is Famous"; Ralph Alan Cohen, "The Most Convenient Place: The Second Blackfriars Theater and Its Appeal"; Mark Bayer, "The Red Bull Playhouse"; and Frances Teague, "The Phoenix and the Cockpit-in-Court Playhouses." Turning to "Other Playing Spaces," Suzanne Westfall describes how "'He who pays the piper calls the tune': Household Entertainments"; Alan H. Nelson, "The Universities and the Inns of Court"; Peter Greenfield, "Touring"; John H. Astington, "Court Theatre"; and Anne Lancashire, "London Street Theater." For "Social Practices," Alan Somerset writes of "Not just Sir Oliver Owlet: From Patrons to 'Patronage' of Early Modern Theatre," Dutton himself of "The Court, the Master of the Revels, and the Players," S. P. Cerasano of "Theater Entrepreneurs and Theatrical Economics," Ian W. Archer of "The City of London and the Theatre," David Kathman of "Players, Livery Companies, and Apprentices," Kathleen E. McLuskie of "Materiality and the Market: The Lady Elizabeth's Men and the Challenge of Theatre History," Heather Hirschfield of "'For the author's credit': Issues of Authorship in English Renaissance Drama," and Natasha Korda of "Women in the Theater." On "Theatrical Practices," Jacalyn Royce discusses "Early Modern Naturalistic Acting: The Role of the Globe in the Development of Personation"; Tiffany Stern, "Actors' Parts"; Alan Dessen, "Stage Directions and the Theater Historian"; R. B. Graves, "Lighting"; Lucy Munro, "Music and Sound"; Dutton himself, "Properties"; Thomas Postlewait, "Eyewitnesses to History: Visual Evidence for Theater in Early Modern England"; and Eva Griffith, "Christopher Beeston: His Property and Properties."

Greg, W. W. *Dramatic Documents from the Elizabethan Playhouses.* 2 vols. Oxford: Clarendon Press, 1931.

Greg claims that "generally speaking it may be said that for every piece in the repertory of an Elizabethan theatre company there must have existed three playhouse documents or sets of documents. First . . . was the Book, or authorized prompt copy. . . . Next there were the Parts of the several characters, written out for actors on long scrolls of paper. . . . Last there were the Plots, skeleton outlines of plays scene by scene, written on large boards for the use of actors and others in the playhouse." In the first volume, Greg itemizes and briefly describes almost all the play manuscripts that survive from the period 1590 to around 1660, including so-called prompt copies, players' parts, and plots. His second volume offers facsimiles and transcriptions of selected manuscripts associated with the playhouses. (For some other kinds of playhouse documents, see the books by Stern and by Werstine, below.)

Harbage, Alfred. *Shakespeare's Audience.* New York: Columbia University Press, 1941.

Harbage investigates the fragmentary surviving evidence to interpret the size, social composition, behavior, and aesthetic and intellectual capacity of Shakespeare's audience. He concludes that commoners, the plebeians, and not the privileged were the mainstay of Shakespeare's audience. In contrast to public theaters like the Globe, private theaters such as the Blackfriars were the domain of the upper levels of the social order. The book's seven chapters are titled "The Evidence," "How Many People," "What Kind of People," "Behaviour," "Quality: Elizabethan Appraisals," "Quality: Modern Appraisals," and "Our Shakespeares and Our Audiences." Two appendices provide, respectively, estimates of attendance and attendance charts. Harbage's view remained uncontested until Ann Jennalie Cook's argument for the privileged (see Cook, above).

Keenan, Siobhan. *Acting Companies and Their Plays in Shakespeare's London.* London: Bloomsbury Arden Shakespeare, 2014.

Keenan "explores how the needs, practices, resources and pressures on acting companies and playwrights informed not only the performance and publication of contemporary dramas but playwrights' writing practices." Each chapter focuses on one important factor that shaped Renaissance playwrights and players. The initial focus is on how "the nature and composition of the acting companies" influenced the playwrights who wrote for them. Then, using "the

Diary of theatre manager Philip Henslowe and manuscript playbooks showing signs of theatrical use,"
Keenan examines the relations between acting companies and playwrights. Other influences include "the
physical design and facilities of London's outdoor and
indoor theatrical spaces" and the diverse audiences for
plays, including royal and noble patrons.

Stern, Tiffany. *Documents of Performance in Early Modern England*. Cambridge: Cambridge University Press,
2009.
    Stern interrogates "two competing current schools
of thought on playscripts: whether surviving playbooks
are ever fully representative of plays as they were performed ('performance texts') and whether playbooks
are ever fully stripped of the theatre to become plays
in an ideal literary form ('literary texts')." Singling
out the label "play-patcher," one of several used to
identify playwrights in Shakespeare's time, she argues
that despite its pejorative connotation, the term accurately depicts the patchwork nature of dramatic texts
"made from separate documents." Stern's extensive
examination of early modern playscripts allows her
to consider the many papers created by authors and
theaters before the actual opening performance of a
play. These documents, each treated in its own chapter,
are as follows: plot scenarios; playbills and title pages;
"arguments" as programs and as "paratext"; prologues
and epilogues (often drawn up on pieces of paper separate from the play they flanked and not necessarily
by the author(s) of the rest of the text); songs ("com-
pleted and sometimes written by composers, and dis-
seminated to be learned separately"); scrolls (including
such property documents as letters, proclamations,
bills, and verses that were to be read aloud during a

performance); backstage plots ("profoundly theatrical document[s]" that hung in the tiring-house and that provided detailed stage entrances, including the properties needed by actors when onstage); and, finally, actors' parts. What lies behind a theatrical production in the early modern English theater, then, was not "any single unified [and authorized] book" but rather a "patch-work" of parts "easily lost, relegated or reused," always open to continual revision and to new configurations for subsequent performances. Taken together, the performance documents explored by Stern were "the play," a conclusion that not only "redefin[es] what a play actually is" but also redefines "what a playwright is"—namely, a "play-patcher." Unlike the "whole artworks [that] poems" were considered to be, "plays had the bit, the fragment, the patch in their very natures." (For accounts of extant playhouse manuscript books and quartos used as playbooks in the theaters, see Greg, above, and Werstine, below.)

The Publication of Shakespeare's Plays

Blayney, Peter W. M. *The First Folio of Shakespeare.* Hanover, Md.: Folger, 1991.

Blayney's accessible account of the printing and later life of the First Folio—an amply illustrated catalogue to a 1991 Folger Shakespeare Library exhibition that showcased twenty-four of the Folger's First Folios—analyzes the mechanical production of the First Folio, describing how it was made, by whom and for whom, how much it cost (probably a retail price of 15s for an unbound copy), and its ups and downs (or, rather, downs and ups) since its printing in 1623. Blayney contends that probably no more than 750 copies were printed. Among the topics discussed are the order of the pages, the importance of casting off (the process of setting a Folio quire by first estimating just what text would fit in the first six pages), stop press corrections, the portrait of Shakespeare, the belated inclusion of *Troilus,* and the activities of Henry Clay and Emily Jordan Folger, the founders of the Folger Shakespeare Library, as collectors.

Hinman, Charlton. *The Norton Facsimile: The First Folio of Shakespeare.* 2nd ed. New York: W. W. Norton, 1996.

This facsimile presents a photographic reproduction of an "ideal" copy of the First Folio of Shakespeare; Hinman attempts to represent each page in its most fully corrected state. The second edition includes an important new introduction by Peter W. M. Blayney, which consists of four sections: "The First Folio and Its Publishers," "The Players and Their Manuscripts," "The Proofreading," and "The Printing" (which includes a table listing the pages of each play in the order in which they were set and the "more reliable compositorial reattributions that have been offered since 1963"). A significant feature of the Hinman facsimile is its "through line numbering" system (TLN), based on the lines printed in 1623 rather than on the acts, scenes, and lines of a modern edition.

Hinman, Charlton. *The Printing and Proof-Reading of the First Folio of Shakespeare.* 2 vols. Oxford: Clarendon Press, 1963.

Prior to the 2012 publication of Eric Rasmussen and Anthony James West's descriptive catalogue of the Shakespeare First Folios (see Rasmussen and West, below), Hinman's attempt to reconstruct how the Shakespeare First Folio of 1623 was set into type and run off the press, sheet by sheet, was the most arduous study of a single book ever undertaken. This two-volume celebration of the 1623 collection—based on a thorough examination of many of the eighty-two copies of the First Folio in the Folger Shakespeare Library—also identifies individual compositors and provides almost all of the variations in readings from copy to copy; it was thus a seminal work for future editors and bibliographical scholars.

Murphy, Andrew. *Shakespeare in Print: A History and Chronology of Shakespeare Publishing.* Cambridge: Cambridge University Press, 2003.

Murphy's comprehensive account of Shakespeare publishing provides a discursive history of the most editorially significant texts of Shakespeare's poems and plays (both single and collected editions) published in Britain and America between the years 1593 and 2002. Focusing on the circumstances surrounding the publication and the reception of these printed texts, the eleven-chapter history begins with coverage of the early quartos and the early collected editions— Folios 1 (1623), 2 (1632), 3 (1663–64), and 4 (1685). Murphy then moves on to the "emergence of a theoretically self-conscious tradition of Shakespeare editing" in the eighteenth century (with its "market-leading 'celebrity-edited'" collected works), followed by chapters on nineteenth-century popular and scholarly editions, the New Bibliography of the early twentieth century (established by W. W. Greg, R. B. McKerrow, A. W. Pollard, and John Dover Wilson in his Cambridge New Shakespeare), and, turning to the later twentieth century, such publications as the selectively modernized *Riverside Shakespeare* and the "bold . . . and experimental" Oxford Shakespeare. The history section of the volume concludes with an examination of the electronic and hypertext editions of the twenty-first century, which reveal technology to be as important as textual theory. An annotated chronology of more than 1,700 editions constitutes the second part of the book, with five helpful indexes organizing the annotated editions by play/poem title, series title, editor, publisher, and place of publication (excluding London).

Rasmussen, Eric, and Anthony James West, eds. *The Shakespeare First Folios: A Descriptive Catalogue.* Basingstoke: Palgrave Macmillan, 2012.

While biographies of Shakespeare, performance studies of the plays, and accounts of the Folio's prepublication history abound, "little has been offered on the relationship of the First Folio's post-publication history to Shakespeare's reception and recognition over the centuries." The editors of this catalog—the result of twenty years of research during which 232 surviving copies of the First Folio were located and carefully examined—seek to remedy this situation by providing "full bibliographic descriptions of each extant copy, including accounts of press variants, watermarks, damage or repair, leaves in facsimile, annotations, bindings, end-papers, bookplates, and provenance [including lists of ownership]." Praising the editors' meticulous description of each copy, Paul Werstine writes in the catalog's preface that Rasmussen and West take their place beside the monumental efforts of Charlton Hinman (see above). Werstine singles out the editors' "greatest gift to Shakespeareans[:] . . . their significant expansion of our knowledge of the extent to which press corrections have interposed themselves between manuscript printer's copy . . . and the early printed texts of the plays."

Because of their labors in producing a complete record of press variants in all accessible volumes, future editors "can provide Shakespeare's readers with editions of the [eighteen] Folio plays based on fully informed decisions about which printed variant has the highest probability of reflecting the manuscript from which the text was printed."

Werstine, Paul. *Early Modern Playhouse Manuscripts and the Editing of Shakespeare.* Cambridge: Cambridge University Press, 2012.

Werstine examines in detail nearly two dozen texts associated with the playhouses in and around Shakespeare's time, conducting the examination against the background of the two idealized forms of manuscript that have governed the editing of Shakespeare from the twentieth into the twenty-first century—Shakespeare's so-called foul papers and the so-called promptbooks of his plays. By comparing the two extant texts of John Fletcher's *Bonduca,* one in manuscript and the other printed in 1647, Werstine shows that the term "foul papers" that is found in a note in the *Bonduca* manuscript does not refer, as editors have believed, to a species of messy authorial manuscript but is instead simply a designation for a manuscript, whatever its features, that has served as the copy from which another manuscript has been made. By surveying twenty-one texts with theatrical markup, he demonstrates that the playhouses used a wide variety of different kinds of manuscripts and printed texts but did not use the highly regularized promptbooks of the eighteenth-century theaters and later. His presentation of the peculiarities of playhouse texts provides an empirical basis for inferring the nature of the manuscripts that lie behind printed Shakespeare plays.

Key to
Famous Lines and Phrases

For government, though high and low and lower,
Put into parts, doth keep in one consent,
Congreeing in a full and natural close,
Like music.   [Exeter—1.2.187–90]

When we have matched our rackets to these balls,
We will in France, by God's grace, play a set
Shall strike his father's crown into the hazard.
                    [King Henry—1.2.272–74]

. . . the mirror of all Christian kings . . .
                    [Chorus—2.Chor.6]

. . . for after I saw him fumble with the sheets and
play with flowers and smile upon his finger's end,
I knew there was but one way, for his nose was as
sharp as a pen and he talked of green fields.
                    [Hostess—2.3.13–17]

The kindred of him hath been fleshed upon us,
And he is bred out of that bloody strain
That haunted us in our familiar paths.
                    [King of France—2.4.53–55]

Once more unto the breach, dear friends, once more,
Or close the wall up with our English dead!
In peace there's nothing so becomes a man
As modest stillness and humility . . .
                    [King Henry—3.1.1–37]

353

I would give all my fame for a pot of ale, and
safety. [Boy—3.2.13–14]

. . . mean and gentle all
Behold, as may unworthiness define,
A little touch of Harry in the night.
[Chorus—4.Chor.46–48]

. . . What infinite heart's ease
Must kings neglect that private men enjoy?
And what have kings that privates have not too,
Save ceremony, save general ceremony? . . .
[King Henry—4.1.244–93]

. . . if it be a sin to covet honor,
I am the most offending soul alive.
[King Henry—4.3.31–32]

We few, we happy few, we band of brothers . . .
[King Henry—4.3.62]

Small time, but in that small most greatly lived
This star of England. [Chorus—5.Ep.5–6]